Celebrating
Difference

Celebrating
Difference

Fifty Years of Contemporary Native Arts Education at IAIA, 1962–2012

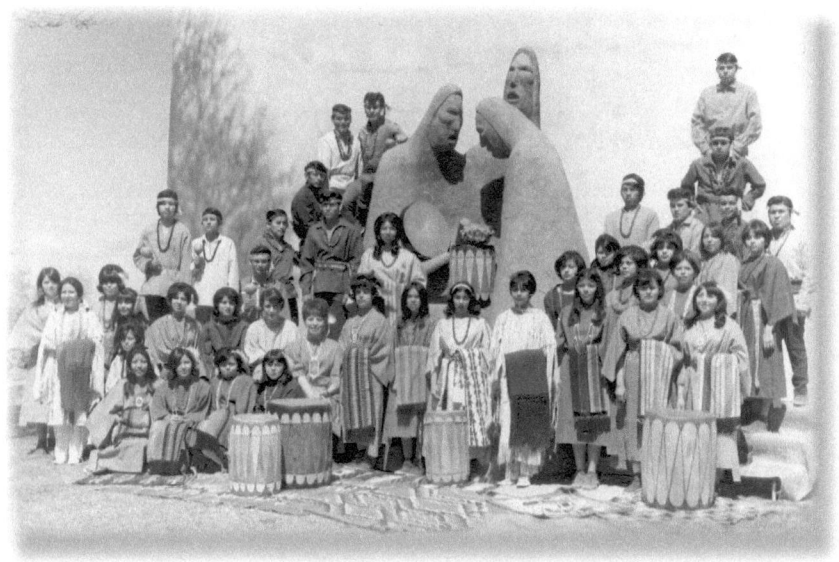

Compiled and Edited
by
Ryan S. Flahive

Essays, Photographs, and Historical Manuscripts
Celebrating the Fiftieth Anniversary of the Institute of American Indian Arts

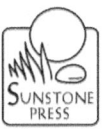

SUNSTONE
PRESS

SANTA FE

Sunstone books may be purchased for educational, business, or sales promotional use. For information please write: Special Markets Department, Sunstone Press, P.O. Box 2321, Santa Fe, New Mexico 87504-2321.

Book and Cover design › Vicki Ahl
Body typeface › Franklin Gothic Book
Printed on acid-free paper

Library of Congress Cataloging-in-Publication Data

Celebrating difference : fifty years of contemporary native arts education at IAIA, 1962-2012 / compiled and edited by Ryan S. Flahive.
    p. cm.
Includes bibliographical references and index.
ISBN 978-0-86534-913-1 (softcover : alk. paper)
1. Institute of American Indian Arts–History. 2. Indians of North America–Education--New Mexico–Santa Fe. 3. Indian arts–United States. 4. Indian arts–Southwest, New. I. Flahive, Ryan S., 1978-
E97.6.I57C45 2012
704'.0397–dc23

                2012036973

WWW.SUNSTONEPRESS.COM
SUNSTONE PRESS / POST OFFICE BOX 2321 / SANTA FE, NM 87504-2321 /USA
(505) 988-4418 / ORDERS ONLY (800) 243-5644 / FAX (505) 988-1025

"To be concerned with the future does not mean to forsake the past, for it is the well from which we draw the strength that serves our present."

—Lloyd Henri "Kiva" New

Contents

We Behold Bright Blessings

by

N. Scott Momaday, PhD

They descend in our clouds
They rise in our harvests
They crackle in our fires
They echo in our prayers
For we are worthy
In the proper way we give thanks
For we are worthy
In the proper way
In the proper way
We behold bright blessings

Acknowledgements

A special thank you is extended to the New Mexico Indian Education Association (NMIEA), namely Leona Zastrow, PhD and Julia Nathanson for their financial support of the IAIA Archives, scholarship on American Indian education, and this publication. From 1981 to 2009, NMIEA worked to improve educational opportunities for Native American students, to strengthen partnerships among schools and tribes, and to identify tribal perspectives. Their mission was to present the school age children of New Mexico a Native perspective of history, and NMIEA published eight volumes of New Mexico history textbooks and teacher guides and distributed copies to local schools the 1980s and 90s. When NMIEA closed their doors in 2009, they generously donated the organization's archives, including manuscripts and drafts of the textbooks to the IAIA Archives. The collection is an excellent representation of research collected to form an Indigenous perspective on history, and the outreach potential of such a project. The collection is open to the public and available for research.

This publication would not have been possible without assistance and support from dozens of people. I profoundly thank the various authors and contributors for using their creativity to apply a new historical approach in assessing the legacy of an educational institution; to my many colleagues at IAIA who have supported this project, particularly Stephen Wall, Richard Sanchez, and Ann Filemyr for editing and planning assistance; to Rose Diaz for facilitating an exploratory meeting outlining the endeavor, for her assistance in conducting the McGrath interview, and her willingness to assist me all along the way; to James McGrath and Dave Warren for inspiration to push forward with the project and the insight necessary to complete it; to Professor Charles A. Dailey for his dedication to preserving the IAIA archives over his nearly forty years at IAIA; to Aysen New, the widow of Lloyd H. New for the donation of the Lloyd H. New Papers to the IAIA Archives; and to the students, faculty, staff, and alumni of IAIA—that the legacy of this important institution continues to shape the future of American Indian education. And lastly, to my wife Cindy and my two children for their unending support of this project and my career.

Preface

As IAIA commemorates its fiftieth anniversary as the birthplace of contemporary Native art, we pay tribute to our illustrious history and the visionaries whose bold ideas and actions resulted in the emergence of an art movement and a truly unique educational institution. It was at IAIA where Native students were encouraged to look to their cultural heritage as a source of creativity and develop contemporary originality in their artistic expression. The captivating vision of the early IAIA staff and faculty was the genesis of our compelling mission to empower creativity and leadership in Native arts and culture and is manifested in our more than 4,000 alumni who have achieved renowned success as artists, writers, scholars, and filmmakers. For example, IAIA graduate and art scholar Gerald McMaster ('74) was selected as the Co-Artistic Director for the 2012 *Sydney Biennale* in Australia; artist Tony Abeyta ('83) was the recipient of the 2012 Santa Fe *Living Treasure Award*, and Santa Clara ceramist Rose Simpson ('07) is currently a delegate to Santa Fe's *UNESCO Creative Capital* sister city of Icheon, South Korea. IAIA alumni continue to make a difference.

As we look toward the next fifty years, IAIA must build upon our rich legacy and strong foundation. By 2017, IAIA plans to double its student body of 400 students, currently representing eighty-four tribes from the United States and Canada. In addition to bachelor's degrees in Studio Arts, New Media Arts, Creative Writing, Museum Studies and Indigenous Liberal Studies, IAIA will soon expand its mission to include graduate degree programs. The IAIA museum will continue to amplify its national and international profile with cutting-edge exhibits, educational programming, and to expand its magnificent collection of contemporary Native art. Finally, a welcome center, a gymnasium, and a performing arts building will be added to our beautiful 140-acre campus with its scenic mountain vistas.

As entrusted stewards for sustaining this national treasure, the administration, faculty and staff are committed to keeping IAIA at the forefront of contemporary Native art higher education and ensuring that the college continues to empower the creative spirit for generations to come.

—Robert Martin, PhD
President

Introduction
by
Ryan S. Flahive

Difference (noun): a point or way in which people or things are not the same

The Institute of American Indian Arts (IAIA) is an educational institution committed to difference. Situated on a 140-acre campus on the high plains south of Santa Fe, IAIA is a world leader in contemporary Native arts and culture education. Published in celebration of the fiftieth anniversary of IAIA, this compilation of historical documents, photographs, essays, and conversations aims to illuminate the history of art education at the Institute. Its purpose is to discuss a few basic questions: How is IAIA different from other colleges? What is it about the history, structure, location, and curriculum of IAIA that makes it a special institution? How did a school that began as an experiment in American Indian arts education progress from a Bureau of Indian Affairs (BIA) high school to a junior college to an accredited non-profit baccalaureate institution in less than fifty years? What does the next fifty years have in store for IAIA?

The larger context of federal Indian policy should be considered if we are to discuss the *difference* between IAIA and other colleges. Since the beginnings of the United States policy to assimilate American Indians into "mainstream America," education has been seen as the primary assimilative tool. Starting with the experiments at the Hampton Institute in the 1870s to the development of the boarding schools in the 1880s, the United States government, acting through the Bureau of Indian Affairs, has controlled Indian education. Through the days of the Indian Re-Organization Act (1932–1945), there were attempts to insure tribal culture and ways of life were part of the educational process, however with the arrival of the termination policy in the late 1940s, the focus came to be one of educating the Indian to leave their tribal community and enter the mainstream.

IAIA was established during the waning years of the termination policy, but still reflected the BIA philosophy of educating Indians to leave the reservation. However, IAIA's gains in prominence paralleled the development of the self-determination policy, a federal policy designed to provide for more tribal authority and self-governance. The roots of self-determination for Native controlled higher education were beginning to blossom. Gradually, tribally controlled colleges began to spring up nationwide beginning with the Navajo Community College (now Dine College) in 1968. In 1978, the Tribally Controlled Community College Act was passed and further urged the self-determination of Native American higher education. Tribes began to develop their own colleges, and presently, thirty-six tribally controlled colleges are in operation, including IAIA.

During the same period, the BIA Department of Education went through a major policy shift under the leadership of education director Hildegard Thompson. Thompson recognized the need to prepare Indian students "for an urban, technological society" during the 1950s, which led to a de-emphasis on traditional vocational training within the BIA boarding schools. Although not fully supported throughout the Bureau, post-high school training, either through vocational schools or colleges, became a focal point of Thompson's efforts until her retirement in 1965. The shift in policy, along with other parallel circumstances, led to the creation of three BIA chartered colleges for post-high school training.

Haskell Junior College (now Haskell Indian Nations University) has served the BIA in Lawrence, Kansas since 1884. Initially a boarding school for younger students, Haskell became a high school in 1921 and later a vocational-industrial school until 1970, when the Bureau chartered the school as a general education junior college. The Southwest Indian Polytechnic Institute (SIPI) was opened in northwest Albuquerque in 1971 and focused on providing a range of career and transfer opportunities for Native learners in science, technology, engineering, and mathematics.

IAIA was opened as a vocational art school for Native students to replace

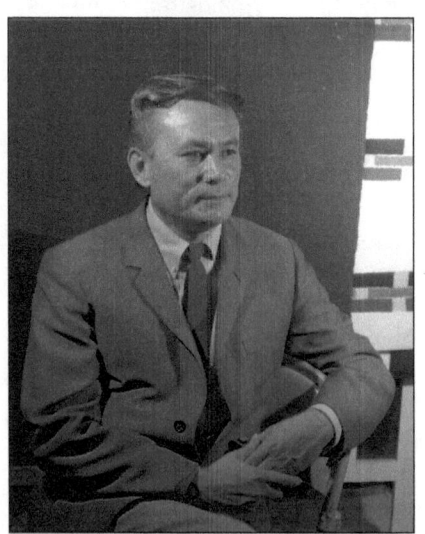

the program at the Santa Fe Indian School in 1962. Its curriculum was based on "cultural difference as the basis for creative expression," a concept developed by Lloyd Henri "Kiva" New and others, and an emphasis was placed on development of the whole individual through academic training and the study of the world's arts and culture.

Lloyd Henri "Kiva" New, 4 April 1968. Photograph by Kay V. Wiest. (Courtesy of IAIA Archives, Santa Fe, New Mexico) (ms 10.002-edit)

Considering their similar goals and structures, Haskell, SIPI, and IAIA were connected and considered the bright lights of BIA-controlled higher education during the 1970s and 1980s. All three shared similar elements; they were not tied to any one tribe and were successful in attracting Native students from tribes across the continent. But by the mid 1980s, IAIA began to differentiate itself from both the tribally controlled *and* the BIA chartered colleges through a dramatic reorganization.

The passage of the Higher Education Amendments in 1986 marked the end of a three-year effort to release IAIA from BIA control. Public Law 99-498, Title XV passed in October of 1986, and the Institute of American Indian and Alaska Native Culture and Arts Development (but still known as IAIA) became a congressionally chartered non-profit on June 1, 1988—an agreement similar in structure to that of the Smithsonian Institution. The charter recognized that the federal government was responsible for IAIA's financial well-being, but allowed the school to run its own operations under a White House appointed board of trustees. Most importantly, the charter granted a great deal of freedom to the Institute in carrying out its cultural and academic goals. No other tribally or BIA controlled college operates under the same organizational circumstances and only two other colleges, Howard University (for African Americans) and Gallaudet University (for the hearing impaired) have similar congressional status.

The newly created board of trustees acted immediately to improve the newly reorganized IAIA. In December of 1988, Rancho Viejo Partnership, a local real estate venture south of Santa Fe, donated 140 acres of its property to IAIA as a permanent home for the college. A few months later, in July of 1989, title to the old federal building on Cathedral Place (prime real estate in downtown Santa Fe) was transferred to IAIA for its museum, now known as the Museum of Contemporary Native Art (MoCNA), which had previously been housed on the Cerrillos campus. It took three years to renovate the federal building into a workable art museum and over twelve years to get the campus built, but the campus and museum are physical testaments to the immense progress of IAIA since reorganization. The new facilities, the campus in particular, provided IAIA with a true *sense of place*, something that lacked during the first thirty years of operation.

But physical and organizational improvements were not the only difference makers for IAIA. The school's unique journey towards accredited baccalaureate degrees is also worthy of discussion. IAIA is one of only seven colleges for Native students in the country that offers four-year degrees, and the world's only four-year college dedicated to contemporary Native art. Others include five tribally controlled

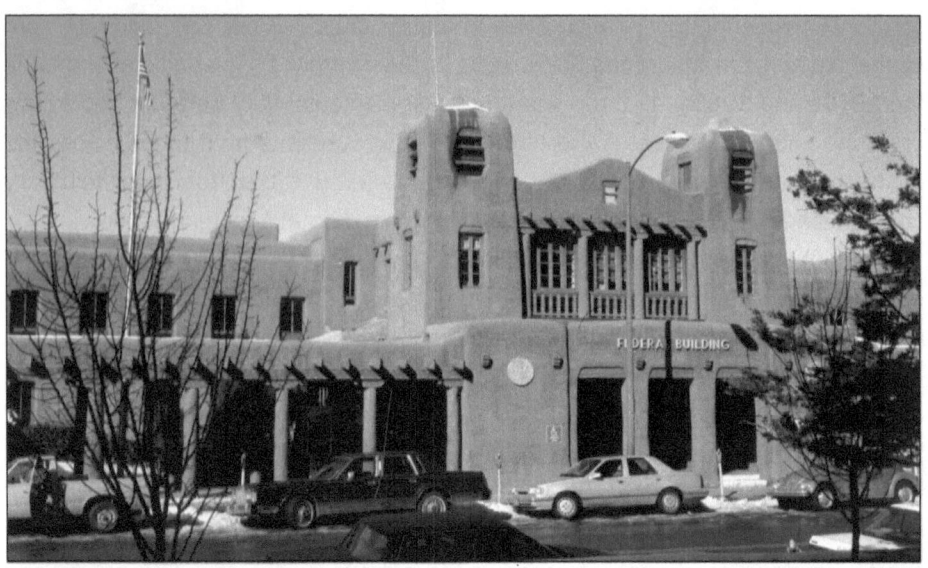

United States Federal Building, 1988. Originally constructed as a post office, the building on Federal Place was used by the General Services Administration prior to its transfer to IAIA. (Courtesy of IAIA Archives, Santa Fe, New Mexico) (box24f13i04)

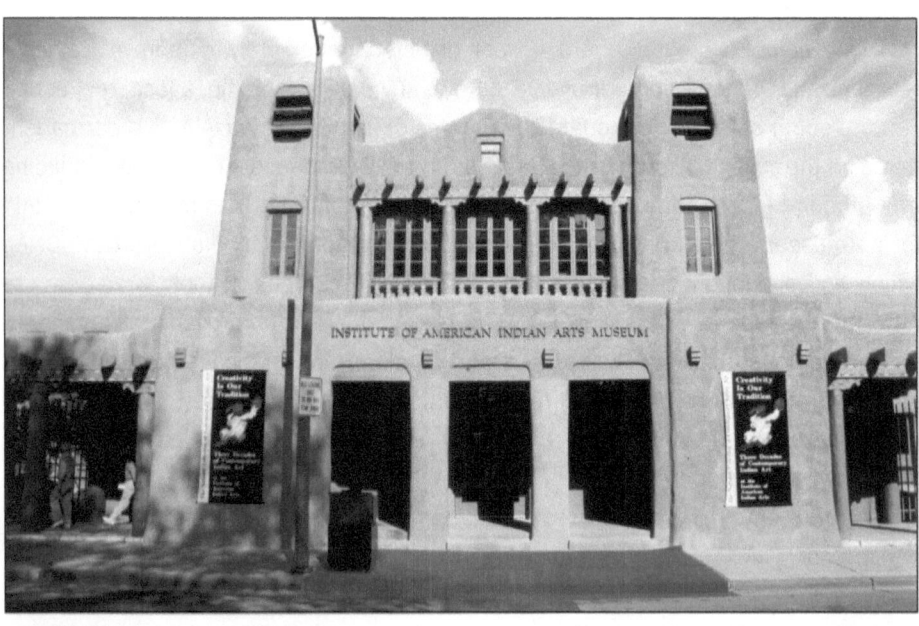

The Museum of Contemporary Native Art, 1992. (Courtesy of IAIA Archives, Santa Fe, New Mexico) (box24f13i02)

institutions: Dine College, Sinte Gleska University, Oglala Lakota College, and Salish Kootenai College as well as the federally controlled Haskell Indian Nations University and the privately controlled institutions Nazarene Indian Bible College and American Indian College. While IAIA and Haskell share similar paths towards accreditation, IAIA's progression has been more complex.

In 1969, the Special Subcommittee on Indian Education in the 91st Congress recommended that IAIA become a four-year college:

> By becoming a college, the Institute could provide a college-wide curriculum for Indians which considers their culture and history . . . the Institute should be expanded into a college curriculum so that the Institute might become a model for Colleges . . . which recognize Indian needs.

Following the recommendation, a report submitted to Louis R. Bruce, Commissioner of Indian Affairs by a special committee appointed to explore the situation at IAIA read "The committee has concluded that the Institute of American Indian Arts has reached a critical point in its history . . . to set the national and international example in American Indian Education." However, the movement towards a four-year college was not sudden; Lloyd New envisioned a junior-college program to precede any four-year program.

The accreditation process was slow for IAIA. In 1974 IAIA began the process with the Higher Learning Commission of the North Central Association of Colleges and Schools (NCA) and also sought accreditation from the National Association of Schools of Art and Design (NASAD). In April of 1978, IAIA received candidacy status to grant associate's degrees from the NCA, and by 1986, received full affiliation status with both agencies. In 1990, a visiting team from the agencies recommended a five-year extension of accreditation.

With the goal of junior college accreditation accomplished, IAIA began the process of gaining accreditation for four-year degrees in 1998. In 2001, IAIA sought approval of BFA programs in Studio Arts, Creative Writing, Museum Studies and Visual Communications and BA programs in Studio Arts and General Education. Following a visit by the agencies in October of 2001, most of the requests were approved by early 2002.

By far the most important aspect on how IAIA differentiates itself lies in its curriculum. The "cultural difference as the basis for creative expression" approach to Native education instituted by Lloyd New and the arts faculty in 1962 led to a flowering of artistic talent from the Institute in the visual and performing arts as well as many talented creative writers. Practically speaking, the original IAIA curriculum was separated into two distinct programs. The high school program was a fairly typical BIA boarding school curriculum with electives in the fine and performing arts as well as traditional 'crafts'. The 'postgraduate' program was open to high school graduates under the age of twenty-three and consisted of art training and college preparation courses.

The arts curriculum urged experimentation with various materials, techniques, and sources of artistic inspiration. The school opened on schedule and the results of the pedagogic experiment were impressive; the combination of unique contextual circumstances and an experimental arts and culture curriculum produced many of the world's great contemporary Native artists and is considered by many to be the birthplace and permanent home of the contemporary Native art movement.

Over the years, the IAIA curriculum has evolved to accommodate the various changes in accreditation status, organizational structure, and physical location. In 1979, the Institute phased out the high school program to enable the growth and strengthening of its new college program. The reorganization of the Institute in 1986 mandated the establishment of a center for Culture and Art Studies and a Center for Research and Cultural Exchanges and built the curriculum around specific arts and culture degree paths.

The curriculum continued to evolve upon its arrival to the new campus in 2001. Studio Arts programming has been bolstered by new facilities, notably a sculpture foundry that provides high quality equipment to enhance woodworking, welding, forging, casting, ceramics and large scale metal, stone, and glass sculpture. Media Arts and the Museum Studies program are hosted in the new Science and Technology Building complete with state-of-the-art digital workspaces, a museum collection storage facility, conservation labs, and our "digital dome." The Creative Writing program continues to grow and add to its impressive resume at IAIA. Students regularly publish their poetry, prose, and screenplay creations. Certificate programs in Business Entrepreneurship and Museum Studies offers students a shorter degree track and the new digital learning initiative has created new ways for students to attend class. In the Indigenous Liberal Studies program students are being groomed for careers as tribal leaders and Native scholars through decolonization theory and Indigenous knowing constructs. IAIA is active in tribal outreach through the Center for Lifelong Education, which is focused on preserving and strengthening Indigenous cultures through educational offerings, technical assistance, and learning opportunities.

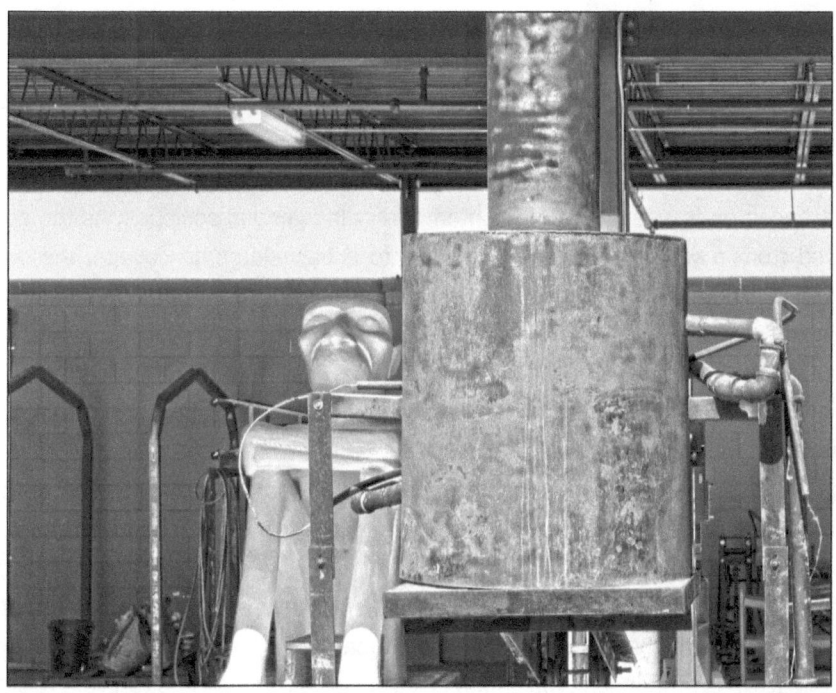

A look inside the Sculpture and Foundry Building, IAIA Campus, 2012. Photograph by Bill McIntire. (sculpturebuilding1)

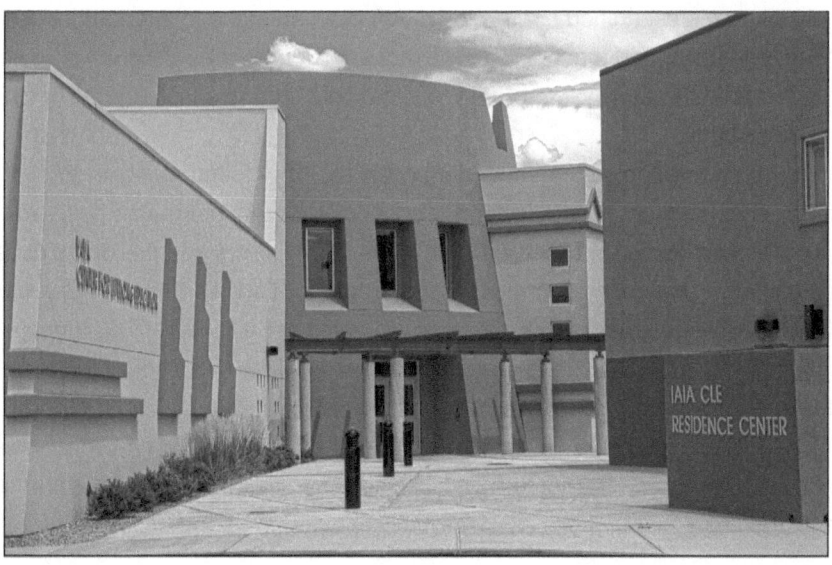

The Center for Lifelong Education, IAIA Campus. Photograph by Bill McIntire. (CLE11)

Perhaps what makes IAIA different from other institutions is it's embracing of *difference*. Celebration of culture is alive and well; each student, staff, and faculty member bring their own cultural identity with them—IAIA is a pluralistic microcosm. Celebration of individual and creative difference is encouraged through social interaction, healthy civil discourse, museum exhibitions, and various events and conferences on issues impacting contemporary Indigenous societies. As the school evolved from a vocational-arts high school to a baccalaureate college, the use of *difference* to enhance student's lives through arts and culture has been maintained to present day.

The gestation of this book was curious. It began with a review of the literature upon my arrival to IAIA in January of 2009. As with any archives job, I had to gain a grasp on the subject matter and its historical context in order to arrange and describe the materials properly. Two books helped me gain a footing; Winona Garmhausen's well-researched *History of Indian Arts Education in Santa Fe: The Institute of American Indian Arts 1890-1962* is an excellent history of IAIA up to 1978 and discusses the school in the overall context of Indian arts education in Santa Fe. It should be noted that the 1982 Garmhausen publication is a truncated version of her University of New Mexico dissertation of the same title. Former IAIA faculty Joy Gritton published *The Institute of American Indian Arts: Modernism and U.S. Indian Policy* in 2000. Gritton's book is also well-researched and explores IAIA in a national and international context of U.S. Indian policy and the history of the modern art movement. These works helped me understand the early years of IAIA, but they did little to satisfy the history of the school past 1986.

I continued to dig for secondary sources, and I found plenty in the library—primarily exhibition catalogs and art history books. Our museum has been active in one form or another since 1963, first as the *Museum Gallery* and then in 1971 as the *IAIA Museum*, titled such by former museum director Charles Dailey. Today, MoCNA is actively publishing books and catalogs including the excellent 2011 publication, *Manifestations*, and IAIA artists and alumni have been written about by art curators world-wide for the past couple decades. After reviewing the secondary literature, I concluded that the unique curriculum practiced by IAIA and its difference has yet to be fully addressed. The force by which IAIA has grown academically and as an organization since 1986 has called for new scholarship on the history of education at IAIA.

Next, I turned to primary sources. My review led me to the stacks; where the IAIA archives live. Reading is an occupational hazard for an archivist, and almost immediately in my survey of the materials in the archives, I began to see the evidential history of IAIA's development: written monographs from Lloyd New, museum reports from Chuck Dailey, committee notes, accreditation self-study reports—the archives provided me with the evidence I sought.

In May of 2010, MoCNA Director Patsy Phillips called a round-table meeting of a number of IAIA staff, alumni, faculty, students, and esteemed former faculty and staff members. We discussed the possibility of publishing a book for the fiftieth anniversary and although the meeting was active and plenty of ideas were tossed about, the project never seemed to get off the ground. Nearly a year later, in February of 2011, I decided to move on this publication project. Has it changed in the past twenty months? Absolutely. But the primary concept has not been compromised: to discuss the history of education at IAIA through various formats of historical information. It's a break from your typical non-fiction prose—it is a combination of recollections, essays, photographs, real conversations, and historic primary source material. I would like to think that this book is, if anything, *different*.

◊◊◊

A few notes about how the book was built. The foundation of the volume is the appendices. Primary source documents form a common denominator for the contributors—each author was provided with a compilation of important writings and monographs from the IAIA archives, and shaped a consistent tone within the subject matter. Essays by Alfred Young Man, Rina Swentzell, and Ted Jojola were generously funded through the New Mexico Indian Education Association fellowship program at IAIA and were the first to be written for the project in 2011. From a historian's standpoint, the oral history transcript of James A. McGrath is of the utmost importance as the conversation adds a human element to the project. The photo essays illustrating the former homes of IAIA are juxtaposed with Swentzell's article on the new IAIA campus to provide a reader with a contextual view of IAIA's *sense of place*. The opening chapter from Dean Ann Filemyr was the final piece of the puzzle and is a fitting homage to Lloyd New and the contemporary issues faced by IAIA in the 21st century. The many moving pieces color IAIA in different ways, but hope to add to an ongoing conversation about the use of historical material in shaping the future.

The first chapter is a an open letter to the philosophical founder of IAIA, Lloyd Henri "Kiva" New, Cherokee (1916–2002) from the current academic dean of IAIA, Ann Filemyr, PhD. Dean Filemyr discusses passages selected from some of New's most important writings (published as appendices) and creates a contextual review of the school's original intentions and its current practices.

Sense of place is paramount in this volume. For that reason, the second chapter is the first of two photo essays devoted to the previous homes of IAIA. "IAIA at the Santa Fe Indian School" is a selection of photographs taken by long-time IAIA photographer and photography faculty Kay V. Wiest between 1964–1975 and presents the facilities used by IAIA on the Cerrillos Road campus.

In the third chapter, Cree artist, scholar, and IAIA alumni Alfred Young Man, PhD, presents his side of the IAIA story from the perspective of a student. Young Man's account offers a glimpse of the social setting of the school and provides the reader with insight into the impact of the unique curriculum on students.

The fourth chapter is an edited oral history transcript from an interview with James A. McGrath, IAIA's first assistant art director and one of its earliest faculty members. The interview was conducted with this book in mind, and addresses questions of *difference* in the IAIA curriculum.

The second photo essay titled "IAIA at the College of Santa Fe" is the fifth chapter. In 1999, Merritt Edson Youngdeer took snapshots of degraded rental facilities and are presented in contrast to our current, permanent campus discussed in the sixth chapter.

Santa Clara artist and architect Rina Swentzell, PhD wrote the sixth chapter of the volume and reviews the goals, composition, and design of the IAIA campus and how it fits the curriculum and philosophy of the Institute.

The seventh and final chapter is an epilogue of sorts by Isleta scholar Ted Jojola, PhD. Through interviews conducted with IAIA faculty, administrators, and students, Jojola presents a valid argument supporting the *difference* of IAIA and its curriculum and offers insight into the future of Indian education.

The appendices of the book are of immense value to the complete understanding of the subject at hand. The historical documents were culled from the IAIA archives and are presented, more or less, in their entirety.

Lloyd New's monograph "Using Cultural Difference as a Basis for Creative Expression," is a masterpiece of modern pedagogical thought. New's concepts complement those of other prominent thinkers of the period including the father of the multiple intelligences theory, Howard Gardner and the founder of the University of Utah's Institute for Behavioral Research in Creativity, Calvin Taylor.

The second and third appendices were also penned by New. "The Role of the Institute of American Indian Arts in the Development of Indian Education and Its

Potential as a Major Cultural Institution," was a report submitted to the Special Sub-Committee on Indian Education, United States Senate. It can be seen as a departure from the vocational art high school model and the start of a push towards becoming a major center for cultural studies, which led to progress in curriculum development and ultimately, baccalaureate accreditation. "The Institute of American Indian Arts: Some of Its Goals, Problems, and Successes" is an unpublished manuscript written by New in 1979 during one of the most tumultuous times in the history of the school which dealt with decreasing student numbers, falling graduation rates, and cuts in federal appropriations.

Appendix four is a drafted statement of mission composed by a special committee in 1988. The "Statement of Mission" compiled by Dave Warren, PhD, presents the basic proposition of what the school should become following its reorganization in 1986. It was the first attempt to build a new college curriculum under its new directive as a congressionally chartered college.

The last appendix looks to the future. "Plan 2015: Building a Foundation for the Next Fifty Years" was written by the IAIA board of trustees in 2010 and offers insight as to the future mission of the school.

It should be noted that the terms Native American, Native, Indian, Indigenous, and Aboriginal are used interchangeably in this volume and represent the Native cultures of North America, including the United States, Canada, and Alaska.

Contributors

Rose T. Diaz, PhD is currently the Research Historian for the Indian Pueblo Cultural Center. Diaz earned a BS and PhD from Arizona State University in the field of American history with a focus on public history. Diaz held numerous administrative and archival positions at the University of New Mexico Center for Southwest Research from 1983 until her retirement in 2008. A well-respected oral historian, Diaz has spearheaded several major projects including the recent New Mexico Centennial Women's Oral History Project and is a former past president of the Southwest Oral History Association (SOHA) and the national Oral History Association (OHA).

Ann Filemyr, PhD is the Academic Dean of the College of Contemporary Native Arts at IAIA. She holds a degree in creative and performing arts from Thomas Jefferson College of Grand Valley State Colleges, Michigan and a MA in English from the University of Wisconsin. Filemyr earned a PhD in environmental communications from Union Institute and University, Ohio. Filemyr's professional activities include assessment, institutional evaluation, and curriculum development as well as the day-to-day administration of the college. As a poet and writer, Filemyr has published several books including her latest effort, *Healer's Diary*.

Ryan S. Flahive is the Archivist at the Institute of American Indian Arts and also serves as support faculty for the museum studies department. Born on the high plains of northeastern Colorado, Flahive studied history and anthropology at Lindenwood University in St. Charles, Missouri and earned an MA in history along with a Graduate Certificate in museum studies from the University of Missouri-St. Louis. Previous employers include Sharlot Hall Museum in Prescott, Arizona where he served as Director of Research, Archives, and Publications.

Theodore (Ted) Jojola, PhD, is a Distinguished Professor and Regents' Professor in the Community and Regional Planning Program, School of Architecture and Planning, University of New Mexico and Director of the Indigenous Design and Planning Institute. He is an enrolled tribal member of the Pueblo of Isleta.

James A. McGrath has dedicated his life to creating and teaching art. He earned a BS from the University of Oregon in 1950 and continued his studies at Montana State University and University of Washington in 1951 and 1952. After teaching high school art he took a position as Arts and Crafts Director for the U.S. Department of Defense's Dependents School in several European countries from 1955 to 1962. McGrath was hired as Assistant Director of Arts at IAIA in 1962 and served the Institute in that capacity until 1973. Concurrently, McGrath served as Native American Cultural Arts Specialist for the U.S. State Department during his time at IAIA. Leaving IAIA in 1973, McGrath held positions in places as diverse as Japan and the Hopi reservation, and returned to IAIA as Dean of the College in 1988 and held that post until June of 1989. James A. McGrath lives in Santa Fe and continues to create and sell art from his private studio.

Lloyd Henri "Kiva" New (1916–2002) was a member of the Cherokee Nation, a famed fashion designer, and the philosophical visionary of the Institute of American Indian Arts. New received his BAE from the School of the Arts Institute of Chicago in 1938 and taught art at the Phoenix Indian School prior to serving in the United States Navy Reserves from 1941 to 1946. After the service, New opened a design/crafts/fashion studio in Scottsdale, Arizona, aptly called the *Kiva Craft Center* in the early 1950s. New left his lucrative business in 1962 to become the Art Director at IAIA and served the Institute in several capacities, including President, until his retirement in 1978. After his retirement, New remained involved in the museum and art business, serving on the boards of IAIA, the Heard Museum, the Buffalo Bill Historical Center, the Indian Arts and Crafts Board and was instrumental in the planning and design of the National Museum of the American Indian. In 1988, Lloyd New returned to IAIA as Interim President during the reorganization period until his departure in 1989. New was a highly praised artist, writer, educator, and speaker who led the way towards a new direction for contemporary Native art education.

Rina Swentzell, PhD was born and raised at Santa Clara Pueblo. She received her BA in education from New Mexico Highlands University in Las Vegas, New Mexico. She earned a MA in architecture and a PhD in American studies from the University of New Mexico. Over the years, Swentzell has taught courses at the Institute of American Arts and the University of New Mexico in various fields. Most of her work experience has been as a cultural and architectural consultant for many institutions including the National Museum of the American Indian, Museum of New Mexico, and the Institute of American Indian Arts. Swentzell is a grandmother of eleven and great-grandmother of five children. She currently lives in Santa Clara Pueblo.

From 1969 to 1989, **Dave Warren, PhD** (Santa Clara Pueblo) held positions at the Institute of American Indian Arts as the Director of Curriculum and Instruction, Acting President, and later, the Director of the Cultural Research and Resource Development Center. In 1994, an award by the New Mexico Commission on Indian Affairs acknowledged his lifetime commitment to the preservation and perpetuation of American Indian languages and cultures. In 2010, the Southwest Association on Indian Arts recognized his lifetime service to the arts with the *Povi Ka* award. He is founding Deputy Director, National Museum of the American Indian.

Alfred Young Man, PhD (Eagle Chief) is an enrolled member of the Chippewa-Cree Indian Reservation in Rocky Boy, Montana and Professor Emeritus of the University of Lethbridge and University of Regina (Canada). Born in Browning, Montana on the Blackfeet Indian reservation, his paternal and maternal Cree grandparent's were from the Duck Lake area reserves in Saskatchewan and the Erminskin and Cold Lake reserves in Alberta. Young Man has had numerous paintings, articles, essays, book reviews and art critiques published in art catalogues, newspapers, magazines, web pages, and peer reviewed journals and has travelled extensively throughout the world presenting at conferences, universities, and symposiums.

Chronology of the
Institute of American Indian Arts (IAIA)

October 1960: Creation of IAIA by the Bureau of Indian Affairs (BIA)

October 1962: Commencement of IAIA program

August 1967: Lloyd H. New appointed Director of IAIA

February 1969: Senate recommends IAIA become a four-year college

April 1975: BIA accredits IAIA as a 'Middle' College

May 1979: IAIA eliminates high school program

August 1981: IAIA moves to leased facilities at College of Santa Fe

October 1984: Commission on Institutions of Higher Education of the North Central Association of Colleges and Schools (NCA) and National Association of Schools of Art and Design (NASAD) accredits IAIA to grant Associate of Fine Arts Degrees

October 1986: Reorganization of IAIA as a Congressionally Chartered non-profit—The Institute of American Indian and Alaska Native Arts and Culture Development under the Higher Education Amendments of 1986

December 1988: Rancho Viejo Partnership donates land for IAIA campus

October 1994: IAIA becomes a land-grant institution through the Equity in Educational Land-Grant Status Act of 1994

August 2000: New IAIA campus opens for operation

October 2001: NCA and NASAD accredit IAIA to grant bachelor's degrees

November 2009: Center for Lifelong Education opens at IAIA

October 2012: IAIA celebrates fifty years of operation

An Open Letter to Lloyd "Kiva" New
by
Ann Filemyr, PhD

Dear Lloyd,

Though we never had the chance to meet, I inherited your energetic vision for what IAIA could be when I began my position as the Dean and Chief Academic Officer in July 2005. I want to take this moment to thank you. You left clear messages about the importance of this unique institution. You projected your experiences and observations into the possibility of what IAIA could become if only your ideas could be set into motion. You understood that the future belongs to those who will reach out and shape it.

In this, our fiftieth year, I thought I might sit down and talk with you. IAIA archivist and editor of this book, Ryan S. Flahive, liked my idea of a dialogue in text between us. He selected a number of your quotes for me to respond to. It is my hope that together we can bridge the distance of time and space, life and death, enacting a truly Indigenous concept that we are all one, one people, and there is only one time. That time is now. I would like to bring you up to date on just where things stand here at IAIA in the beginning of the twenty-first century. A time you imagined clearly.

So let us begin. I will respond to the quotes from your writing as if we are sitting together in a sweet, cool evening breeze on the wide veranda overlooking the central plaza of our campus. The bright New Mexican summer sun sinks behind the indigo peaks of the Jemez Mountains coloring the sky with the most vivid pinks and golden orange. I know these fabulous desert colors once inspired your fabric designs, for you were an artist first and foremost. Out of your commitment to Native art grew your commitment to education.

Let's start with your ideas about the future of Indian art.

The Future of Indian Art.

It is generally assumed that the future of Indian art lies in an ability to evolve, adjust, and adapt to the demands of the present, and not upon the ability to remanipulate the past.[1]

We wholeheartedly agree with you. Further we have found that in order, "to evolve, adjust and adapt to the needs of the present," we must incorporate technology into our artistic disciplines. Successful artists today must utilize digital media, at the very least in the form of a website, CD, or DVD. In the past three years, we have taken major leaps in bringing new technology to our campus for our students and faculty to explore as part of their creative expression.

Today we house the world's only articulating digital dome. This large half-circle is like looking up inside a tennis ball, only the dome is twenty-five feet in diameter and creates an immersive environment in which both audio and visual material can be communicated. The viewer sits beneath and is surrounded by the artist's vision. We can lower it into what we call "the kiva position," and viewers stretch out on their backs as if lying on the earth herself looking up at the sky. The dome utilizes multiple projectors to seamlessly stitch together multiple images into a 360-degree full circle. It leaves the viewer with the feeling of being inside something and not simply watching a film. It is the experience of being within nature.

We decided to incorporate dome technology into our curriculum because of the importance of the circle itself. The flat screen as a place for projected imagery may not always serve a cultural imperative. The round interior spaces of wigwams, sweat lodges, kivas, and other cultural spaces signifies many things, perhaps most importantly, the appropriate expression of inter-relationships, as all beings exist in an equal way within the circle.

In the past, dome technology was used primarily in planetariums. Today artists are beginning to create unique and original works for this environment. The IAIA dome was recently featured on the cover of a College Art Association (CAA) publication. We continue to seek unique opportunities to showcase the abilities of this new arts technology. But that is only one of our new innovations.

IAIA is also expanding its use of three-dimensional (3-D) technology. We have purchased and are learning to use a motion-capture system that would allow us to record movements, such as the traditional dance steps of an elder, in a 3-D environment. Another project is using a new 3-D scanner that allows us to digitally record the shape of a pot or a piece of sculpture and reproduce it on a 3-D printer. This technology could be used by tribal museums and cultural centers to scan fragile objects and shared in appropriate educational and cultural settings. Children could handle the reproductions and learn about it without endangering the original object.

We believe tribal communities can make excellent use of these new technologies. We also believe individual Native artists may find these tools to be significant in shaping new forms of artistic expression. The twenty-first century has only just begun. We want to be at the forefront of innovation in artistic expression. We are committed to providing our students the tools they need to become artistic innovators. We do not know what they will create; we just know we want them to create. In creation is life.

Incoming IAIA students will learn about and be able to utilize tools that blur the boundary between art and technology. In addition to the digital dome and motion-capture system, we have the "fab lab" (3-D scanners and printers), the broadcast studio, and several high-end computer classrooms loaded with the latest software for digital artists. Students are required to create and update individual electronic portfolios (ePortfolios) to keep digital records of their development as artists and scholars. Faculty members review student ePortfolios as part of an on-going assessment and program improvement initiative.

Here is what we say about this in our 2011–2012 college catalog.

Art & Technology at IAIA

IAIA is beginning to explore the field of STEAM (Science, Technology, Engineering, Arts and Mathematics) and develop a unique curriculum to serve Native American students and further the relationship between Art & Technology as a vital crossroads for creative expression.

Together the new The Digital Dome, Motion Capture System, Broadcast studio, Sculpture/Foundry Center, and the Fab Lab at the Institute of American Indian Arts provide new opportunities to research, experiment, develop content and expand the possibilities for artistic expression.

Strategies to utilize these tools for cultural preservation and service to Native communities are being explored.

IAIA is moving forward and serving our students' unique needs with innovation and dedication. Details about these facilities are located in the

Academic Resources section of our catalog as well as under the facilities descriptions in each major program. We are expanding our campus resources in order to provide amazing facilities for our students. These new facilities allow us to move forward with our commitment to excellence in teaching and learning.[2]

In summary, the Institute of American Indian Arts is embarked upon a program, with many steps yet to be taken, the early outcomes of which are indicative of significant discoveries in education. The Indian student is being inspired to new personal strengths in dimensions heretofore unrealized. He can be oriented to his own cultural background, enabling him to function constructively in tune with the demands of today's culture, without sacrificing his cultural self on the alter (sic) of assimilation, as so often is the case.[3]

Culture

Let us explore your challenge to continue the ongoing discussion regarding the role of culture in the IAIA curriculum:

. . . the school will constantly work on the development of techniques for bringing through to the general stream of culture those unique qualities that Indian society has to offer. This will come about in an educational program that looks not only at Indian culture, but can instill a realistic awareness of the general cultural milieu. The student will learn about the world in which he will function.[4]

Our ideas of culture shape both the content of our courses and our course delivery methods. In 2011 we revisited this idea of culture as central to an IAIA education. Central to this discussion was the question, *what does it mean to be engaged in an educational model that is not mainstream but successfully prepares students to achieve in both their own Native cultural contexts as well as mainstream cultural contexts?*

It seems this question was the same one you articulated for us at the very beginning. For example, we require all Studio Art majors to study both European art history and Native American art history; student filmmakers study both American

Indians in cinema and world cinema. However, it is not just exposure to these content areas that infuses a sense of our multicultural mission. We recognize the great diversity *within* Indian country as well.

Ultimately we crafted a statement specifically examining this notion of culture, and what culture means at IAIA in the second decade of the twenty-first century. We agreed that this statement was directed at the faculty who deliver the curriculum, for they shape the learning environment most intimately in their classrooms and through individual relationships with the students. Therefore, we framed this statement on culture as "Principles of Practice for IAIA Teachers."

The purpose was to define our uniqueness as the only Native-centric, arts-based higher education institution in the country. How are we different from mainstream art and design schools? How are we different from other tribal colleges? What is central to our pedagogy, the method by which we transmit and inspire the quest for knowledge, skills and ways of being and understanding the world as Native artists and scholars? What is central to our epistemology, and what do we believe undergirds our work?

IAIA realizes its unusual position. We serve a federal mandate through our congressional charter and are accredited by the same higher education body as every other school of higher learning. Yet we do not serve a strictly assimilationist purpose. We believe Indigenous knowledge systems arising from traditional place-based life ways are vital in reshaping mainstream attitudes and practices. We live in a time of change, and IAIA wants to assume a leadership role in this change.

Below is the final statement, which was incorporated into the 2011–2012 college catalog:

Principles of Practice for Excellence in Teaching at IAIA

Definition

We define excellence in teaching at IAIA as the ability to create a stimulating learning environment for Native American students and other students to thrive, take creative risks, and learn from each other, from their teachers, and from the materials and experiences presented in the class.

Philosophy

There is no such thing as an *acultural* environment, situation, person or position. Each one of us is the result of cultural influences and a contributor to cultural influences. It is this acceptance of culture as a pervasive and profound shaper of human experience that underlies our educational philosophy at IAIA. We do not teach culture here, as we are a multicultural, multitribal institution. However, our educational model seeks to reinforce existing cultural foundations primarily through the study of the arts, Indigenous knowledge and literature. We recognize that we may be knowledgeable about our own cultures, but we are not experts of each other's cultures. Therefore every student and teacher at IAIA is open to learning about culture and actively supports respect for and appreciation of our cultural diversity.

Principles of Practice for IAIA Teachers:

1. An IAIA education supports students to have an awareness of the importance of the Native American story as a counter-narrative to the dominant narrative. We support this principle by actively engaging with our students to understand and analyze the underlying assumptions that are communicated through art, culture and story.
2. An IAIA education supports active self-reflection as part of developing a deeper awareness of and appreciation for cultural differences. We support this principle by being self-reflective learners aware of our own cultural influences.
3. The IAIA classroom promotes an environment in which multiple voices and viewpoints are encouraged and students are safe to share their experiences, perceptions and creativity. We support this principle through actively engaging with our students in critical and creative dialogues about art and art-making.
4. In an IAIA education collaboration is valued over competition. We support this principal through facilitating collaborative learning.
5. In an IAIA education attention is given to whose culture and whose voice is privileged. We support this principle through an engaged examination of texts, speakers, knowledge systems, institutions, or experiences.[5]

We have embedded these core principles into our annual teaching evaluations. During the 2012–2013 school year, we will begin a regular process of visiting each other's classrooms. By observing our peers teaching techniques, we can assess how well we are embodying these unique core principles in the classroom.

Beyond the classroom, we are interested in reaching out into the world to challenge historic practices and processes that invalidate Indigenous cultural worldviews. Our Museum Studies program is advancing a theory and practice of Indigenous curatorial practice in which curators are collaborative partners with individual artists and communities and not simply subject experts imposing interpretations on artistic work.

Our Indigenous Liberal Studies program actively challenges the status quo definition of research. It is an attempt to integrate Indigenous research methods at both the undergraduate and graduate level by calling into question the purpose of research if it does not serve the community being studied.

Finally, our Essential Studies program has brought a discussion of ecological, environmental, social, and cultural sustainability into our science, math, and English classes as well as into our *Freshman Seminar* foundation course. In 2012, and for the first time, they will offer a course on Indigenous strategies to address global environmental issues. This course arises from the highly successful conference organized this past year by the student sustainability leaders, "Climate Justice and Indigenous Solutions."

National and international Native leaders on these issues came to our campus to engage our faculty, staff, students, and the wider community to address the future of life. The question of how we will live together as nations of people in relationship to the water, soil, air, plants, and animals of earth and sea is perhaps the most pressing cultural question of our time. Who better to make a truly significant contribution to this global discussion than those Indigenous peoples of the world who remain committed to healthy and sustainable practices that honor "all my relations."

This discussion of culture is never-ending and will remain a vital part of our campus conversation. I would like to end this part of the discussion with a vision you shared that we have yet to realize:

> Imagine if you will, how rewarding it will be when Indians and others begin to tap their rich and mystical world for contributions to the fields of literature, theater, music, and dance. Conceive, also, the flow of 21st and 22nd century philosophy when enriched by the ecological and spiritual beliefs of Native Americans, a philosophy that is bound to come into its own as the world finds itself faced with the need to know that which Indian religious

leaders have preached for centuries. Dream, if you will, about the many contributions that could be made about an environment enhanced by a form of architecture developed by indigenous artists who have not yet forgotten what real plasticity of form is, because of their particular sense and feel for nature.[6]

Youth, Identity and Self-Actualization

At the Institute, emphasis is given to Indian traditions as a basis for creative expressions in the fine arts, including sculpture, painting, the written arts, the performing arts such as drama, music and dance. The approach used, stressing cultural roots as a basis for individual creativity, is a unique development on the world scene and in our national dedication to the enhancement of minority contributions. As a result of this approach, students find new directions and gain self-confidence.[7]

Most young Indian people now share similar educational experiences with the typical teenager of today. They no longer wear the tribal costume, and they speak the common language. They, also, are victims of televisions and followers of the latest fad. They have all the problems common to the youth of the country, and in addition, the special problem of making satisfactory psychological reconciliations with the mores of two cultures.[8]

For the person who stems from a special cultural ethos the latter proviso can only be met if he is encouraged to feel deeply about himself for what he is and have access to the special vehicles that will allow him to express those feelings. Practically speaking, for the Indian students at the Institute these vehicles are: classes in cultural studies, traditional techniques, Indian history, and an opportunity to mingle with peers in an atmosphere of honor for Indian people and Indianism in general.[9]

This area represents some departures from your original vision and some similarities. In the beginning IAIA exclusively served Native American high school and post-graduate students. They were youth engaged in the first stumbling stages of becoming adults and were between the ages of fourteen and twenty-three. Today, our average student is twenty-seven years old. Many are parents. Some are grandparents.

Many of them know *who* they are as Indian people in a modern world. They come to IAIA to accumulate new skills, refine their talents, learn more, and return to the world where they have already worked, better able to realize and manifest their dreams and ambitions.

Age is not the only factor that differentiates today's Institute from the early years. Today IAIA is open to all students. Students, staff, and faculty of all races, ethnicities, and nationalities are part of IAIA, but this does not dilute the mission, "To empower creativity and leadership in Native arts and cultures through higher education, lifelong learning and outreach." IAIA welcomes a diverse community to serve this clearly focused mission.

This diversity enhances meaningful dialogue about contemporary society. It also acknowledges the rich hybridity of contemporary identity. For example, we have students, faculty, and alumni who identify as Mandan-Hidatsa-Norwegian; or Mestizo; or Metis; or Seneca-German-Irish; or Choctaw-African American; or Navajo-Filipino; or Apache-Appalachian or Kiowa-Hopi-Mexican; or Native Hawaiian-Chinese-Japanese; or Comanche-Maori and the list goes on. An individual may hold such a diversity of Native ancestry (someone may be Chippewa-Blackfeet-Otoe-Missouria-Osage-Pawnee) that they are not recognized as tribal members in any single tribe due to the blood quantum requirements of each individual tribe. In fact, the critique of the system of identity ranking and tribal identification cards based on blood quantum is quite lively. One student created a vivid 3-D piece in metal that was a mock blood quantum-measuring tool for tribal police to use.

So what is our role amidst this lively debate on identity? We acknowledge it. We encourage our students to recognize the complex political, social, and economic factors shaping both the history of identity and the contemporary identity debate. We want them to be empowered to be fully themselves; to honor the unique stories, courage, and convictions of their ancestors. We want them to feel as well as think their way through the sometimes-tangled web of relations. Our students and faculty may write their stories, sing them, paint them, film them, sculpt them, exhibit them, and perform them. Through art, they are visibly removing the stigma of silence, moving from the background, and placing identity on center stage.

The students of today are two-and-a-half generations removed from the first students of IAIA. Yet some of those first students are now teaching now at IAIA. Their story and IAIA's story of identity and self-actualization is ever-evolving. Our task is to recognize and support their efforts without dogma or judgment so that the fullness of these experiences can be translated from pain or joy into art.

Central to campus culture is the celebration and recognition of the enduring power of Native art and culture. We host an annual pow-wow. We begin administrative meetings as well as the academic year with prayer. A sweat lodge is used regularly on campus for spiritual and physical purification. Our student body today is eighty-three percent Native, our faculty is fifty-seven percent Native; staff and administration is fifty percent Native. Over thirty percent of the full-time faculty is IAIA alumni. This remarkable continuity helps impart the deeper meaning of this educational experiment.

Currently IAIA offers five majors, two certificate programs, and a range of college courses developed to meet the needs of students in particular tracks of study. A common core of thirty general education credits is required for all entering freshman. Of these courses, only one explicitly addresses Native identity; *Introduction to Indigenous Studies* offers a series of exercises designed for each student to explore the cultural norms of his or her Native community.

The diversity of cultural backgrounds creates an interesting dialogue in the course. Some students are active participants in their tribal communities, having participated in their ceremonies and reared by relatives close to the culture. Some are the children or the grandchildren of American Indian Movement (AIM) activists and Native arts luminaries, the second or third generation of a cultural resurgence following 1960s civil rights movement. Others have never lived near their tribal communities or seen their ceremonies, and may be third or fourth generation Native people to be raised in urban centers such as Los Angeles, Oakland, Cleveland, Chicago, or Seattle. This is the real meaning of twenty-first century Indian diversity, and these are the real stories of our students today. It is best not to make assumptions about their experiences but instead give them the tools they need to speak for themselves.

The next generation of students must work diligently to address imbalances in educational, social, and economic access. We need our students to know *whom* they are, to be excellent communicators and advocates, to be prepared to engage meaningfully as artists and cultural leaders empowered to make radical change and honor the past.

Economy

> ... the school fully realizes the importance of the urgency towards proficiency in the arts and crafts, and finding a sound place for the artist in the economic world. It will offer significant learning opportunities, and experience, in

marketing, production techniques, cost accounting, finance, promotion and sales practice.[10]

IAIA offers courses that address some of the issues discussed in your statement above. The college offers the *Portfolio* course and *The Business of Art* to Studio Arts majors while New Media Arts offers *Career Focus & Specialization* and *The Business of Movies* to support student career development. The National Association of Schools of Art & Design (NASAD) accredits our BFA degrees in those areas and our programs meet rigorous standards for professional arts schools. The purpose of the BFA degree as accredited by NASAD is to prepare students for careers in the art and designs fields. Both programs offer internships for students to get hands-on experience in professional settings.

However, it seems this still was not enough for our students. They asked for additional preparation in marketing and promotion, finance and accounting, and for an understanding of entrepreneurship so they could begin their own home-based, family-based, or community-based arts businesses. In Santa Fe, Native people run only one or two of the numerous galleries and there are very few Native-owned and operated businesses in the city. We realized we needed to do more.

With funds from the Lilly Foundation secured by the American Indian College Fund for the Woksape Onate (Wisdom of the People) initiative, IAIA successfully garnered financial support to begin a Certificate in Entrepreneurship. This fifteen credit, five-course program is designed for any student at IAIA to add to their major field of study or students may choose to focus solely on the certificate program.

The initial results have been tremendous. Students begin with an introductory course, *Money, Wealth & Personal Finance*, to explore their own relationship with money, their feelings about it and learn how money works in the economy. They move on to take four other core courses: *Financial Accounting, Marketing*, and *Small Business Development*, and complete the program with a capstone course in *Entrepreneurship* in which they create a formal business plan that they can use to launch their own business.

Our four-year start up and pilot program concluded June of 2012. We have absorbed this important initiative into the operating budget because we are committed to its continued success. You would be pleased to know the final report for the pilot project concluded with this quote from you:

... students simply have to learn that artists have to earn their own way, and that there are no special dispensations right now in being an "Indian artist" – certain real advantages, but no dispensations. How does the new institute plan to deal with this problem? What emphasis will be put [on] entrepreneurship, and how is it incorporated in the students' outlook?

Remember, a lot of people have the idea that to become a real artist student artists should not be encouraged to sell their works, they become commercial too early and art development stops. I personally think that good artists can be guided around this pitfall. Incidentally, Native American artists have a leg up on the Art market – but strictly on a regional basis. It will take some changes, to crack the big established market, but its worth the go.[11]

The Power of Material Culture & Indigenous Intellectual Traditions

A unique educational curriculum needs to be developed at the higher education level expressly to meet the specific needs of Indian students, covering professional development in the arts, supported by in-depth exposure to the Humanities and Science as related to the contemporary educational needs of Indians. The Institute's goal is to become the national center of an institutional move toward the collection and collation of hard and soft cultural material to levels that presently do not exist to the benefit of Indian students or others who seek a better understanding of Indian culture. The advent of such a cultural repository and research center would overcome the deplorable historical lack of culturally relevant material that has hampered the healthy self-knowledge of Indian youth for generations.[12]

They will be exposed to the arts of the world, to give them a better appreciation of the artistic values of their own cultural contributions by comparison and contrast. They will gain an awareness of the value and the place of art as an important factor in the fundamental needs of mankind. They will sense the need for contributing to the beauty of environment. They will learn to live up to the best in themselves in their roles as creative artists, evolving personal criteria of judgment for their conduct in the realm of the art world.[13]

In the past two years the faculty and I revisited and revised the *Academic Program Vision Statement*, the *Values of the Academic Program*, and the *IAIA Core Competencies* we expect every student in all five of our major academic programs to demonstrate.

I think you would concur that these program directives are central to our educational model. Here they are, excerpted from the 2011–2012 college catalog:

Vision Statement of the Academic Program at IAIA

Providing a strong educational foundation for future leaders who will be prepared to utilize the power of art and culture to enrich communities.

Values of the Academic Program

Creative expression
Respect for diverse cultures
Ethical behavior
Effective communication
Excellence in creating and maintaining a positive environment for teaching and learning
Honoring the power of place as a foundation for cultural and creative strength

IAIA Core Competencies

Students will develop the art of critical thinking
Students will explore the power of place as a foundation of cultural and creative strengths
Students will communicate effectively
Students will engage effectively in communities
Students will produce original work that demonstrates learned skills and practices
Students will articulate the value of diverse cultural perspectives
Students will develop an understanding of ethical practices.[14]

We value a holistic approach to education that incorporates intellectual, physical, emotional, and spiritual health. We now support a fitness & wellness program and a diabetes prevention program on campus and require courses that encourage a healthy lifestyle. We have a full-time counselor and numerous student success programs to provide emotional and spiritual support. We are a small campus community, and we care about each other.

We value exposure to the art world and see travel as an important opportunity for experiential learning. Although IAIA does not have a formal education abroad program, IAIA has taken advantage of opportunities to expose our students to the larger world of art. In 2005 a group of students attended the World Indigenous Peoples Conference on Education (WIPCE) and the World Indigenous Nations Higher Education Consortium (WINHEC) in New Zealand. In 2010 we sent students to Turkey to live and work at Samsun University to create a site-specific work concerning the drilling of oil in the Black Sea.

In 2011 a group of students studied art at the Venice Biennale. During the summer of 2012 we sent a student with the museum director and the IAIA president to the Sydney Biennale, a large exhibition of contemporary visual art curated by one of our alumni, Gerald McMaster, PhD. The students' Culture Club raised money for student trips to New York, Hawaii, and Los Angeles to visit museums, galleries, and cultural organizations. President Robert Martin recently returned from a trip to Mexico with an agreement with the Indigenous universities of Mexico for student and faculty exchanges. With increased funding, we could stand to do more in the area of international education.

You set in motion the collection of contemporary Native Art for future study. The permanent collection of the Museum of Contemporary Native Art now contains over 7,000 art objects. Housed in a visible, state-of-the-art, and climate-controlled facility on our campus, it can be a vital resource for students, faculty, and outside scholars.

As for scholarship, we successfully secured funds to create a high-end art book featuring sixty contemporary Native artists edited by one of our alumna, Nancy Marie Mithlo, PhD. Fifteen Native art curators/scholars compiled sixty essays, each covering a different artist, and the new book entitled Manifestations: New Native Art Criticism in a required text for Issues in Contemporary Native Art, an upper level course for Studio Art majors. Manifestations demonstrate we can now produce the Native American art textbooks our curriculum demands and continue to help shape dialogue in the field. Our ambition is to redefine the conversation concerning Native art; we want to impact not only our communities but also affect mainstream universities and art organizations. This new scholarship puts us in a favorable position to maximize our impact.

However, it is not only in the visual arts that we have this ambition. Our Creative Writing program has significantly impacted contemporary Native American literature and is the incubator—the home turf—of the majority of new and emerging

Native poets and writers. This literary movement needs to be documented and perhaps one of our faculty or graduates will write the story of the Native American literature movement. When they do, they will note decades of service that poet and IAIA Faculty Emeritus Arthur Sze and his colleagues gave to shape this program.

The growth of tribally controlled museums and cultural centers across the continent owes much of its success to the IAIA Museum Studies program. Faculty Emeritus Charles Dailey's impact on Indian country in this regard is immeasurable. IAIA seeded the field by training and graduating dozens of future tribal cultural officers, repatriation officers, tribal museum staff, cultural center directors, collections managers, exhibit designers, and curators. Our museum's chief curator is an IAIA alumnus, as are the two full-time faculty in the Museum Studies program. We have truly made a difference in this area.

Our most recently developed four-year academic program is a BA in Indigenous Liberal Studies (ILS). Graduates of this program have moved on to either graduate school or tribal leadership roles. In May 2012 a formal campus gathering of recent ILS alumni sparked a fascinating discussion on the need to identify and develop Native intellectual scholarly traditions. Alumni proposed the development of *Vizenorians* who further develop the intellectual work of Gerald Vizenor, or *Delorians* who commit themselves to the development of ideas initially laid out by Vine Deloria, Jr. We could have *Newians* who review your writing and speeches, Lloyd, and engage them as texts for an important intellectual tradition in culturally centered arts education. This discussion is a mark of our maturity. It is a coming of age for Native American cultural development; our thirty-year-olds are entering graduate schools with a thirst to develop ideas, theories, and possibilities they were exposed to at IAIA.

We have been besieged in recent years by requests from Native American doctoral students who want to come and study IAIA as the subject of their research and we arranged an Institutional Research Board (IRB) to formally review and approve these requests. We want to be studied. We want to be documented. We want to support the intellectual development of new Native scholars studying Native institutions. We also want to have our needs met in this process. I think these developments would fascinate you.

IAIA has contributed to the development of a contemporary Native aesthetic. It is the birthplace of contemporary Native art and all of this is part of your legacy. But we are not done. We have unmet ambitions. We want to be the center for the next generation of Native artists utilizing digital media. We want to be a center for new and emerging filmmakers. We would like to have a performing arts center and bring back dance, music, and theater to our curriculum. We are working on the conceptual design of a Native-centered arts entrepreneurship center. We have our dreams.

As you can see, what you started is not yet finished, but it is still going strong. A friend of mine defines education as 'the ability to set in motion.' Lloyd, you were a brilliant educator; look what you set in motion! It has been truly delightful to sit and chat with you as Nokomis Tibik Giizis (Grandmother Moon) rises in the east shedding her coppery light on the purple shadows of the Sangre de Cristo Mountains. I know that any number of topics we have briefly touched on here could be the subject of a future Indigenous scholar's doctoral dissertation! I hope that this quick overview sparked your interest. Keep an eye on us; you still inspire us to do better.

There is much more to say and I know there are probably many important things we have forgotten. Thank you for everything you did out of your profound and abiding love for future generations of Native artists. I hope I have been able to share a little of what we are doing today, building upon your legacy. Be proud. You will not be forgotten.

With my deepest respect,
Ann

2

Photo Essay: IAIA at the Santa Fe Indian School

The Bureau of Indian Affairs assigned IAIA to the Santa Fe Indian School (SFIS) Campus on Cerrillos Road in early 1961, and after construction of new facilities, IAIA opened in October of 1962. The beautiful, serene setting inspired composer Louis Ballard to write the IAIA Alma mater, "Home in Santa Fe":

Oh, the Cottonwood trees are swaying
All a-round us here to-day.
And all our thoughts are straying
To our Home in Santa Fe
I-A-I-A, we sing to you,
The school where dreams come true.
Within these halls our hearts will stay,
Though we are far, far a-way
　　　　　　　　　　　—Louis Ballard, 1962

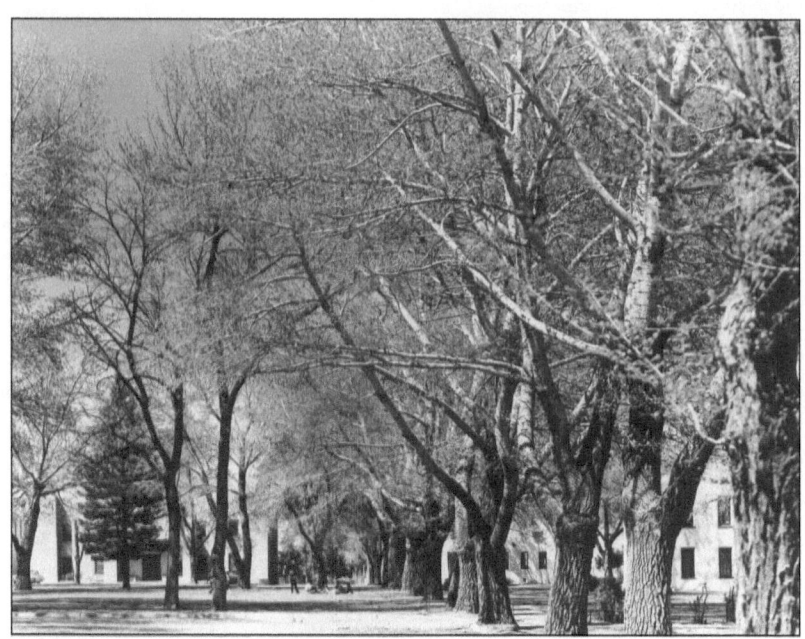

Tree lined sidewalks of the IAIA campus, c. 1968. Once covered with cottonwood trees, today the campus is virtually devoid of any foliage. Photograph by Kay V. Wiest. (Courtesy of IAIA Archives, Santa Fe, New Mexico) (rg03box9f04i06)

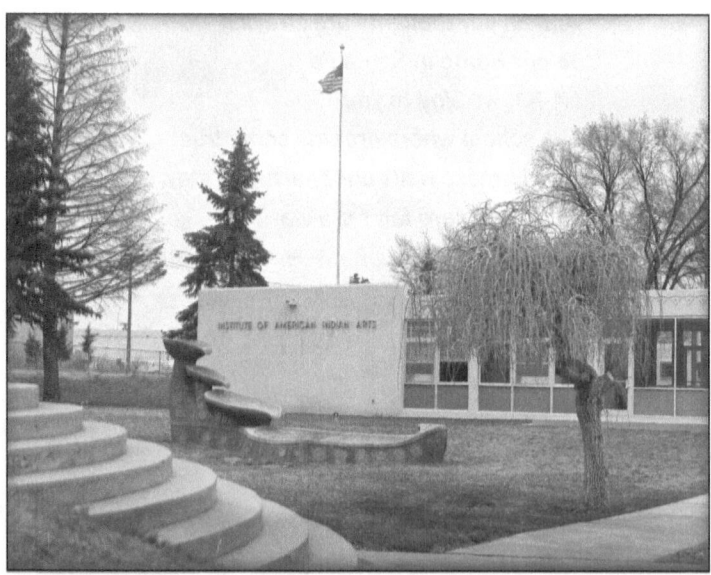

IAIA administration building, c. 1964. The building and ornate fountain were demolished by the SFIS in 2012. Photograph by Kay V. Wiest. (Courtesy of IAIA Archives, Santa Fe, New Mexico) (MS010.002.01)

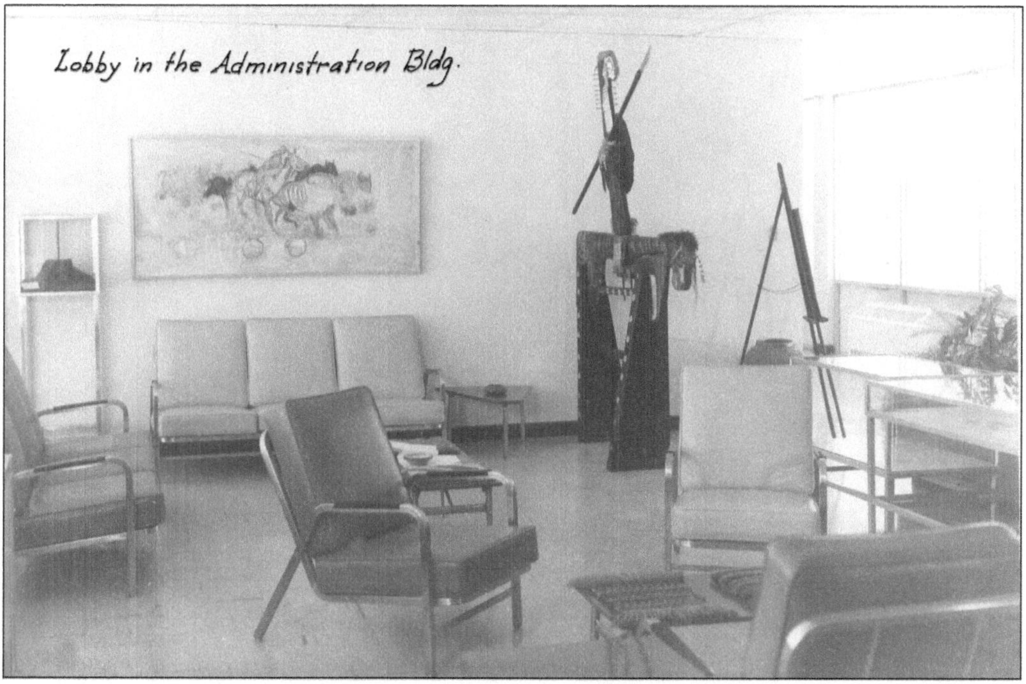

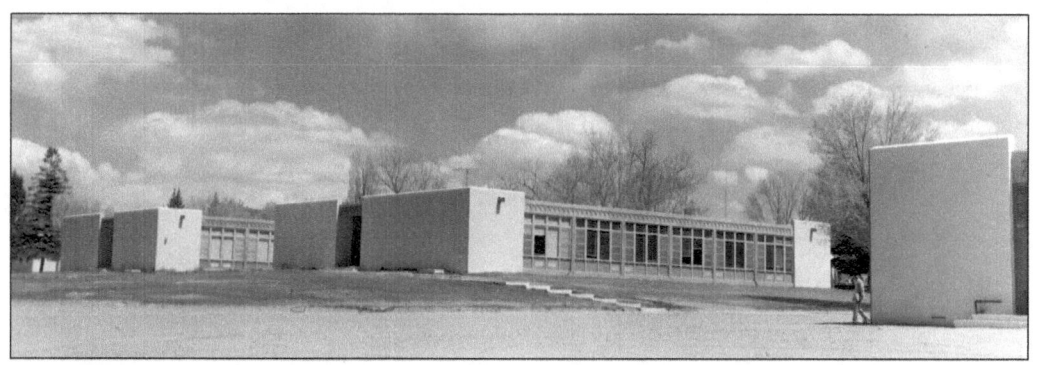

Lobby in the Administration Bldg.

Lobby of the IAIA administration building, c. 1964. Photograph by Kay V. Wiest. (Courtesy of IAIA Archives, Santa Fe, New Mexico) (rg03box24f01i03)

Exterior of the academic buildings, c. 1966. The majority of academic and art courses were held in these buildings. Studios were located on another section of campus. Photograph by Kay V. Wiest. (Courtesy of IAIA Archives, Santa Fe, New Mexico) (rg03box24f02i01)

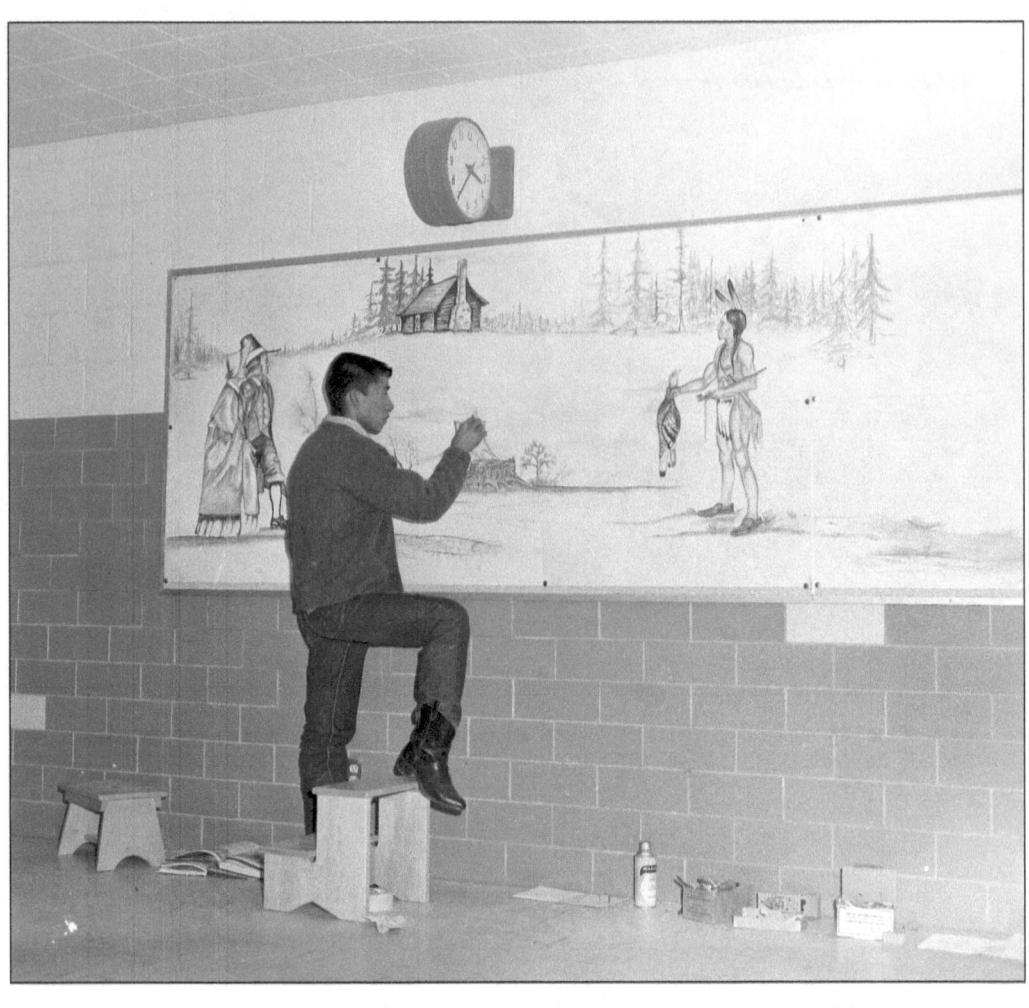

IAIA student working on a Thanksgiving Day mural in a hallway of the academic building, c. 1966. Photograph by Kay V. Wiest. (Courtesy of IAIA Archives, Santa Fe, New Mexico) (MS10.003.042)

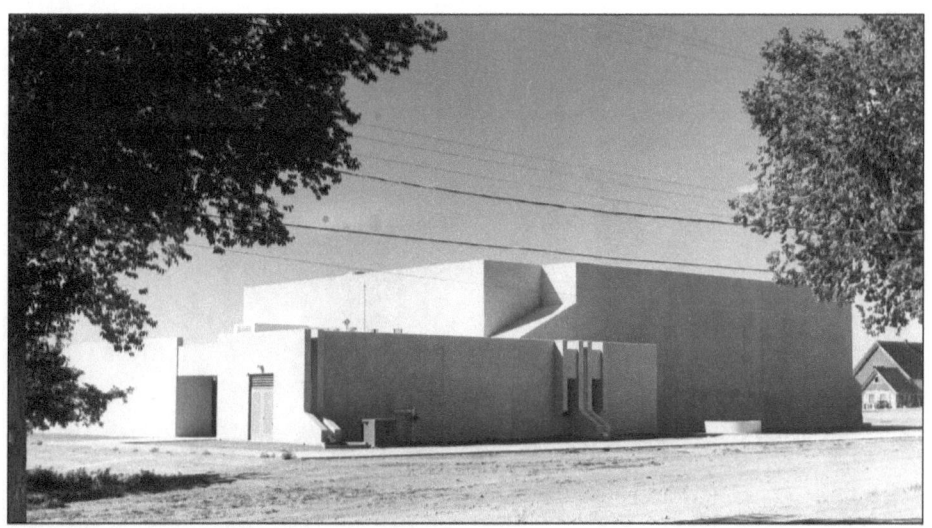

Gymnasium, c. 1965. School dances and socials were held here as well as events for the IAIA boy's and girl's basketball teams and pow-wows. Photograph by Kay V. Wiest. (Courtesy of IAIA Archives, Santa Fe, New Mexico) (rg03box24f04i01)

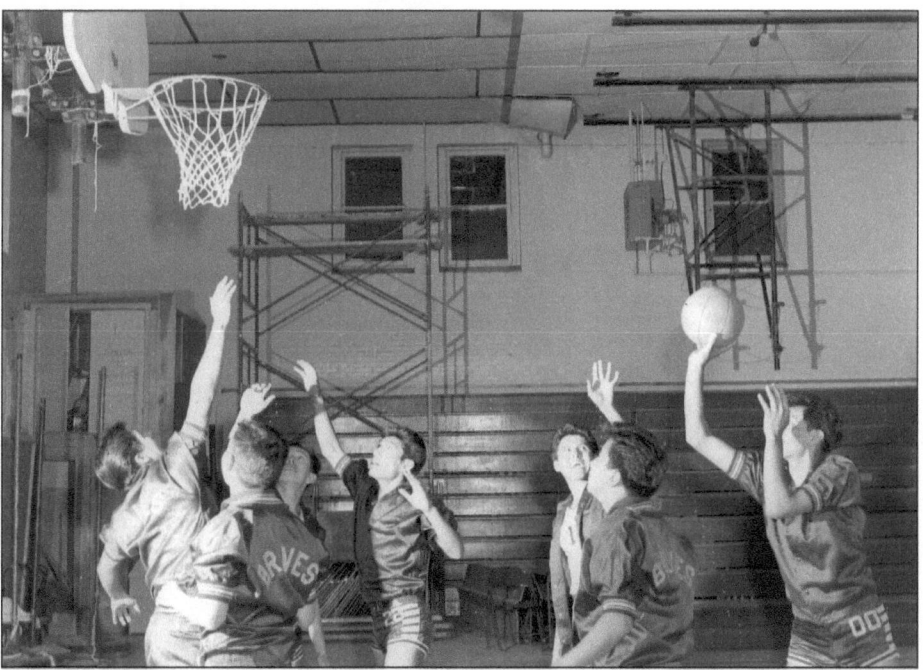

The IAIA "Braves" basketball squad warming up for a game, c. 1966. Photograph by Kay V. Wiest. (Courtesy of IAIA Archives, Santa Fe, New Mexico) (rg03box10f01i05)

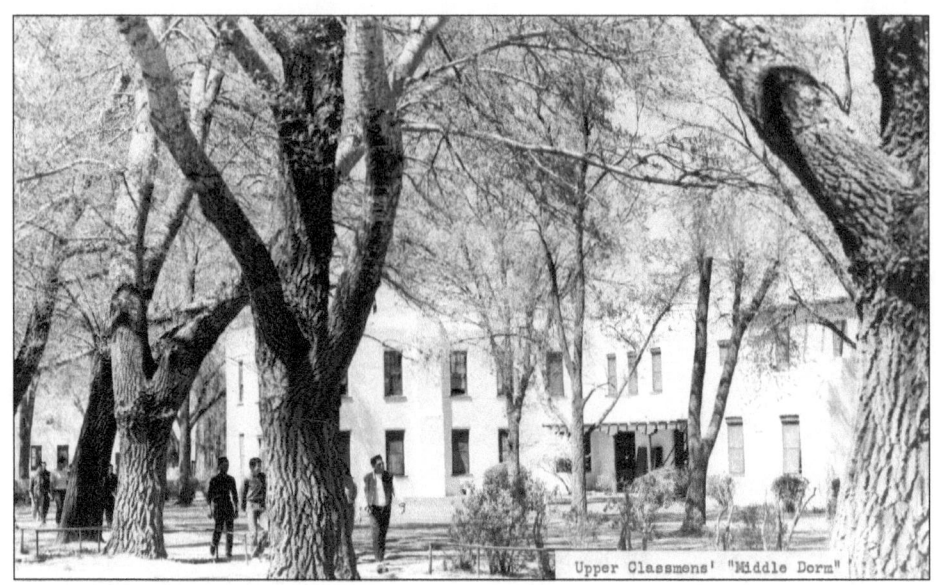

Middle dorm, c. 1968. The middle dorm was the home of most of the junior-college aged men on campus. Photograph by Kay V. Wiest. (Courtesy of IAIA Archives, Santa Fe, New Mexico) (rg03box24f08i01)

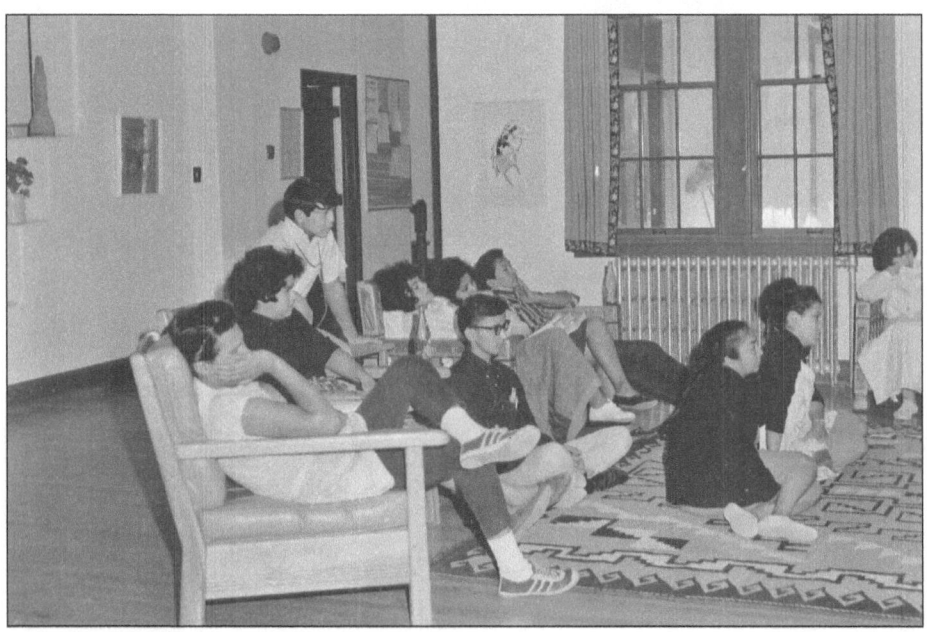

Students lounging around the middle dorm living room, c. 1965. Photograph by Kay V. Wiest. (Courtesy of IAIA Archives, Santa Fe, New Mexico) (ms10.015.004.07)

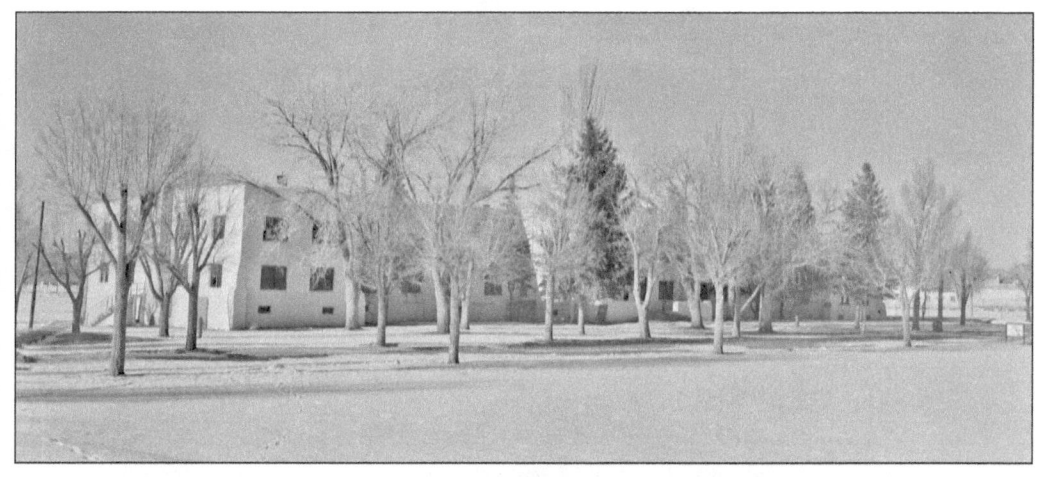

Boy's north dorm, 1964. The north dorm was home to the high-school aged male students. Photograph by Kay V. Wiest. (Courtesy of IAIA Archives, Santa Fe, New Mexico) (ms010.034.021)

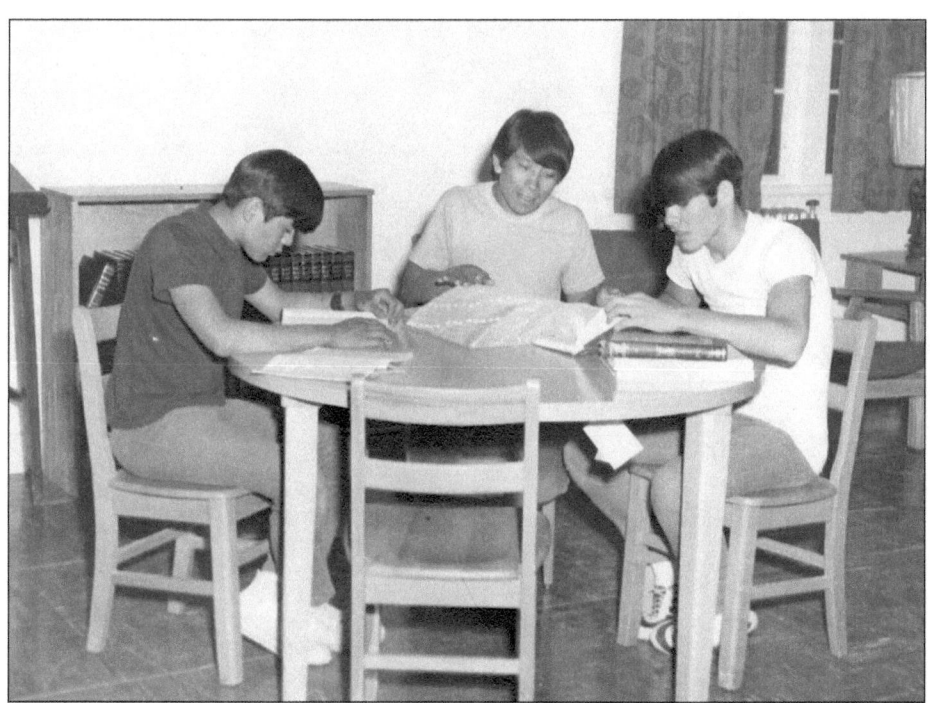

Left to right, Virgil Marchand, Alfonso Sakeva, and Martin Martinez studying in the boys north dorm, c. 1965. Photograph by Adrian Pushetonequa, (Courtesy of IAIA Archives, Santa Fe, New Mexico) (rg03box24f08i03)

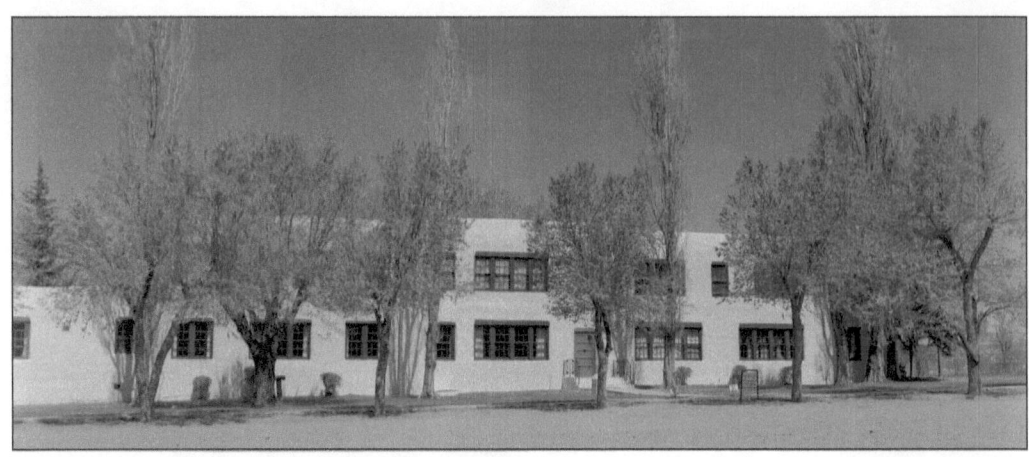

Girl's south dorm and family housing, 28 April, 1968. The south dorm was home to the junior college aged women at IAIA. Photograph by Ruth Charles. (Courtesy of IAIA Archives, Santa Fe, New Mexico) (ms10.034.017.03)

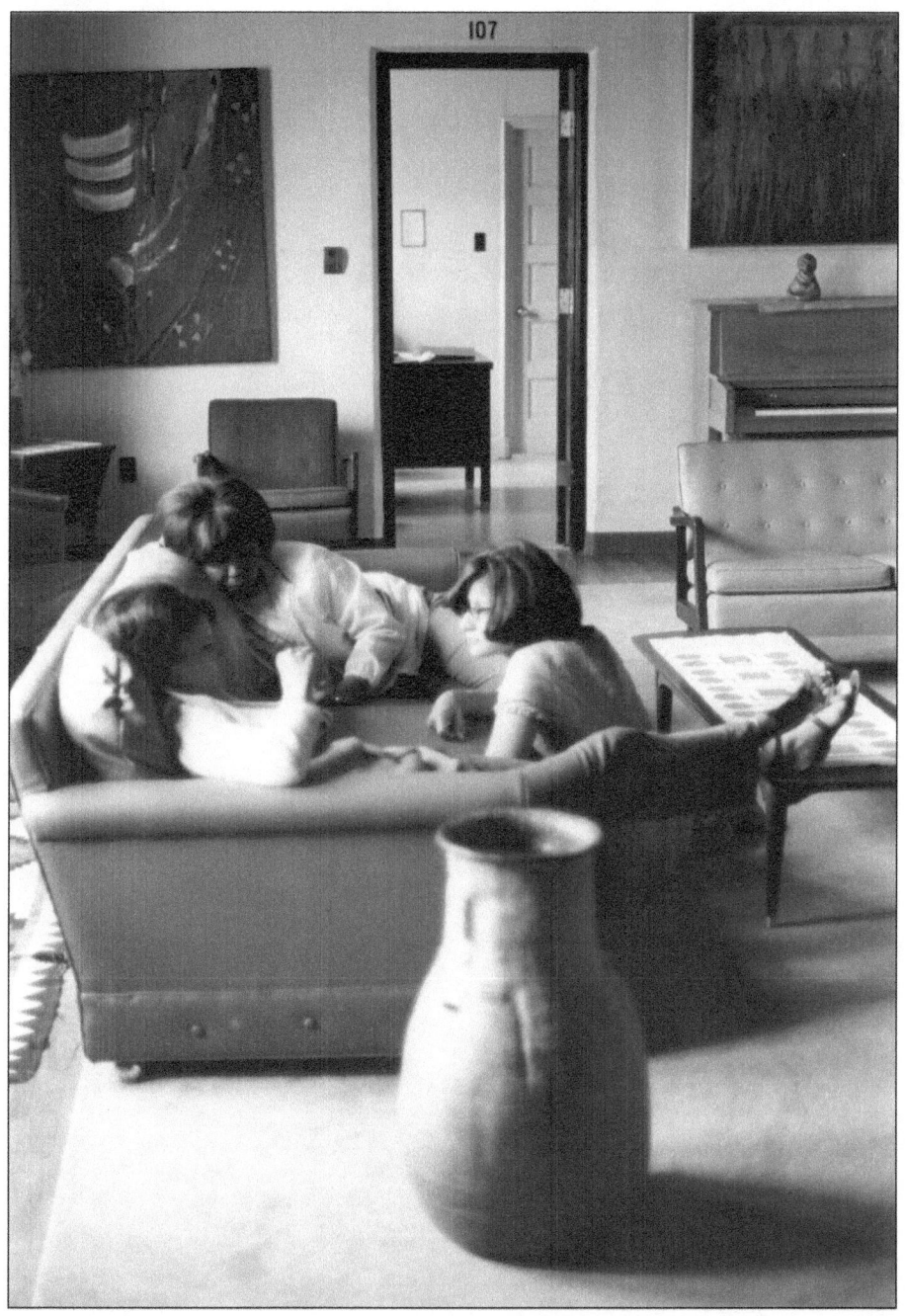

Female students lounging in the girl's south dorm. Photograph by Kay V. Wiest. (Courtesy of IAIA Archives, Santa Fe, New Mexico) (rg03box24f08i04)

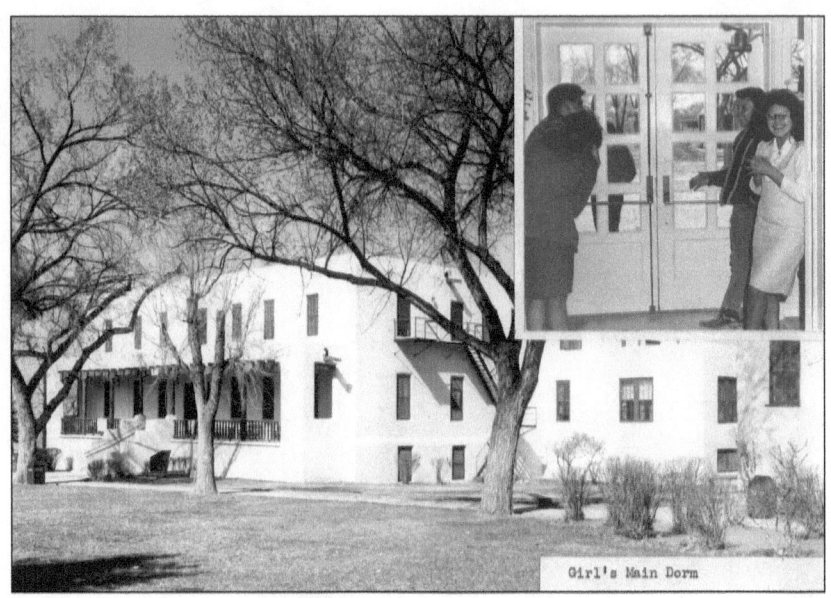

Girl's main dorm, c. 1968. This dorm was home to the high-school aged girls on campus. Photograph by Kay V. Wiest. (Courtesy of IAIA Archives, Santa Fe, New Mexico) (rg03box24f08i02)

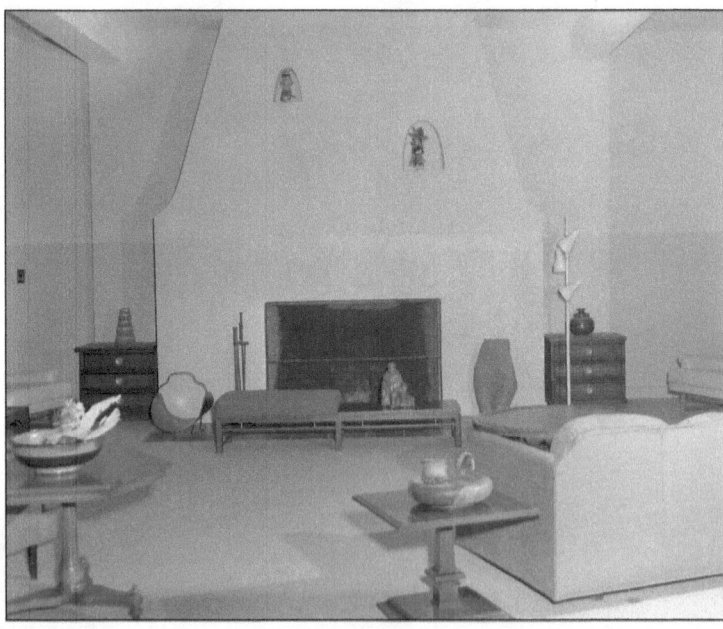

Living room of girl's main dorm, c. 1966. Photograph by Kay V. Wiest. (Courtesy of IAIA Archives, Santa Fe, New Mexico) (ms10.015.001.03)

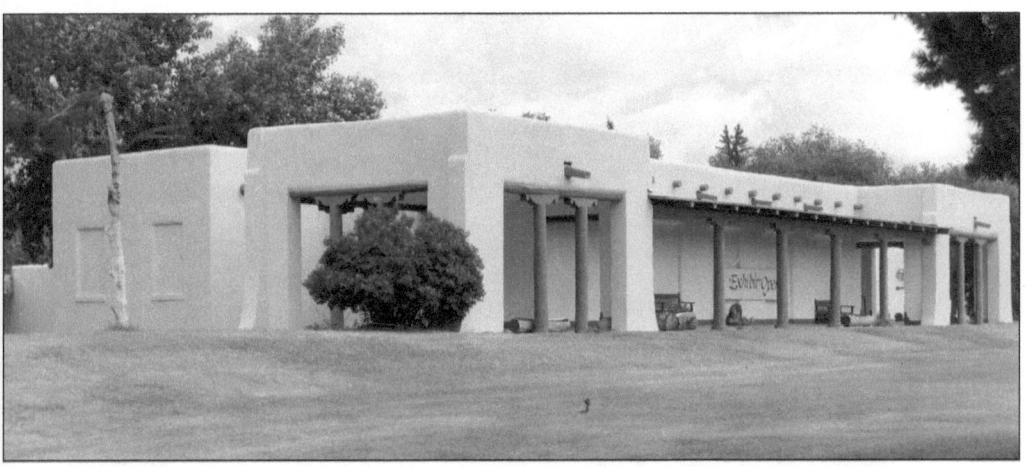

The IAIA Museum Gallery, c. 1967. Later known as the IAIA Museum, the facility was used to exhibit not only student work but also traveling exhibits. This building was used by IAIA until 1992. Photograph by Kay V. Wiest. (Courtesy of IAIA Archives, Santa Fe, New Mexico) (rg03box24f12i01)

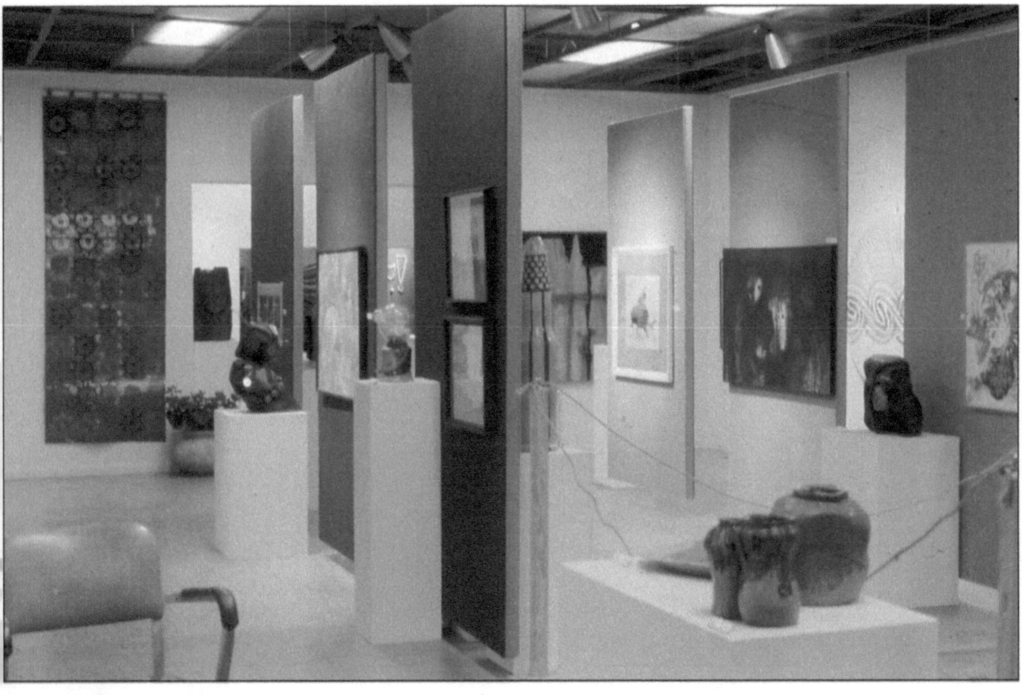

Interior of the IAIA Museum, 1972. (Courtesy of IAIA Archives, Santa Fe, New Mexico) (art_gallery_interior)

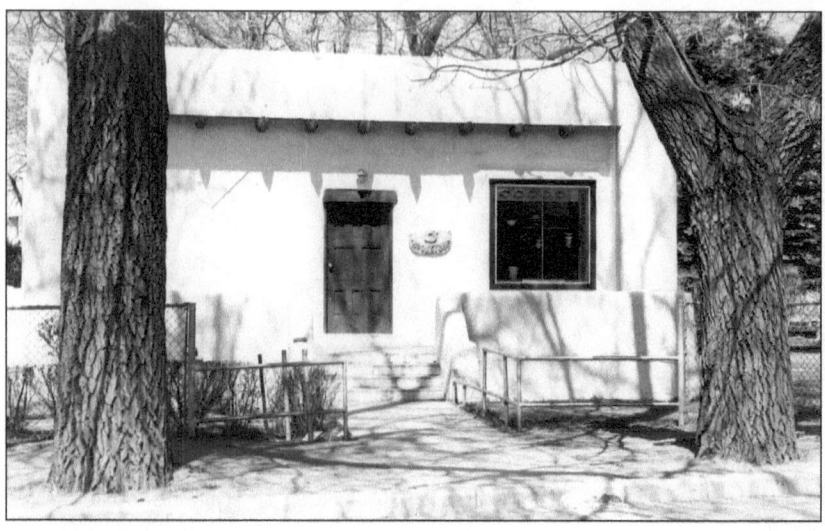

Hookstone Student Sales Center, c. 1967. Hookstone was managed by IAIA students and facilitated the sale of their artwork. (Courtesy of IAIA Archives, Santa Fe, New Mexico) (rg03box24f11i02)

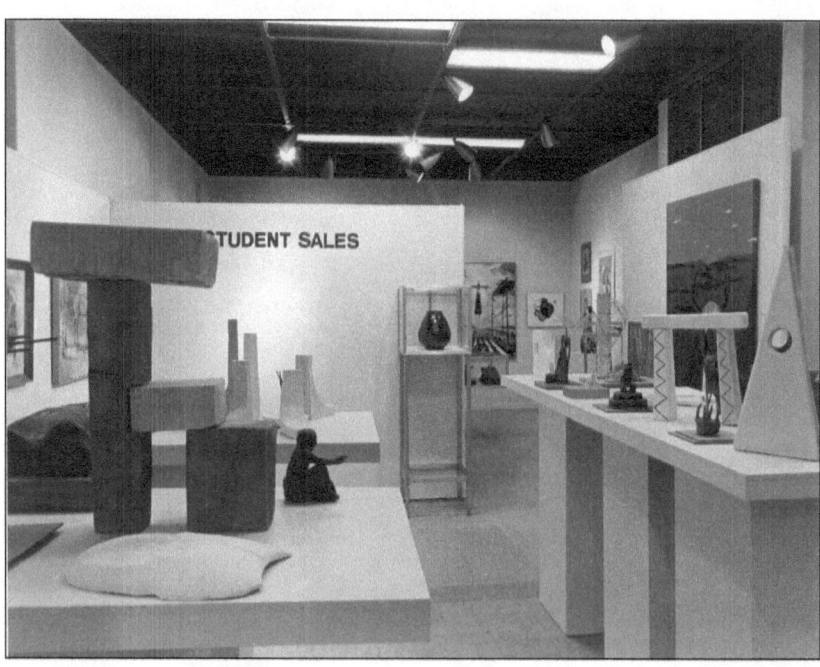

Interior of Hookstone Student Sales Center, c. 1970. (Courtesy of IAIA Archives, Santa Fe, New Mexico) (rg03box18f27i01)

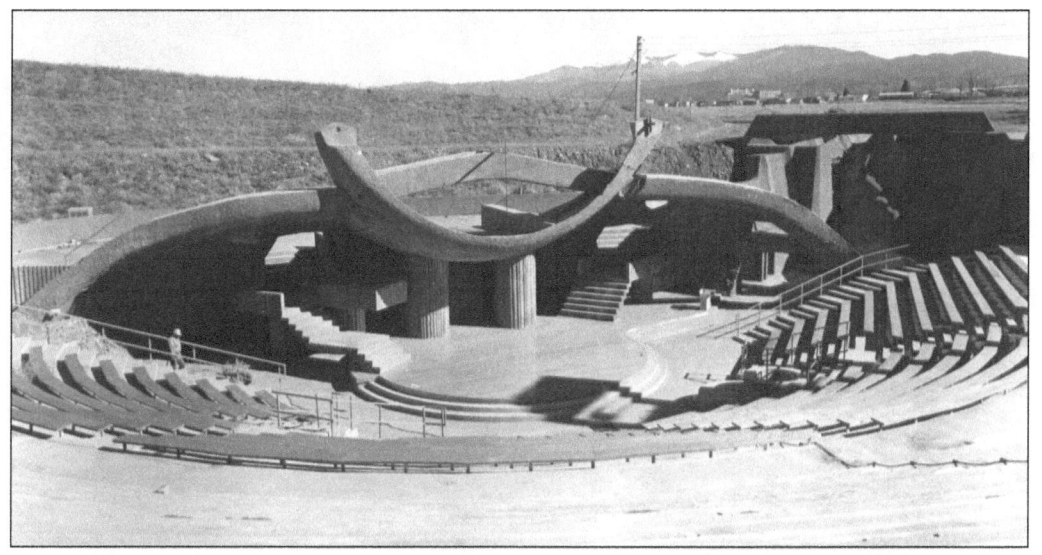

Construction of the Outdoor Bowl Theatre, c. 1970. Later named after the architect of the theatre, Paolo Soleri, the outdoor bowl theatre design was commissioned by IAIA in 1965 and opened in 1971. The Soleri Theatre became a premier music venue in the Southwest until it was closed by the Indian School in 2010. Photograph by Kay V. Wiest. (Courtesy of IAIA Archives, Santa Fe, New Mexico) (rg03box24f03i04)

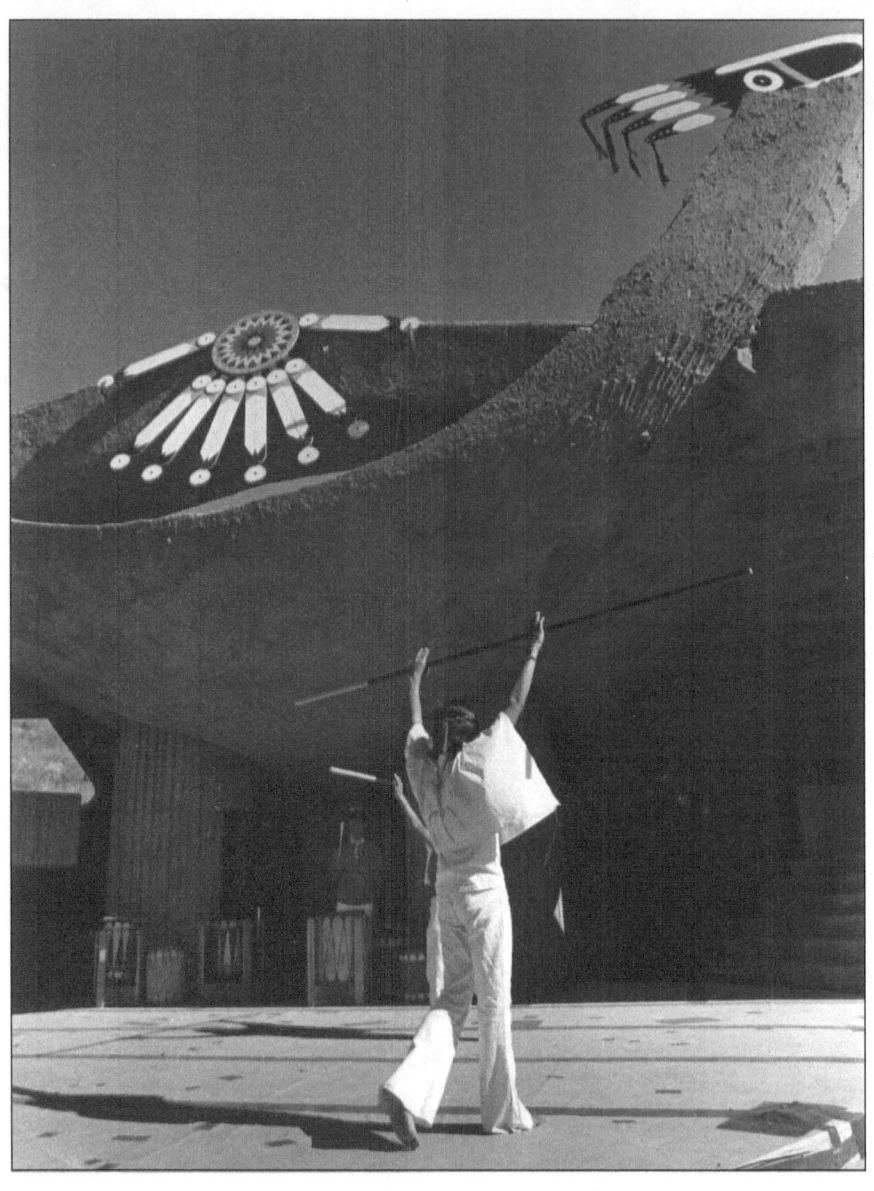

Student performance in the Paolo Soleri Theatre, c. 1975. (Courtesy of IAIA Archives, Santa Fe, New Mexico) (rg03box19f03i20)

3

Institute of American Indian Arts 1962–1972
Where It All Began

by

Alfred Young Man, PhD

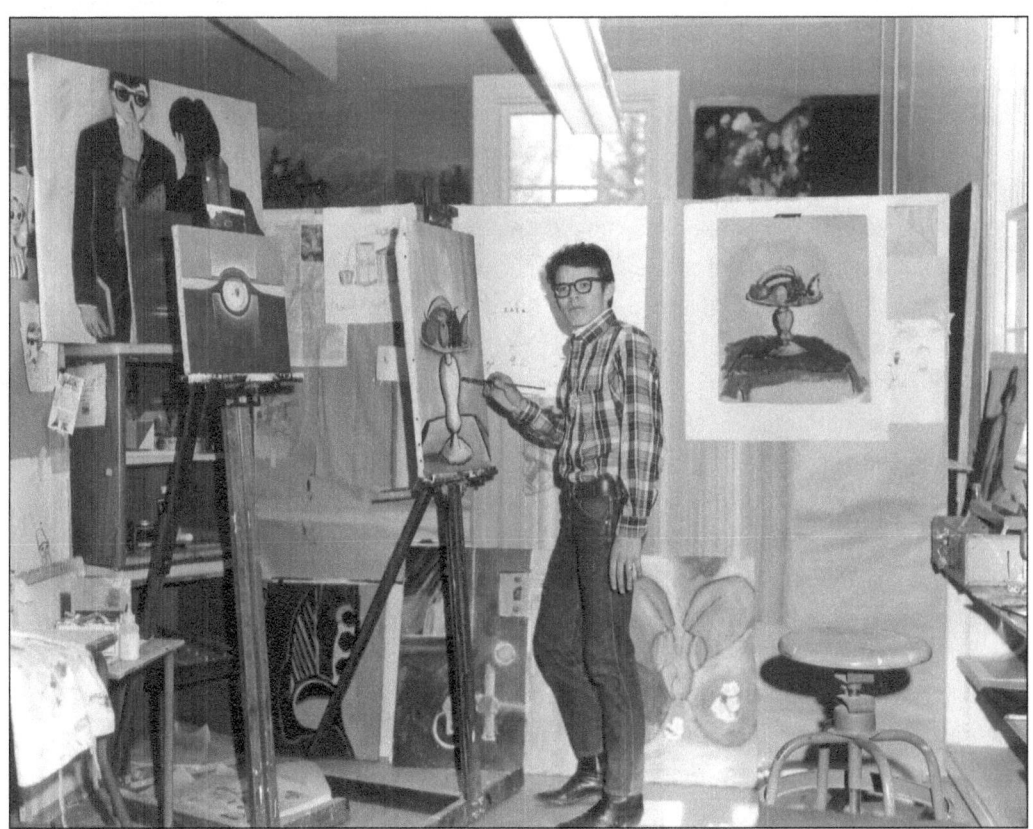

Alfred Young Man, 1968. From 1963 to 1968, Young Man was a blossoming painting student at the Institute of American Indian Arts. Photograph by Kay V. Wiest. (Courtesy of IAIA Archives, Santa Fe, New Mexico) (rg03box04f66i01)

L ike many of my generation who came to the Institute of American Indian Arts (IAIA) in the early 1960s, I was born and raised in another era on the Blackfeet Indian Reservation in Montana on the eastern foothills of the Rocky Mountains. It might have been in another century; I grew up at a time when an individual could still ride a horse across the width and breadth of the reservation and seldom encounter a barbed wire fence. The pristine earth ground had not yet been turned by a plow or plundered by the hooves of sheep and cattle. Our people had suffered through a century of injustices: the taking of our lands and resources, forbidding Sun Dances and other religious practices, and denying us the right to speak our languages. We must also include the collecting of Native cultural patrimony, called "art objects," as a part of the pattern of injustice. Collected by trade or theft, these millions of art objects and artifacts were taken from our communities and warehoused at such places as the Heye Foundation in New York City, in the storage vaults of the vast Smithsonian Institution on the outskirts of Washington, D.C., and in hundreds of museums, vaults, and art centers around the world.

The students at IAIA had come from everywhere across North America and we shared the fact that by the time of our arrival in the early 1960s at IAIA the injustices our people suffered were not ceasing. It was against this politically charged historical and cultural environment of the early 1960s that the improbable idea of establishing a school for artists of American Indian heritage began. Lloyd "Kiva" New has been credited as the philosophical founder of IAIA through a curriculum developed though an alliance with the Rockefeller Foundation and born out of a workshop in Arizona.[1] IAIA developed into a unique experiment to develop young Native artists and its success was based in how their art became intellectual, historical, and political fact; the truth of a fundamental loosely defined idea of a American Indian fine art movement and aesthetic. As a mark of New's vision and IAIA's early success, over eighty-seven Indian languages and nations were represented at the height of the 1960s, a United Nations of Indians, all united by one idea, the *Indian art movement.*

It was the belief that by exposing students to a wide range of art and academic subjects, they would be enabled to benefit from and to contribute to both.[2] Through such opportunity many Indian students could then make significant cultural contributions to the world: in other words, empowerment.[3] To that end IAIA was established as a school with a unique curriculum and educational program at a time in which American Indian culture was seen to have little value. As a Bureau of Indian Affairs (BIA) school, IAIA was almost antithetical to the educational philosophy of the BIA.

The school's faculty showcased some of the most talented, gifted, and dedicated contemporary and traditional Native art, drama, and music instructors anywhere. This included Chiricahua Apache sculptor/painter Allan Houser, Hopi jeweler Charles Loloma, Hopi ceramicist Otellie Loloma, Blackfeet painter Neil Parsons, Comanche traditional techniques instructor Josephine Wapp, Cherokee/Quapaw musician and composer Louis Ballard, and Blackfeet modern dancer Rosalie "Daystar" Jones. A number of non-Indian art instructors also played a critical role in the dissemination of IAIA's arts philosophy. Painters James McGrath and Seymour Tubis, potter Ralph Pardington, and jeweler Michael McCormick all player their part along with writer/creative writing instructor Terry Allen, painters Leo Bushman and Fritz Scholder, the latter resolutely insisting to his last days that he was not an *Indian artist* per se but that in fact he was a German painter.

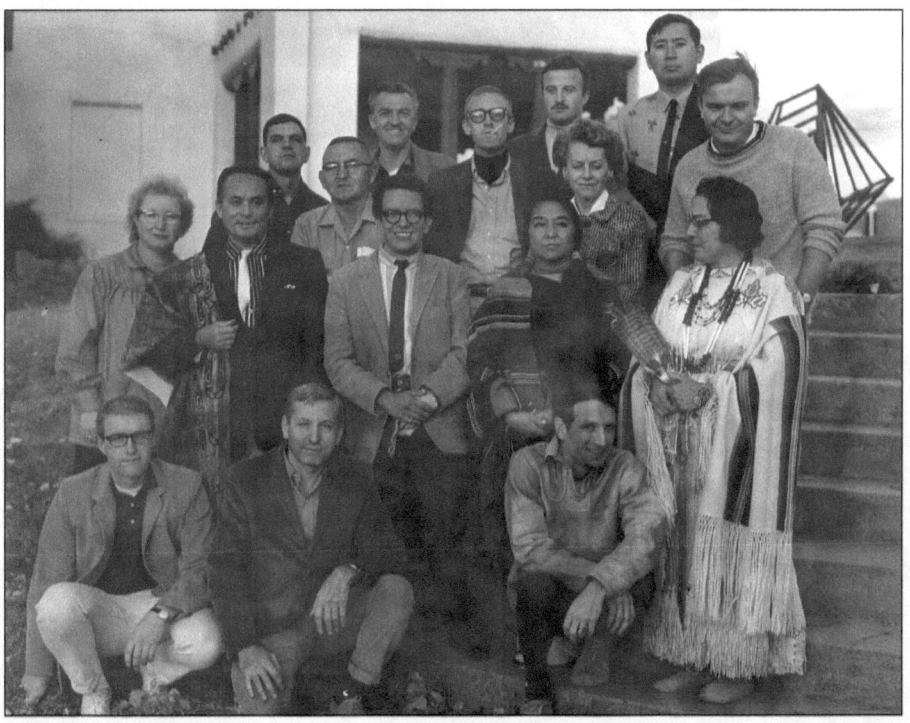

IAIA arts faculty, c. 1967. Front row, left to right: Metal Arts Instructor Terence Schubert, Graphics and Painting Instructor Seymour Tubis, Assistant Arts Director James McGrath; Middle row, left to right: Commercial Arts and Photography Instructor Kay V. Wiest, Art Director Lloyd New, Painting Instructor Fritz Scholder, Ceramic Sculpture Instructor Otellie Loloma, Traditional Techniques Instructor Josephine Wapp; Top tier, left to right: Painting Instructor Neil Parsons, Sculpture and Painting Instructor Allan Houser, Painting Instructor Leo Bushman, Jewelry Instructor Michael McCormick, Ceramic Instructor Ralph Pardington, Creative Writing Instructor Terry Allen, Music Instructor Louis Ballard, Drama Instructor Rolland Meinholtz. (Courtesy of IAIA Archives, Santa Fe, New Mexico) (rg03box13f03i01)

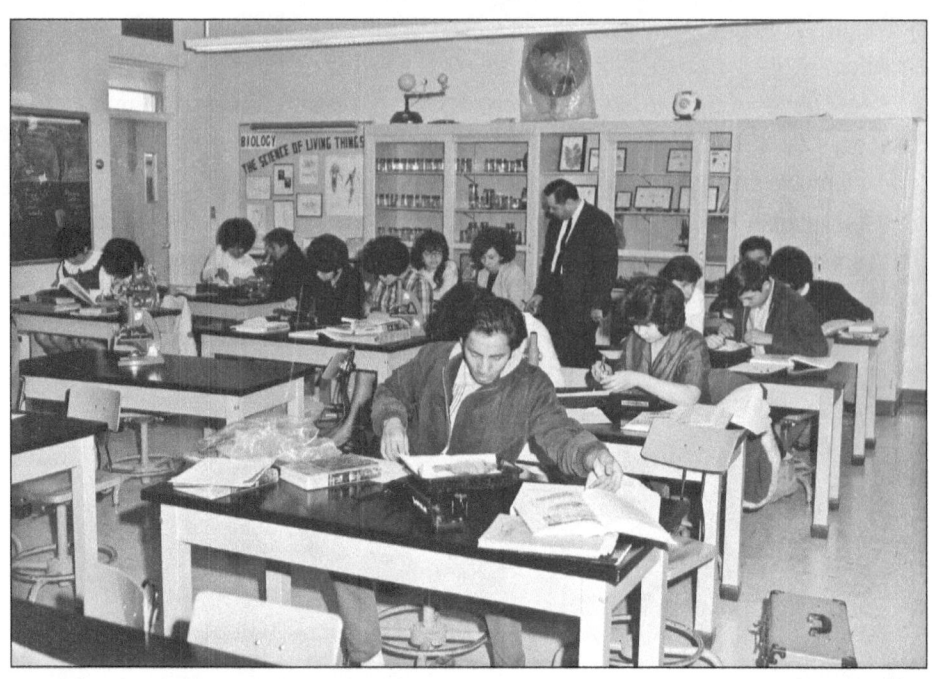

Biology class, c. 1964. Photograph by Kay V. Wiest. (Courtesy of IAIA Archives, Santa Fe, New Mexico) (ms10.003.031.01)

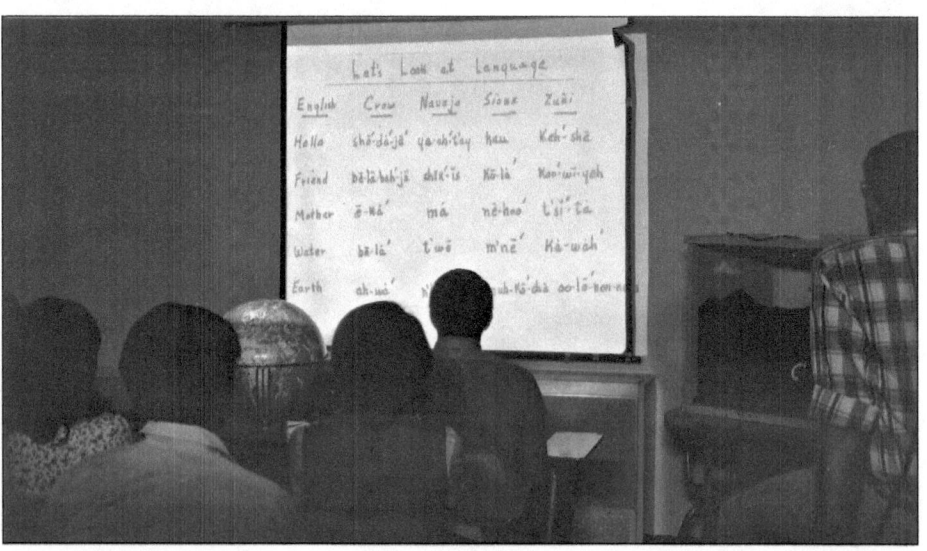

Language arts class, c. 1964. Photograph by Kay V. Wiest. (Courtesy of IAIA Archives, Santa Fe, New Mexico) (ms10.003.036)

In its first decade IAIA offered the typical high school courses in biology, world history, English, American history, business mathematics, algebra, and geometry. Courses were offered in the aesthetic survey of Indian arts and culture that included areas of philosophy, literature, dance, costume, music, and visual arts in both the North and South American continents. Courses in elements of design and principles of art were offered, looking closely at design as used by Indians to the concepts of design in a more universal sense.

The essential dichotomy between Indians and non-Indians was what informed our art. We reveled in the popularity of pop and op art, abstract expressionism, and the southwest painters who painted Indian life in New Mexico. Students loved how the French impressionists painted. Students were exposed to a variety of artistic traditions. As they learned about the historical traditional culture of their own nations, they could not wait to get into classes that covered Central and South American Indian art. It mattered not that the material presented was largely ethnographic and anthropological in character.

The majority of books in the library with Indian art subject matter were written by non-Indian authors. Unlike today, at that time in history there was very little in the way of books, articles, or films authored by American Indians. None of the non-Indian authors were able to articulate with any great degree the purpose, clarity, meaning, or integrity of the Native perspective, which is what the students should have been learning. Yet, the students were able to extract important concepts from the materials available.

One might say the most basic curriculum at IAIA in the 1960s was the interaction between the students themselves. It was very natural for them to share, and with so many students on campus from so many places, reflecting so many cultures, student discussions became an educational tool. The fact was, that as artists, these students had sensitivity to those impulses of art, culture, justice, and expression that created a fertile environment for discussions.

Students spoke of their tribal cultures and history, sharing their perspectives on everything including spirituality, ceremonial life, and unexplained occurrences in their communities. The students often related stories that might better be suited to the likes of the *X-Files*. Stories where people could change into wolves or deer, that UFOs were a part of family history, where huge serpents, ape-like men, little people, and spirits of the forest existed. Stories were told that reflected a time when spirits and their impact upon the Native people were accepted as an everyday occurrence.

As students we were being politicized and acculturated at an ever-accelerating pace, our art reflected those social and political changes. Students talked endlessly about their people's living conditions back home on the reservation, about mythologies, prophesies of the elders, and what life used to be like before Columbus. They spoke of history—of family as well as their own people's history. They exchanged oral stories about actual events that occurred amongst themselves from Maine to California, Florida to the Aleutian Islands in Alaska. Stories in which ancestors made long journeys at the point of a gun as the U.S. Army trailed them in close pursuit.

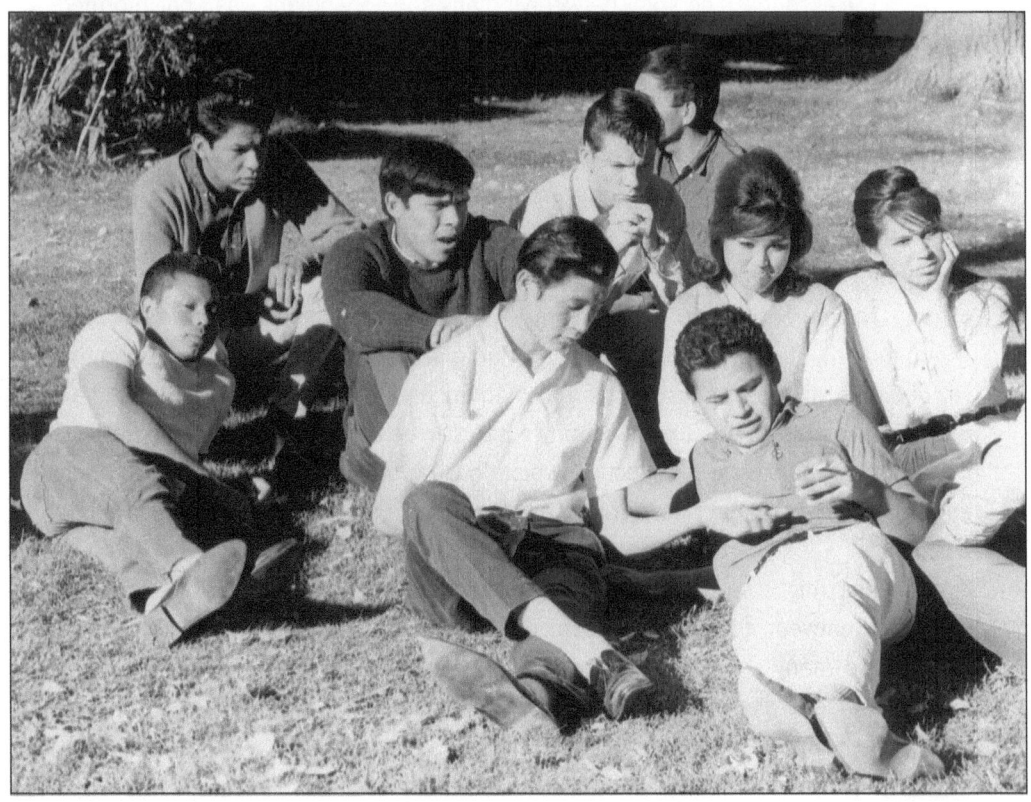

Group of IAIA students relaxing between classes, c. 1965. Photograph by Kay V. Wiest. (Courtesy of IAIA Archives, Santa Fe, New Mexico) (rg03box09f04i04)

The intensity of political and historical art discourse amongst the students was inspirational. Issues that affected our lives were discussed routinely like the war in Vietnam, racism, and communism. Often discussed was the prison-like atmosphere of our campus, how the chain link fences seemed to be more like that of a penitentiary than a school. At the extreme end of the spectrum, some students compared the fence to those found in Nazi concentration camps. They spoke of how the fence acted to symbolically separate us from our families, off-campus friends, or from the ordinary people of Santa Fe. Students spoke of how they felt disliked by the Mexican and white people, how they had a sort of inter-tribal rivalry going amongst themselves that sometimes led to fights on campus. The students worked determinedly to overcome that rivalry, to defeat those cultural and linguistic prejudices and stereotypes found amongst ourselves and in other races of people. No doubt naively, since as a group they saw themselves as being different than other people. They understood that they were on the cusp of a new chapter in American Indian art history.

Racism was a topic often discussed by the IAIA students. Many students suffered the same discrimination as African-Americans since they came from southern states where racist politics were a fact of life. In the northern states students experienced prejudice and bigotry too, with many of their people imprisoned in off-reservation jails, perhaps arrested for some minor offense.

The social science research of the time often reflected the racism of the times. The scientists taught that Indians were some kind of primitive people who were categorized, technologically, as living in the Stone Age, 10,000 years behind Western civilization. In reality, with these paradigmatic discussions, IAIA students were exploring alternative perspectives of the reality described by the social scientists. When the students came to learn how some anthropologists acquired government funding in the thousands, and sometimes hundreds of thousands of dollars to study the very things the students talked about and took for granted, they marveled at how efficient the American system was at disenfranchising Indians from our own world. Students could not understand why the scientific establishment was still writing about Indian people as being inferior. It simply did not add up, except that racism was a normal part of our lives so it was tolerated and food for thought.

Although students did not get to the point where extreme articulation of these important political and historical issues was found in everyday conversations, they intuited these realities as a part of their political conscience. The student's political conscience informed their art. Certainly there was no author anywhere, white or Indian, who thought about or articulated a political and historical consciousness shared by the IAIA students. Not until Standing Rock Sioux author Vine Deloria, Jr. came on the scene and wrote *Custer Died For Your Sins*[5] in 1969 was there anything like the truthful analysis of the state of affairs for American and Canadian Indians expressed by the IAIA students. Such personal and racial experiences had a cause and effect element, resulting in students having an overwhelming incentive to continue as artists. They had plenty of motivation and desire to paint paintings, write stories, cast jewelry, spin pottery, sing songs, and dance.

Many of the students were gifted musicians and they formed and named their own rock bands, amongst these were the *Fauves* named after the European art movement, the *Playboys* and the *Jaggers* who appeared in the article "Rediscovery of the Redman" in *Life* magazine December, 1967.[6] T.C. Cannon, who played with the *Fauves,* went on to open a stage performance by the 1960s folk group, *Peter, Paul and Mary* some years later. Louis Ballard had his E-Ya-Pah-Ha singers chanting original songs, touring such places as Washington, D.C. to perform for government dignitaries. Rolland Meinholtz produced original dramatic stage performances in the fine arts theatre by drama students that were later performed in the outdoor Paolo Soleri Amphitheatre which would in its own lifetime see the likes of such celebrated artists Leonard Cohen and Lyle Lovett perform.

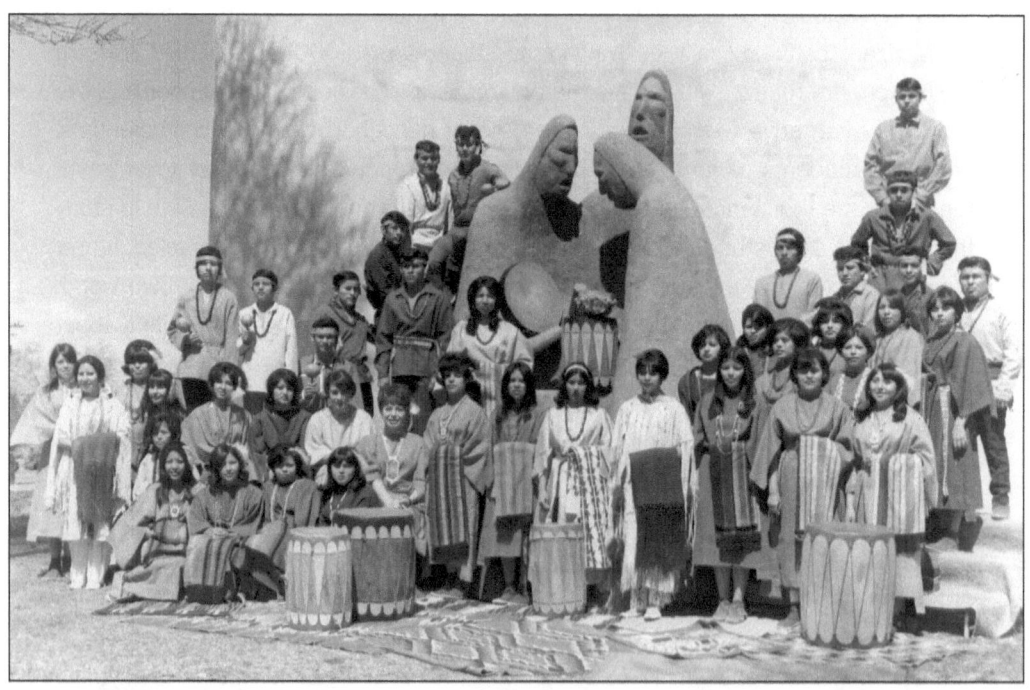

IAIA E-Yah-Pah-Hah Indian Chanters, c. 1966. In English, the name of the chorus means "The Town Criers." Photograph by Kay V. Wiest. (Courtesy of IAIA Archives, Santa Fe, New Mexico) (rg03box08f02i05)

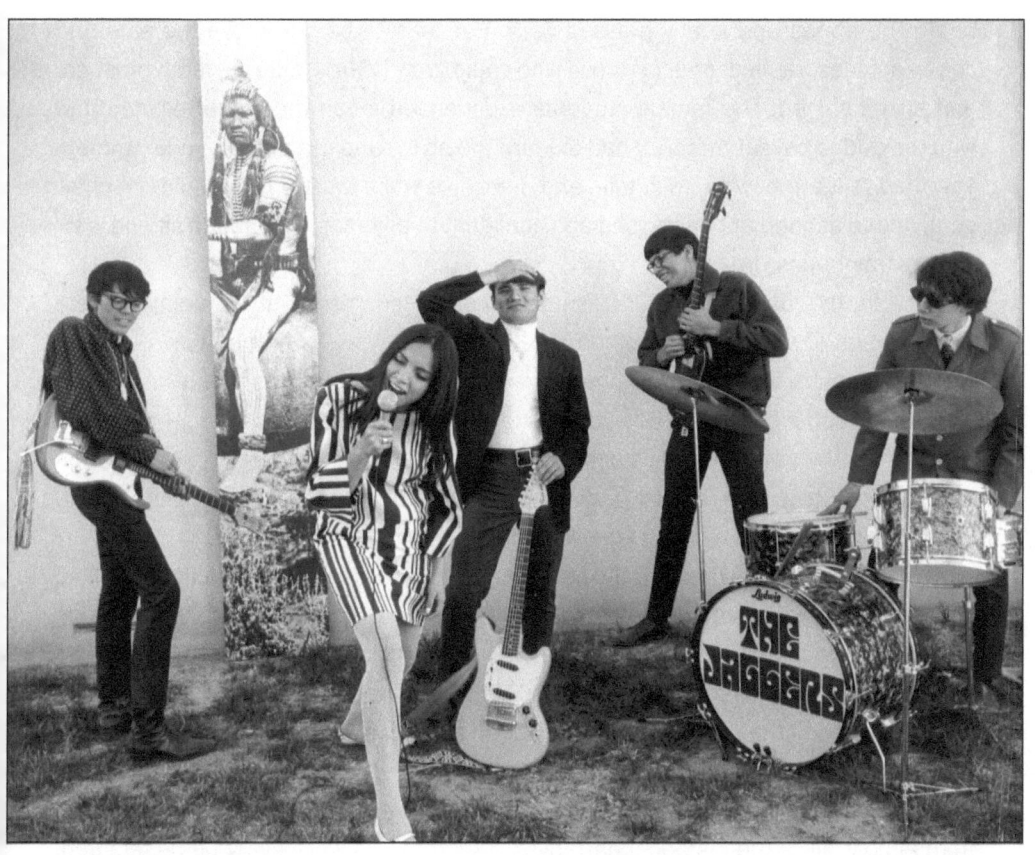

"The Jaggers," an IAIA student band feature in *Life* Magazine. Left to right: Alfred Young Man, Rosemary Peas, Dennis Stover, John Gritts, and Loren Moore, 1967. Photograph by Steve Schapiro. (Courtesy of Steve Schapiro)

As with all BIA schools, the curriculum was seen as extending into the whole experience of IAIA. Education took place, not only in the classrooms or places of socializing, but also in the daily life at IAIA. Students had to keep themselves and their individual living spaces and public spaces scrupulously clean. Hallway floors of the dorms were swept and mopped daily, waxed on Saturday. Beds made every morning before breakfast. Clothes were to be neatly pressed and hung on hangers in closets and folded in dresser drawers. Bedtime was before 10 P.M. every night of the week, up at 6 A.M. Smoking or drinking was forbidden and daily showers had to be taken.

Hygiene was a major concern and smart personal appearance was stressed. For the male students shirttails were not to be worn outside jeans or trousers. Clothes had to be ironed and neatly pressed daily. Hair was to be cut above the ears and combed, faces washed, and, for those who could grow beards, shaven, teeth brushed, and shoes shined. The female students experienced much the same regimen, but with the added caveat that they had to learn the styles and manners of white women. They had to learn how to walk, talk, and dress like white ladies. They could not chew gum, had to act and appear poised and confident at all times, and had to sit and walk with a straight posture.

In the dining hall, 300 students practiced "family-style dining" where small groups of six men and women dined together, typically at one table. Students were assigned to work in the kitchen as assistant cooks, dishwashers, waiters, and waitresses; serving food, washing the dishes, and mopping the floors after each and every meal. The stainless-steel cooking stoves, giant cooking pots, and air circulation vents in the kitchen had to be polished sparkling clean, ready for the next meal, with not so much as a fingerprint left in evidence.

Relationships between the male and female students were strictly controlled. There was a physical separation between the male and female students. Men lived in three separate dormitories at the mid and north end of campus and the women lived in two separate dorms at the south end. Dating was firmly regulated and was subject to consequences that were not normally found at most schools.

The most important ingredient in documenting IAIA's genesis and pedagogy is the story of IAIA as told by the art students themselves, an ingredient missing from almost all of the historical narratives. The students were every bit as talented, intelligent, artistic, motivated, energetic, innovative, and enthusiastic as art students found anywhere else in the world, be it the Slade School in London, the San Francisco Art Institute, Cooper Union in New York City, the Rhode Island School of Art and Design, Chouinard Art Institute, or the Art Institute of Chicago. IAIA students were producing work at such a high standard of creativity and excellence that by the time they applied and were accepted into these world-class art schools, most were thought to be advanced students. IAIA painters, printers, photographers, ceramicists, jewelers, and sculptors had created a tremendous body of artwork by the time they departed campus as late as 1968, art that could compete contemporaneously with the best anywhere.

The problem encountered by the early art students was that the uniqueness of IAIA and the quality of art being produced was not truly appreciated and celebrated at that time. Therefore art students and patrons could not come to understand and value themselves in relation to this place of genius, except in retrospect. Few advanced scholars have been incisive or inclusive enough to do the research needed to fully describe the degree of genius at IAIA during the 1960s. Decades later some serious attempts were made to correct that shortfall, mainly short monograms and exhibition catalogue copy, such as in Charleen Touchette's 2001 exhibition, *IAIA Rocks the Sixties* and subsequent book *nDn Art: Contemporary Native American Art,*[7] and the relatively late *Scholder: Indian not Indian,*[8] a 2008 retrospective at the National Museum of the American Indian in Washington, D.C.

About as close as those early artists ever got to receiving the accolades they deserved was when the famed Peggy Guggeheim of the New York's Guggenheim Museum came to Santa Fe and visited the IAIA art studios in the mid-1960s. She declared that the level of energy generated, dedication, innovation, perspective, purpose, enthusiasm, and originality equaled anything being done at the time on the east or west coast. This included comparisons with important movements as the ash can school, dada, pop art, and other American art movements. Although the students from the 1960s may have not received the acclaim they deserved at that time, history has shown that the accolades and recognition was to come for the students and for IAIA as a whole.

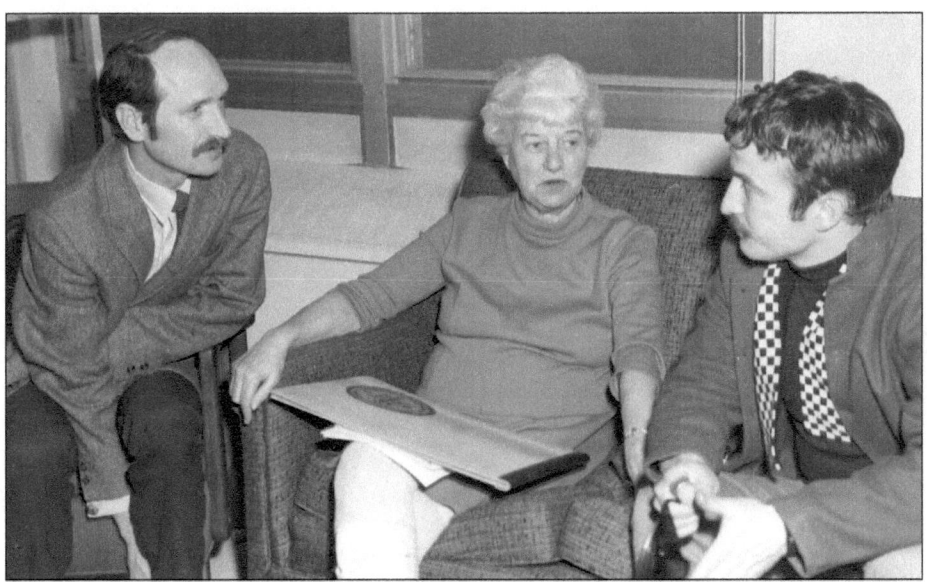

Peggy Guggenheim (center) reviewing the IAIA publication "Four" with Assistant Art Director James McGrath (left) and ceramics instructor Ralph Pardington during her visit to IAIA, c. 1965. Photograph by Kay V. Wiest. (Courtesy of IAIA Archives, Santa Fe, New Mexico) (rg03box16f11i01)

As IAIA celebrates its fiftieth anniversary, its contribution to the creation and development of the contemporary American Indian art movement is unrivaled. IAIA's success can be seen as serendipitous. The combination of Lloyd New's vision, a faculty with exceptional skill and credentials, and exemplary students created the foundation for the development of a new reality for American Indian art. Even though the BIA educational policies at the time were still trying to assimilate Indian people into the American mainstream, IAIA provided a counterbalance. The unique recipe of art education and cultural expression has produced generations of artists, activists, teachers, business and political leaders, and others who have contributed to the revitalization of American Indian communities.

From those students who arrived in 1962 to the most recent graduates, IAIA has provided a unique educational opportunity. IAIA has grown from being a high school program to offering associate's of fine arts degrees, and now bachelor's of fine arts and bachelor's of arts degrees. Through these transitions the curriculum has changed. However, the nature of the curriculum changes has not altered the unique IAIA experience. Through the curriculum, IAIA continues to integrate art and culture in a way that encourages and celebrates cultural expression.

Though it can be said that the curriculum of the 1960s did not so much spawn the art—that the art came into being regardless of the curriculum—but that for all intensive purposes, IAIA allowed for something greater than itself to occur most unexpectedly.

4

A Conversation with James A. McGrath
by
James A. McGrath with Rose T. Diaz, PhD
Edited and Annotated by Ryan S. Flahive

Oral history narratives often reveal details and perspectives not always found in traditional academic sources. The following piece is an edited and annotated oral history transcript highlighting the narrative of James A. McGrath (JM). McGrath is a working artist, an active arts educator, and served IAIA as the first assistant art director of IAIA from 1962 to 1967. He became art director of the school in 1967 and held that position until his departure in 1973. McGrath returned to IAIA on an interim basis in 1988 as the academic dean of the school during its reorganization.

Oral historian Rose T. Diaz (RD) conducted the interview at McGrath's home in Santa Fe on June 27, 2011 alongside IAIA archivist and oral history project coordinator Ryan S. Flahive (RF). The full transcription was completed by WorldCenter, Inc. and Origins and Legacies Historical Service, and is available for research in the IAIA Archives.

In an attempt to amplify and further explain parts of the transcript, primarily people, events, and programs, discursive notes from the editor have been provided to the reader in the notes section of this publication.

In the following selection, the conversation picks up after a discussion regarding McGrath's childhood in Washington state and his time in Europe while exhibiting his art and teaching science, health, and art for the U.S. Department of Defense in Italy, Germany, and France during the 1950s.

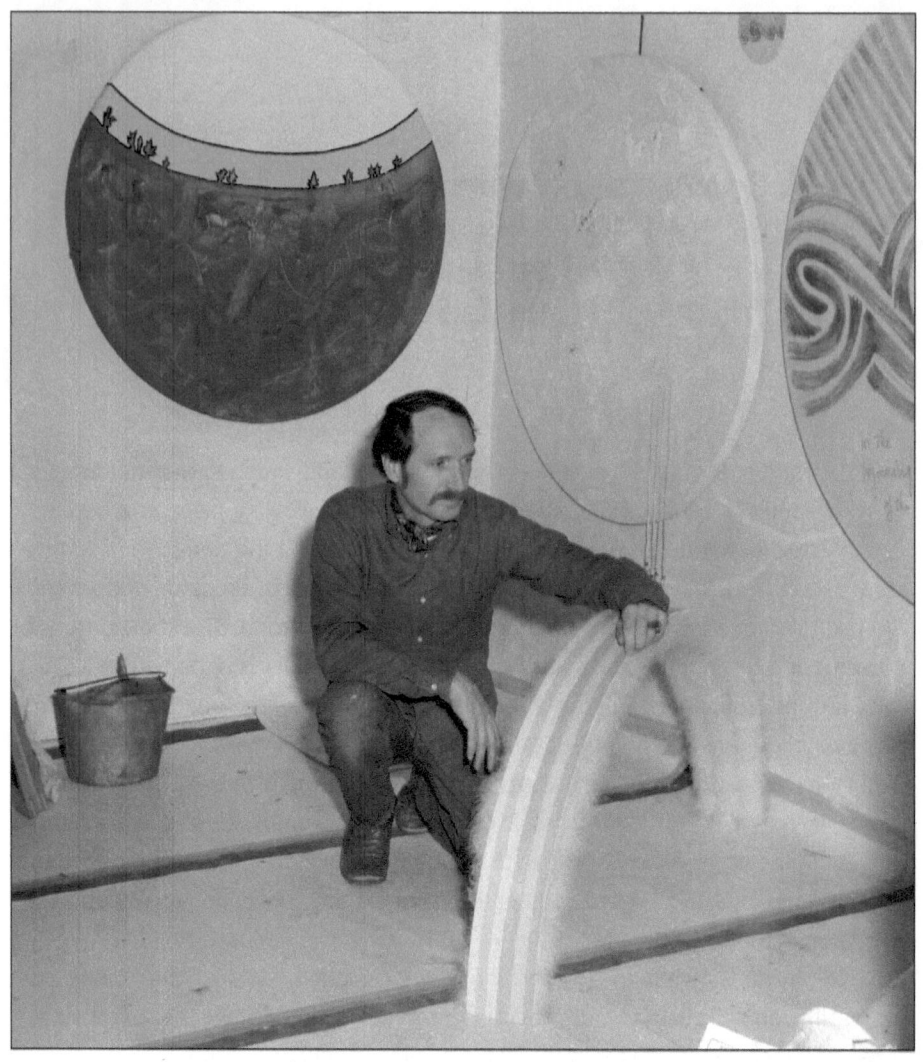

James A. McGrath, 1971. Photograph by Kay V. Wiest. (Courtesy of IAIA Archives, Santa Fe, New Mexico) (rg03box11f36i07)

RD: Under what circumstances did you leave Europe?

JM: . . . I got a letter from Pauline Johnson, who was the art education person I worked with at the University of Washington, and she told me about a new school that was opening up in New Mexico called the Institute of American Indian Arts, and they were looking for an art director. I said, "Ooh, that sounds like that might be very interesting.

I think I may apply." So I wrote a letter to Dr. (George) Boyce[1] and told him a little bit about my background and applied and had some people write recommendations for me. And lo and behold, I got a letter back saying that they were interested. But, the art director job had [already] been selected—Lloyd New.[2] But, Lloyd had looked at my credentials and felt it might be nice if I was his assistant, and I thought, "Well that's probably even easier, and I think if they'll accept me I'll take it." So I wrote back and said exactly that, that if they were interested I would take the job. This being a government job as a BIA school, I could make what was called a lateral transfer, I think they called it.

RD: So it didn't mean terminating one and then going to another?

JM: That's right, that's right. I mean . . . that wasn't all that important to me. The important thing was the job and what it meant. I remember some of the questions they asked me. "What is Indian art to you?" Well, there were some other interesting questions. "How would you work with young Indian kids?" I think my answers were of the type that was acceptable because I got the job. So I came in May of 1962, and at that time the campus was being refurbished and I lived in the dorm. So, I had another single room in the dormitory! Lloyd was in Tucson with the Rockefeller project,[3] and my instructions were to get the studios together . . . get some supplies, look at the students' applications that were coming in, set up a library if you can . . . I mean, it was an enormous thing to get the school going!

RD: Under what circumstances did the school become part of the Santa Fe Indian School, or was the school closing? What do you recall from that?

JM: Well, as I recall, the school had closed.[4] I remember the one building that is still left—we used for the music building. There were still projects in there—student projects, and I remember seeing those. There were no teachers around. People were just working and painting and getting things ready. I don't know if the academic building had even been completed . . .

RD: So you inherited the whole of the campus then?

JM: Yeah. I think Wilma Victor did come in during that period when I was there. She was the principal of the academic department; she was Choctaw. I remember her coming in, and I think maybe Oleta Merry—who ultimately married Dr. Boyce—came to student services. So there was the academic principal, Wilma, myself, and Oleta. These were the three main people that were there at the time . . . and also a registrar. Ruth Duncan was there to get student files and things ready. Alvin Warren, Dave Warren's father, was there and was the recruiting officer . . . Lloyd, as I say, was in Tucson. So we had our own unique jobs, [but] also tried to get some things going together as well.

RD: How did that work . . . to integrate all of those components?

JM: We didn't have any models.

RD: Right.

JM: That was another problem. I mean we just had to work from the top of our heads and from our hearts to figure out what we were going to do. Wilma . . . I think she came out of Intermountain,[5] [and] I believe, Oleta did too. So we [all] brought different backgrounds, but somehow they worked together—it was *very* congenial. I don't think we ever had an argument. It was like a family thing happening.

RD: How did Dr. Boyce tie into all this?

JM: Well, he was in the building. He had us in meetings frequently, [he] wanted to know how things were going, and he had certain expectations to get things done. I don't ever remember anything about budgets though. It just seemed like we had the money to do things with, and I think he gave us support. He respected our own experiences and knowledge and gave us the support we needed. It seemed to work out okay.

RD: What did you instinctively feel his philosophy was about the school?

JM: I have to admit I bit my tongue several times . . . I wasn't quite sure always what he was after. I felt that he really wanted this assimilation business. That seemed to be uppermost [in his mind], and I think the rest of us felt that whatever the *student* really wanted to develop in his life is his business and his right to do that . . . But, I remember with Lloyd . . . we wanted really good materials, top-grade materials. We wanted the studios to be really good. We didn't have the best facilities like they have now. I was teaching in the old bakery where we had ovens, and I kept students' work stored in the ovens. A lot of us just didn't have any modern facilities . . . but I felt that wasn't so important. The important thing was to get the students working and getting them involved. I would say most of the faculty had the same feeling. The only exception was in the [student] scheduling. We did schedule art classes like three or four hours long, which was *not* exactly what the academic people liked. They felt we were taking too much time out of the day for the arts as they wanted to have for math, science, and English. So it took a while to get all that worked out in the curriculum, but we got it done that first year. Well, it seemed like we were changing quite a lot along the way to change some of the [core].

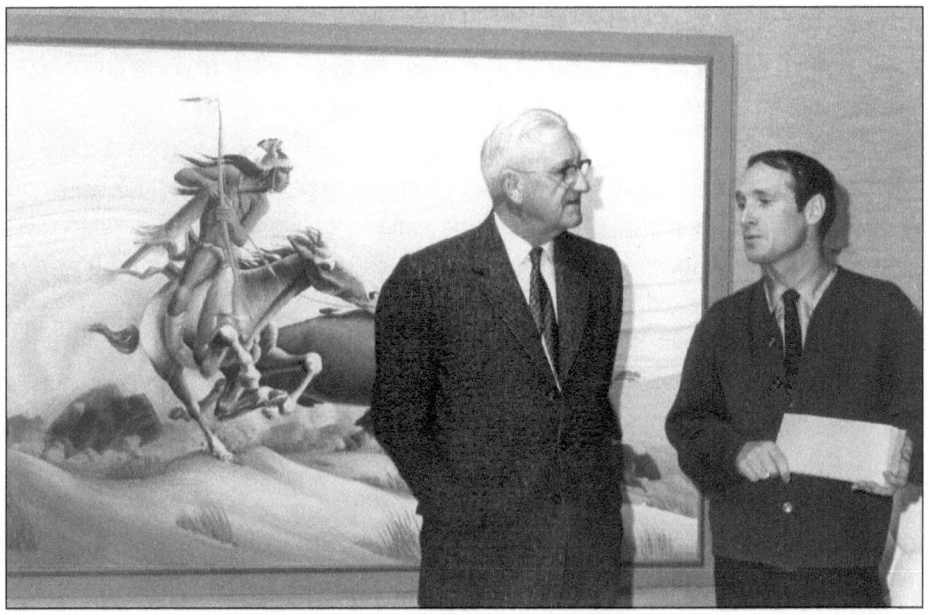

James A. McGrath with IAIA Superintendent George Boyce, c. 1965. Note the Allan Houser painting "When Meat was Plentiful" on exhibit behind them. Photograph by Kay V. Wiest. (Courtesy of IAIA Archives, Santa Fe, New Mexico) (rg03box11f36i01)

RD: So it appears that Dr. Boyce did appreciate the flexibility.

JM: I think so.

RD: And he gave that to the administrators and coordinators . . . [the ability] to do that?

JM: I think so, right. Also, it was early that Lloyd and I felt (well, both of us had been teachers and we loved teaching) that was a part of our heart—so, we also taught [along with administration duties]. Lloyd taught his *Printed Textiles*, and I taught *Painting* and *Museum Training* in the museum that we set up in that building . . . I also [taught] *Design* and *Creative Writing*. So, I had four classes to teach along with this other aspect. And, [I] lived on campus, so I was right there in the middle of it all.

RD: So you were a *real* house parent?

JM: I was a house parent, right, and it made all the difference—just all the difference.

RD: Well, I was curious with so many of the key people coming from Intermountain how that influenced what was structured for the school.

JM: Well, I think [for] those of us who hadn't had that experience . . . I think we kinda looked up to them because they had some experience we didn't have—[staff like] Allan Houser,[6] Ann (Houser) in the office, and of course Wilma (Victor). So they had an experience that we didn't have and that was important to us. There was a certain amount of conservatism, shall we say, as compared to those of us who may have come in from the outside without that base, and I [definitely] saw that difference in the classrooms. Like Allan Houser would teach [in an] apprentice style where he would work in the classroom along with the kids; whereas another teacher would never do that that didn't have that experience. Charles Loloma[7] and Otellie [Loloma][8] would also do that. So, I saw a difference in teaching styles that came out of people that came there with more experience with the kids.

RD: So a more institutionalized way of [teaching]?

JM: There seemed to be—but it worked. There was quite a variety of what went on in the classrooms.

RD: Which was probably good for the kids.

JM: Oh, it was excellent!

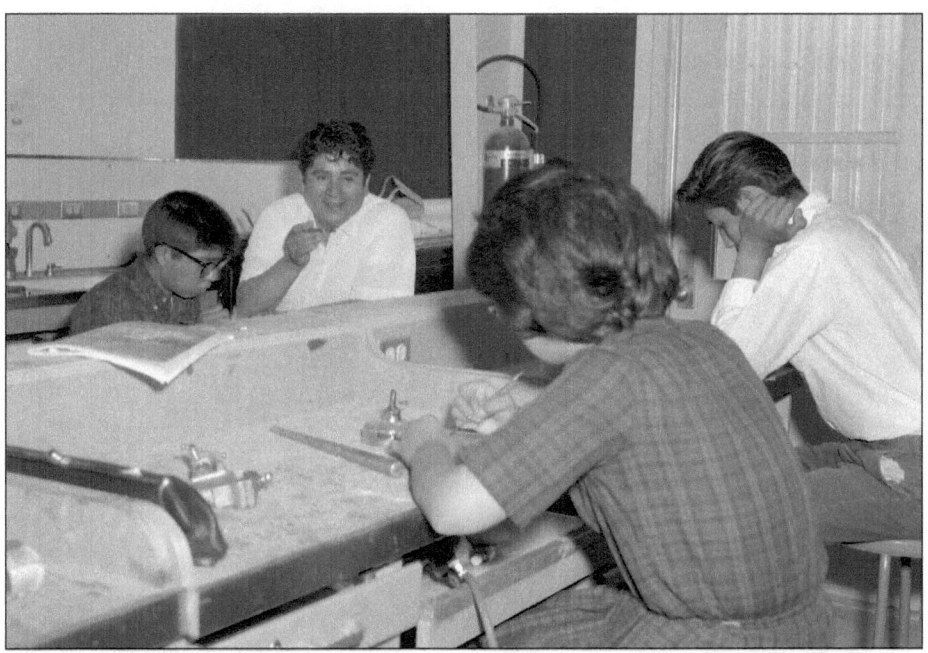

Charles Loloma (center), c. 1965. Photograph by Kay V. Wiest. (Courtesy of IAIA Archives, Santa Fe, New Mexico) (ms10.loloma)

RD: So they could see different models at work.

JM: Exactly, yeah, because Ralph Pardington,[9] who was teaching clay, came from Cranbrook in Michigan with a master's degree, and Otellie came from Hopi without a degree . . . yet, they were both teaching clay, but they were different, and it worked. And I think they had a deep respect for each other, too.

RD: Well, that seems to be a theme as well—not only a relationship of respect between the superintendent and the faculty, but among the faculty there didn't seem to be too many jealousies. I don't think there can be [many] in the beginning, because you're all just one step forward, two steps back.

JM: I did sense . . . one thing Dr. Boyce did though, is he really looked at it as being a family. I think that was part of it that we all got very early [on], and that was maintained all through the years, that I was there anyway. Even in our art staff we all had a number of students that we felt were kind of *our* students that we would take on trips or have in our homes for holiday periods or something of that nature. There was always that sense of family, which I thought was *extremely* important, and I think very cohesive. It built up trust early enough and built up a sense of belonging for all of us.

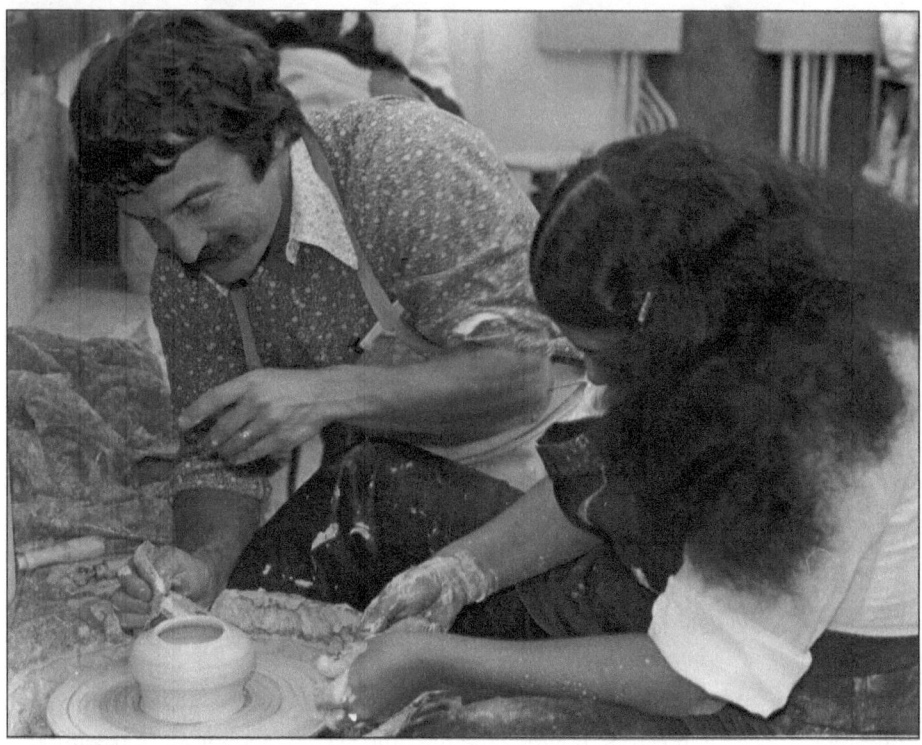

Ralph Pardington, c. 1970. Courtesy of IAIA Archives. Photograph by Kay V. Wiest. (Courtesy of IAIA Archives, Santa Fe, New Mexico) (rg03box12f03i01)

RD: I'd like to move now to really talking about the curriculum and the development of the curriculum [since] you're all thinking about new directions. [With] some people coming from institutional backgrounds, [others] coming from a more flexible or art background . . . since everything is focused on Indian art and identity—these helped to shape the curriculum that I want to talk about.

How did the staff conceive of that curriculum that included the school philosophy? (The school philosophy, based on various primary source readings, can be summarized into three basic ideas. While at school: 1) Students gained a better understanding of the world-at-large outside of their own tribal affiliations or the school, 2) There was an encouragement of creative expression, and, 3) That expression was incorporated in whatever you did within the school [based on] cultural traditions.) So how did faculty frame around those three ideas?

JM: Well, there were two basic classes. One ended up being called *Indian Aesthetics*, which was the study of Indian culture in the broad sense, but particularly through the sense of beauty and the sense of the arts—that was a required course. We all met together in an auditorium and divided the student body up according to geographical locations in the country. [Each group] would do a program for the rest of the student body during the year sometime about their cultures, their tribal groups, and their affiliations, particularly about the arts.

I remember in the wintertime some of them were storytelling times. There was a stage there and there was a big auditorium. Some of them did things where they showed slides, some did dances . . . but each group during the year would do something special for the rest of the class, and it was also a team-teaching event. There was Josephine Wapp,[10] Otellie (Loloma), myself, Allan Houser, and, I think Louis Ballard.[11] I think maybe those were the five main people, and we picked themes for the times when the students weren't doing something. We might talk about architecture, music, or about Plains culture related to the horse. There might be something that we felt might be universal enough so that everyone could have some input in it. That was a no-graded course, but the kids always seemed to show up and they always did [the activities]. I think that was the most important class probably at the school.

In the non-Indian world, with Ralph Pardington and Otellie (Loloma) doing the clay work and [teaching]. Otellie always taught out of her culture, I know. Ralph, not having that would do the other thing. I taught painting and Allan Houser did some painting, and it was a time when Fritz Scholder was there and he did a style of painting.[12] There were several painting teachers and they brought in different viewpoints as well. Music . . . Louis (Ballard), if you know his work at all, developed a chorus—a wonderful chorus where they would sing and recreate traditional music in new forms . . . mostly through the voice and maybe through some basic instruments— drum or rattle or something of that nature. Josephine Wapp was the main [one in] traditional techniques. In fact, her class was called *Traditional Techniques*. They did the finger weaving and a number of works with [different] leathers and just different things using the more traditional materials. So I think that was the main way we did this was through the classes.

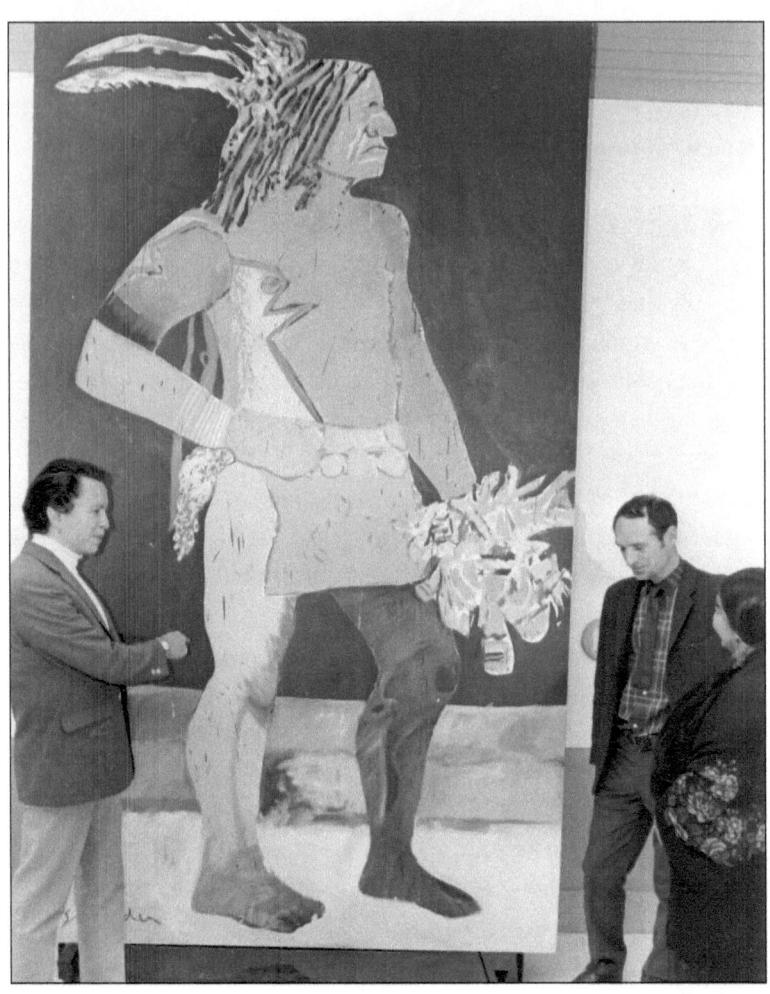

Fritz Scholder (left) with James McGrath and Otellie Loloma, c. 1968. (Courtesy of IAIA Archives, Santa Fe, New Mexico) (rg03box12f14i06)

But then there were other activities, like the big *Indian Foods Day* in the spring. [A time when] students just had freedom from the academic classes and we, students and art faculty, developed three to four days of activities and events. We would order traditional foods from Alaska, some of the kids went deer hunting—it was an amazing event—some built wikiups and hogan units—just different things and events to really bring the cultures together. That was like the final [event] of that Indian Aesthetics program.

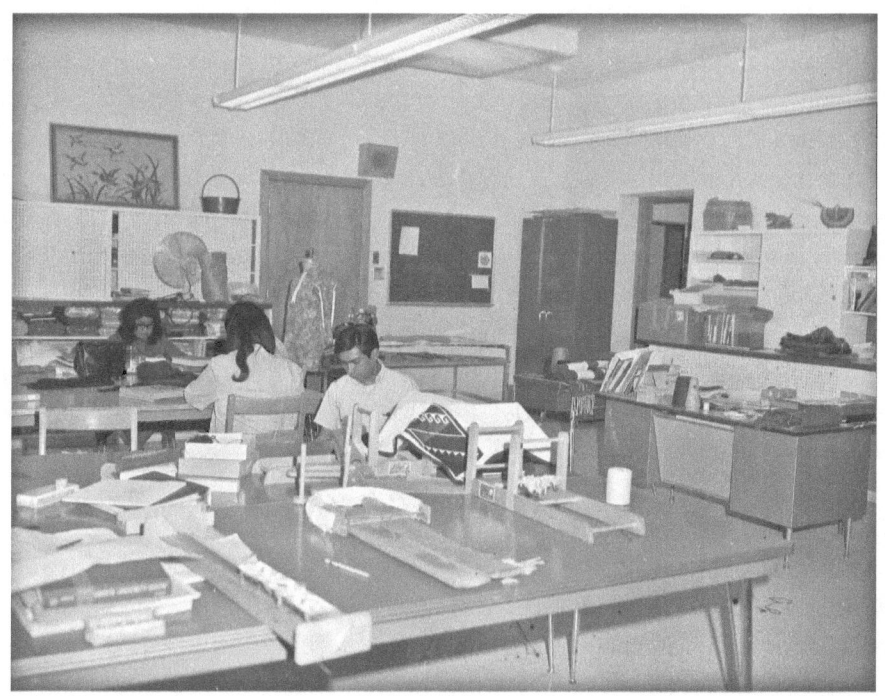

Josephine Wapp's Traditional Techniques classroom, c. 1966. Photograph by Kay V. Wiest. (Courtesy of IAIA Archives, Santa Fe, New Mexico) (ms10.001)

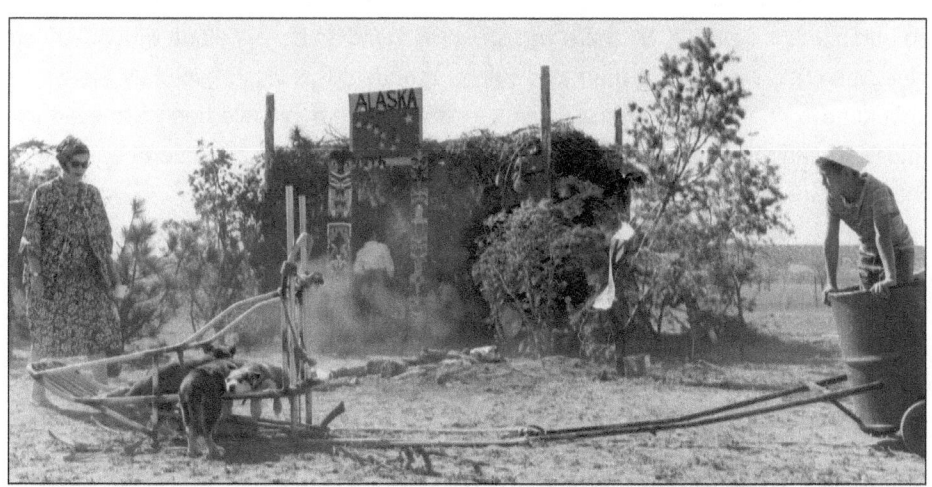

The Alaska exhibit at *Indian Foods Day,* 1965. Photograph by Kay V. Wiest. (Courtesy of IAIA Archives, Santa Fe, New Mexico) (rg03box08f04i25)

Then there was a *Basic Design* class, which was another required course for everybody. I had to teach that one, and I remember [for] the very first class we had an invasion of grasshoppers on the campus. I remember not having an awful lot of materials [to work with]—they hadn't come in yet. [The classroom] was in the north dorm, not in the hallway, but in a room there, because the [regular] classroom wasn't set up yet. I wanted to find out (subtlety) what the [various] differences were among the students—so we [worked] with the grasshoppers—torn paper grasshoppers. I saw that the Eskimo kids, the Pueblo kids, the Cherokee kids, and the Plains kids were doing different images. Well, that immediately—thank God I did that—I immediately saw these visual differences going on! So, that became another way of doing things in that *Basic Design* class—to give a unit or an idea and letting them express in their own way.

RD: So how did the academic units and the art units come together?

JM: . . . We had students with very low reading levels. We did do some testing, and we had maybe, oh, particularly some areas where they came in with third and fourth grade reading levels. I don't know who did this, but I felt a way to do it. Let them read about Indian subjects, none of this Dick and Jane business and these other things that most kids read in their schools.

It was best to read stories and things maybe that they have written or about things they have had in their backgrounds. Well, the reading levels started going up, so that made a big thing. So there was a course in Indian history along with American history, so this was part of their curriculum. I thought this was absolutely the way it should have been. I think in the science classes there may have been some similar things. I wasn't that involved with that so I don't know, except I do remember some of these instances.

RD: Did the curriculum standards have to fit a model [under] state or federal [guidelines]?

JM: Fortunately we didn't have a board, and we didn't have a real connection with the (New Mexico) State Department; otherwise we probably wouldn't have had Otellie (Loloma) there or Allan (Houser) there. We wouldn't have had certain teachers, because they did not have college degrees, and that made a big difference, so we didn't have to do that.

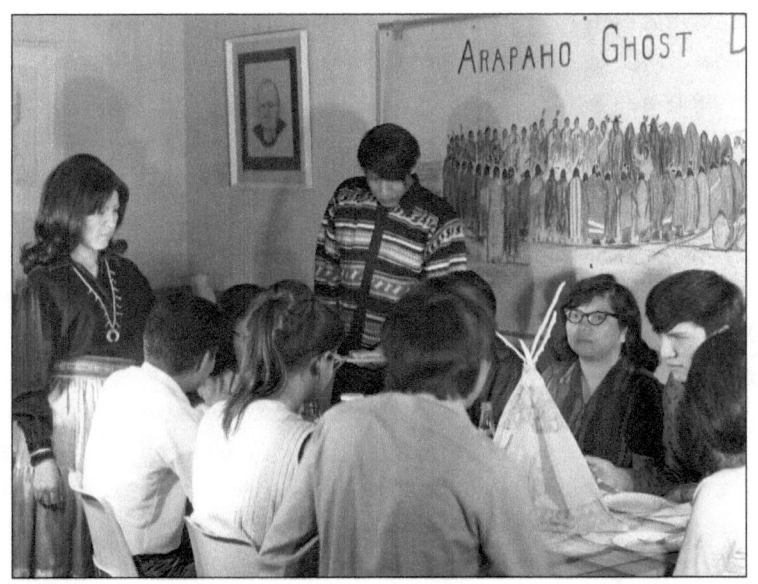

Indian history class, c. 1966. Photograph by Kay V. Wiest. (Courtesy of IAIA Archives, Santa Fe, New Mexico) (rg03box20f02i01)

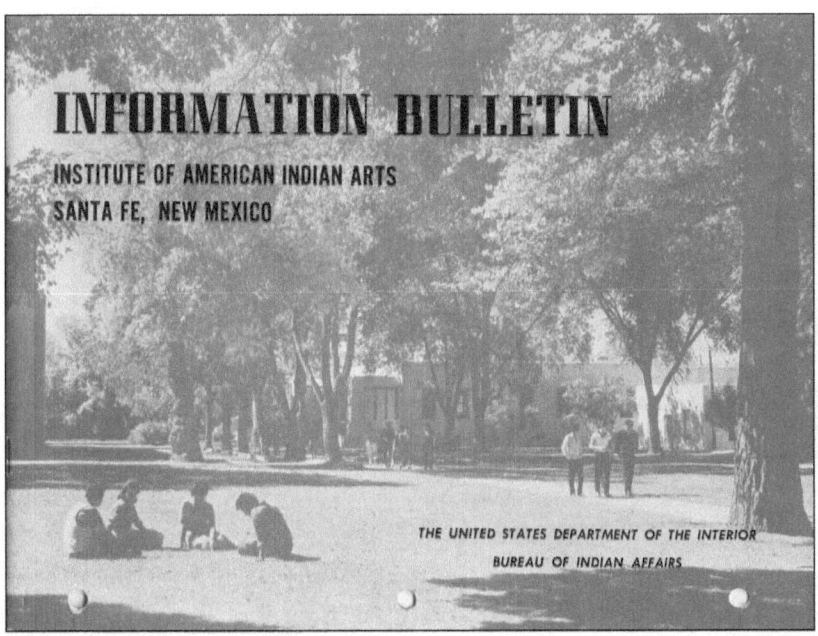

Information Bulletin, Institute of American Indian Arts, Santa Fe, New Mexico. 1961. 24 pp. (Courtesy of IAIA Archives, Santa Fe, New Mexico) (ms01box11f06)

RD: Well, from this early curriculum development of the design courses and aesthetics courses, how did you use this to recruit students? How did you use those philosophies or those examples of work?

JM: I think I may have given the IAIA Archives Alvin Warren's booklet that he sent out to recruit. It was very basic. I think it had pictures, what the school was about, and this is how you apply. I think that was the first thing that went out, and they had to send in examples of their work. I was one of the people that had to go through all of that, and I think we decided . . . I think with Lloyd we decided we'd take *everybody*. We didn't care anything about grades. That was completely unimportant. If they sent in a poem, or a drawing, or a painting, or wanted to do music—good. That's why we want you there.

That went on for quite a few years. I know it's changed now, but that's how it was; otherwise we wouldn't have got Kevin Red Star[13] and Earl Eder,[14] and a lot of these young people at that time are now well-known artists. They just didn't have the background or the grades. The registrar didn't like that, because she came from a more academic area too, and she felt they really should have better grades. So we did have a few conflicts, but we stood our ground and did it anyway. So that's how we recruited.

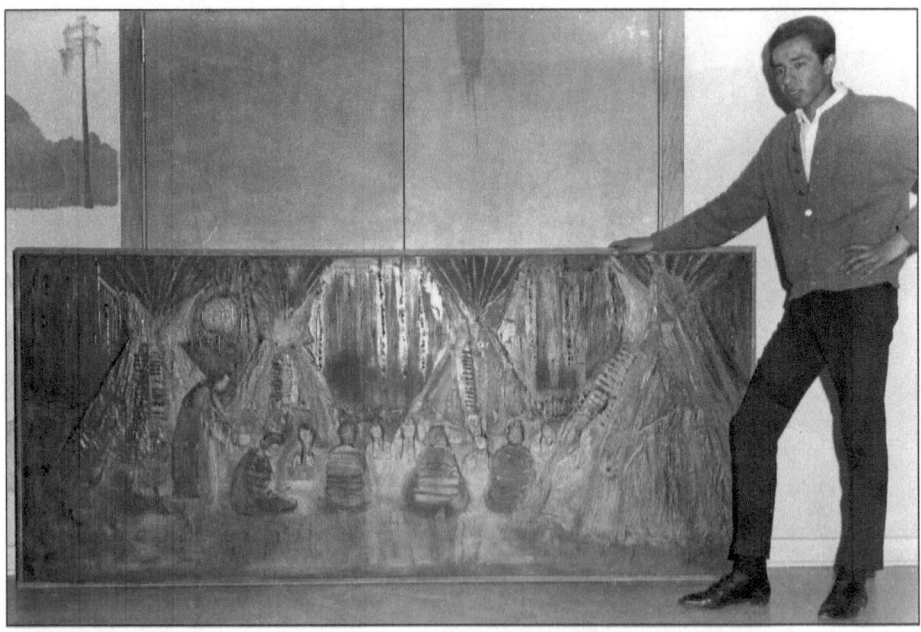

Kevin Red Star, 1965. (Courtesy of IAIA Archives, Santa Fe, New Mexico) (rg03box03f63i02)

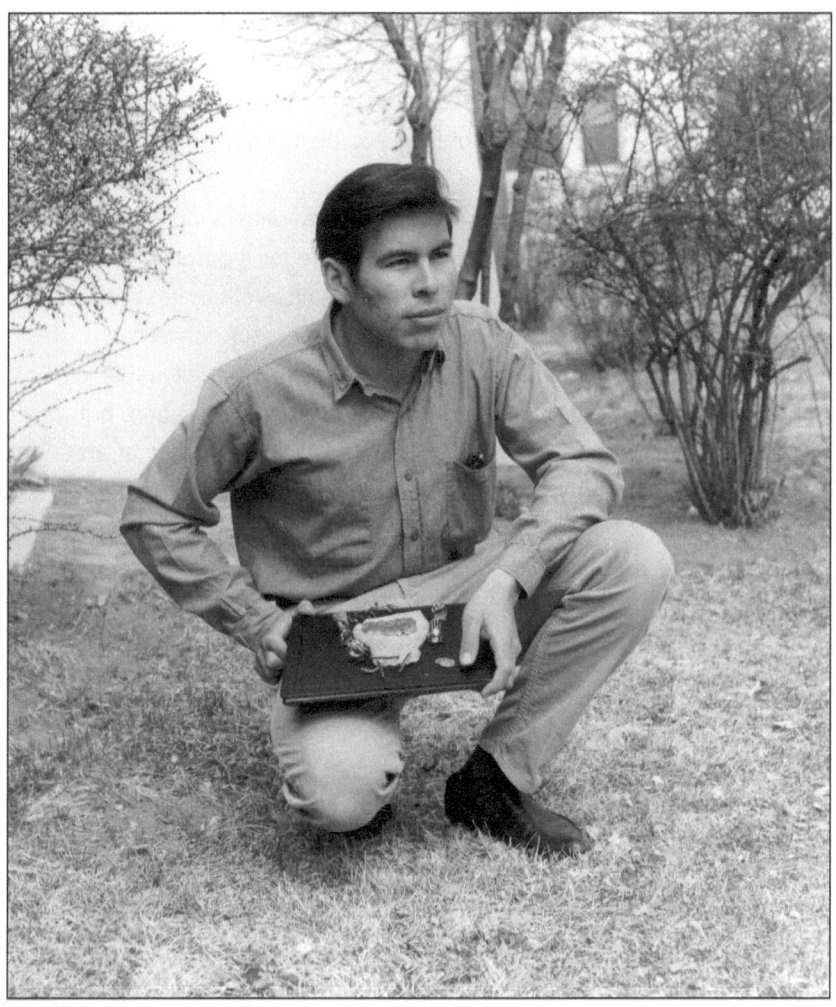

Earl Eder, c. 1967. (Courtesy of IAIA Archives, Santa Fe, New Mexico) (rg03box02f06i01)

Then later on when we tried to get students from here into other schools they also wanted test scores, and we had a woman, Dr. Anna Martin, who gave all of the tests. We got her convinced that if we could do a non-verbal test along with the verbal tests and send them both these tests that they would see that there's some interesting differences. That's how we started doing that so we could get them into these other schools for their advanced training such as the San Francisco Art Institute and Chicago Art Institute.

RD: Well, coming in at the ground level of building the school, you talked about how students with poor grades would, by reading about their culture, improve their reading grades. How else did students flourish that maybe didn't have very solid backgrounds—both academically or creatively? How did you see them flourish?

JM: Well, I think they flourished because they were with people of creativity and with the Native cultural base—people who were there for a purpose. I think that was probably one of the main things. There was a lot of talk about that . . . talk about what they were doing, and how they were doing it, what these differences were. This might be a Crow interpretation compared to somebody else and how valuable is this? They were learning from each other, so there was a real cross-fertilization, but they really maintained who they were as individuals. I didn't see any real style of art . . . except maybe some of the newer styles that came in when they became more interested in being active, like the AIM (American Indian Movement) group that came in. There were some real explosions then that were quite different, but that was the time when it was happening, but I think part of it was because they were being nourished with each other and supported with each other and the staff and the teachers.

RD: What response did you get from parents?

JM: We didn't get a lot of response from parents, because so many of them were out of state. I know we did have some problems with some of the Pueblos here, some very difficult ones.

RD: Can you talk about that a little bit?

JM: I wasn't terribly involved with it, except at the beginning I knew it was in the newspapers. Some Pueblo leaders felt that art was to be taught at home, this was no place to have it . . . that there wasn't a need for an art school. This was very much from the Pueblos, and yet we had some pueblo students coming from Santo Domingo, San Ildefonso, and Jemez [Pueblos]. Some of the Institute staff people were Pueblo, and there were just a few that were from the original school. There weren't very many that stayed, and I think they were still kind of critical because of what we were doing.

RD: Well, it seems like the Pueblos would be probably more conservative than most other people.

JM: Exactly.

RD: And is that where the conflict was—the traditionalists versus [the progressives]?

JM: I would say that's exactly where it lay.

RD: And was anyone on the staff more of a traditionalist?

JM: Well, that's always the thing . . . what is tradition? Certainly Otellie, Charles, Louis, and Josphine were traditional, but they were also open to new ideas.

RD: We're going to switch a little bit now, because I'd like to get your recollections about individuals that came in with you at the same time. I'm interested in what strengths did each of them bring and if you have any particular stories or recollections as you think through the names. So let's start with Dr. Boyce.

JM: Well, of course his strength was being an administrator, and also having years and years of experience as to what students needed. I suppose [it was also] his philosophy, and he expressed what he felt they needed and wanted to be sure that happened. He was personable and warm and seemed to be caring as far as the staff and the students. I think everybody liked him, because he was open and friendly, but I think he definitely had an agenda and he let us know what it was. We tried to go along with it because that was our job.

   Dr. Boyce was also out and about and didn't stay in his office all the time. He would come out into classrooms, he talked with students; he'd meet the faculty and students—*that* made a big difference. Again, that was part of that family approach to things, I think. He was definitely a gentleman [and] didn't put up with any hogwash.

RD: Let's move to Lloyd New.

JM: Lloyd was, again, a person who had, I thought, a great background in art and teaching and in [dealing with] people—he really knew people! I think he knew the staff's strengths and selected people for the jobs based on what he felt they could do with the students and let us do it. I think that was his biggest strength—letting us do the job that he felt we could do. He also was one that spent a lot of time with the students. He was off campus quite a bit, because of a lot of things going on that he had to do.

I think he did more in Washington than probably Dr. Boyce did. Again, he was a very personable person, a gifted person . . . very involved with lots of good ideas, and *very* supportive. He was very trusting, and I think all of us respected him for what he could do. He was there with us and for us all the way through.

He was very successful with his business in Scottsdale (Arizona).[15] He was a fashion designer and a textile printer, so he almost moved there as a studio, even though we had to recreate the whole thing. He was down in the studio a lot with the students. I found that an artist would come in there with their skill and their expertise and get it going and have *great* success and then if they left—it stopped.

That's what happened with the textile fashion area . . . nobody really came in after him, just like with Otellie (Loloma) and the ceramic thing. Her style and her work in a certain way when she left that [method] stopped. I think in Lloyd's case, he was quite disappointed that it did not happen. He wanted fashion, he wanted textiles, he wanted design to come out of Indian culture and really become nationwide. He had contacts in New York and Scottsdale and Los Angeles to do this . . . but it just never quite got to that. I think that was a disappointment for him.

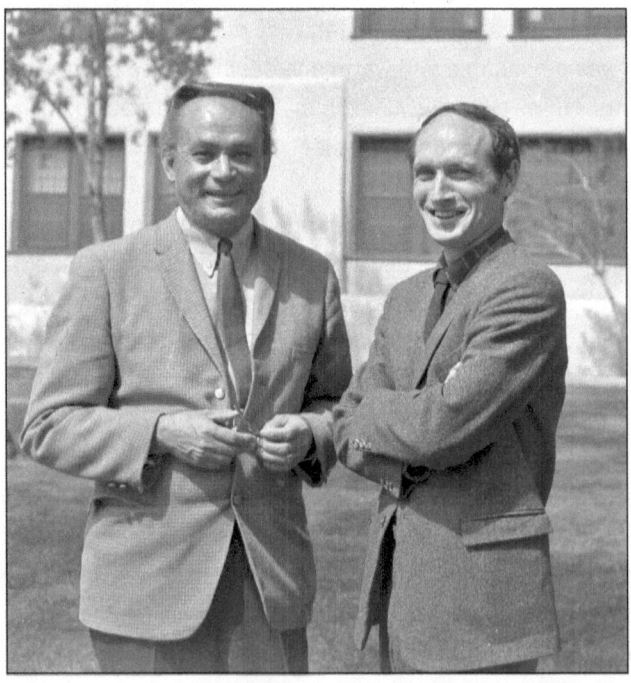

Lloyd New and James McGrath, c. 1970. Photograph by Kay V. Wiest. (Courtesy of IAIA Archives, Santa Fe, New Mexico) (ms10.003)

RD: Do you know the circumstances under how he was hired, how he came to IAIA?

JM: I suspect it was his success with the Phoenix Indian School.[16] He also wrote—he would write articles and he knew people. He may have known Hildegard Thompson.[17] He certainly was on the Indian Art and Crafts Board with Royal Hassrick,[18] [Vincent] Price,[19] and Rene d'Harnoncourt[20]—people that were very influential. I don't know all the ins and outs, but I suspect that had a lot to do with it.

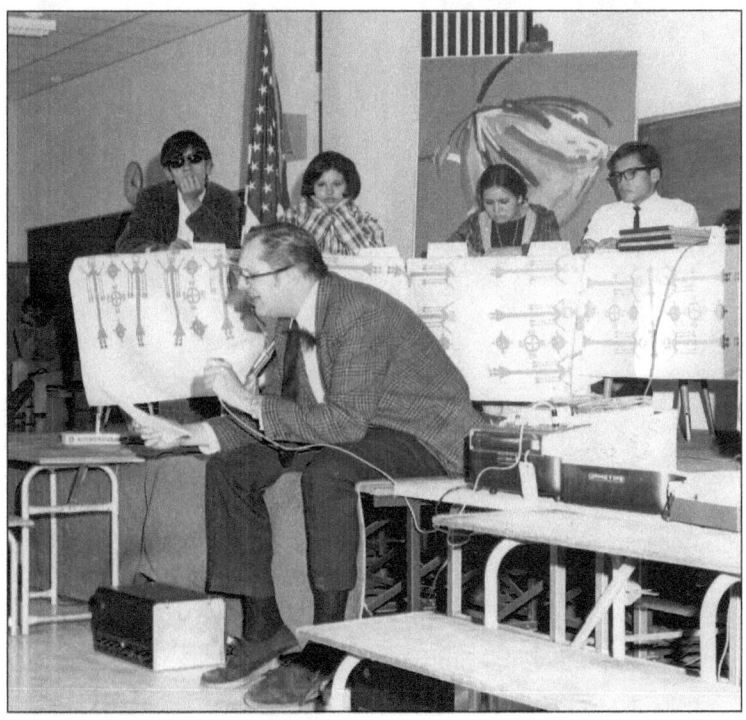

Vincent Price reading poetry at IAIA, c. 1967. Photograph by Kay V. Wiest. (Courtesy of IAIA Archives, Santa Fe, New Mexico) (rg03box16f26i02)

RD: How about Louis Ballard?

JM: I felt Louis was a *very* gifted musician and very contemporary but always had the roots in Indian music and got his students involved in—again, new forms of music based on Indian culture and Indian music traditions . . . As a teacher he was *excellent*. He taught guitar, piano, and voice. He knew the whole thing and he also did some important educational materials for other schools and for other institutions for Indian music. He, again, was always willing to do extra things and to get the students involved . . . He had a building of his own and he really developed it in a very, very successful way. I think when he left, again, the music program just failed to evolve.

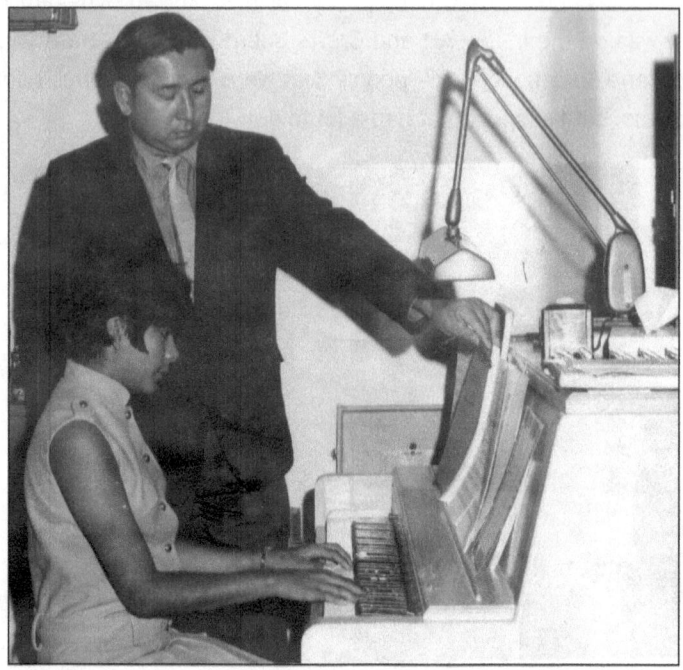

Louis Ballard, c. 1965. (Courtesy of IAIA Archives, Santa Fe, New Mexico) (rg03box11f03i01)

RD: Now I know that he probably prepared the students for all of these tours that you went on.

JM: He did *very* well, right.

RD: Can you talk a little bit about that work?

JM: Well, I remember the big one was a major exhibit to Scotland, Berlin, and all through South America. I wanted to be sure that there was music in there, so he'd prepare [it and the students]. Also he worked very closely with either Mr. (Rolland) Meinholtz[21] who usually did the drama [productions] or the ones that went to Washington and different places. They worked closely together on the music and the theater.

RD: Let's turn [now] to Allan (Houser).

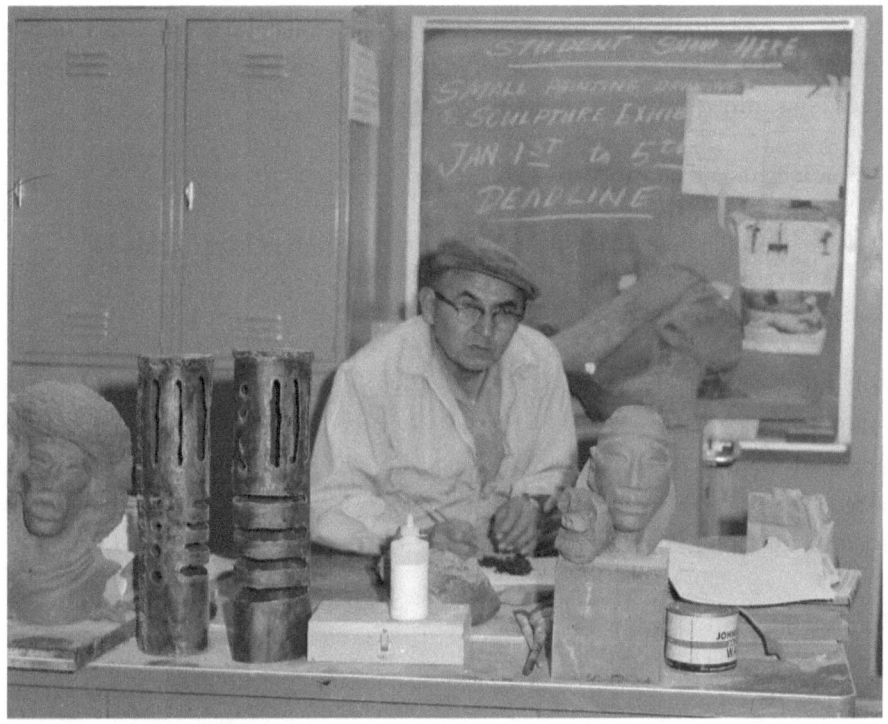

Allan Houser, c. 1968. Photograph by Kay V. Wiest. (Courtesy of IAIA Archives, Santa Fe, New Mexico) (ms10. box10.07)

JM: Allan's method of teaching was working in the classroom. I remember Lloyd and I mentioning once that his student's work looked a lot like his work. [Then we thought] . . . well, he works in the classroom, and that's kind of what happens when you are strong and you encourage students [in their] work—there is some similarity. Now we would talk with Allan about this occasionally, but it was his method and it was respected.

But, he also was willing to bring in new materials . . . and was willing to try different things, and he would do that in class. With the kids he would sculpt metal things using a can of liquid metal, he'd do welding, and work with wire. They didn't do much with clay, because that was in the other area. You know his work now is very refined and very elegant. Once in a while it would just burst [open] . . . he had these flares [of creativity.] That was his way of doing things.

RD: Well, probably his students influenced him as much as he did them.

JM: Exactly. Well, that's what happened to all of us there. We'd get *deeply* influenced by our students. It was really wonderful, yeah, but he was a good teacher. I mean, he got students involved and they really did wonderful work.

RD: How long did he stay with the school?

JM: He was still there when I left in '73, so I don't know how long he stayed.

RF: 1975.

JM: It was '75? Well, he was making big breakthroughs himself. He had the galleries in town (locally) and his work . . . he had some good commissions in Oklahoma. I think he needed—wanted—to be on his own, I think . . . That was another thing. We all grew. The staff was growing as much as the students were in some ways. People had to make decisions. "Are you going to stay there or not stay there?" . . . and things like that.

RD: What about Otellie Loloma?

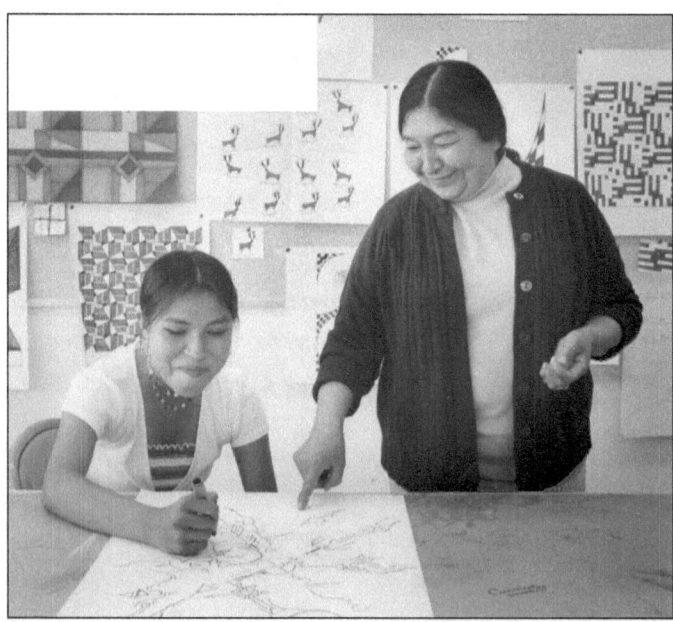

Otellie Loloma (right), c. 1976. (Courtesy of IAIA Archives, Santa Fe, New Mexico) (rg03box11f30i05)

JM: She was another *amazing* artist. She could do things with clay that was just unbelievable—and she was a very generous [person]. I mean for me being a non-Indian she was so generous with sharing with me. I would go home (to Hopi) with her and Charles (Loloma) to some of the ceremonies. They always would take me places that I knew were very special and [they] would share that on a personal level. In the classroom, she would work along with the students. She was just a devoted woman with clay . . . a devoted woman with her students.

She had really good students, and whenever it came to the Indian Foods Day or something she was always there—cooking and always there involved. She and I would take people to Zuni—to *Shalako*—and we would go to the dances. We would be able to get out of school to do some of these things, and she was always there to go places with the kids. Some of the teachers didn't like to do that very much, but she was one of them [that did]. She felt how important that was to do.

RD: There are a couple of people—not necessarily faculty—but certainly influential in terms of the creation of the school and sustaining the school. I'm specifically talking about Secretary of Interior Stewart Udall[22] and his wife, Lee (Ermalee).[23] I'd like for you to talk a little bit about your relationship with them and their relationship with the school.

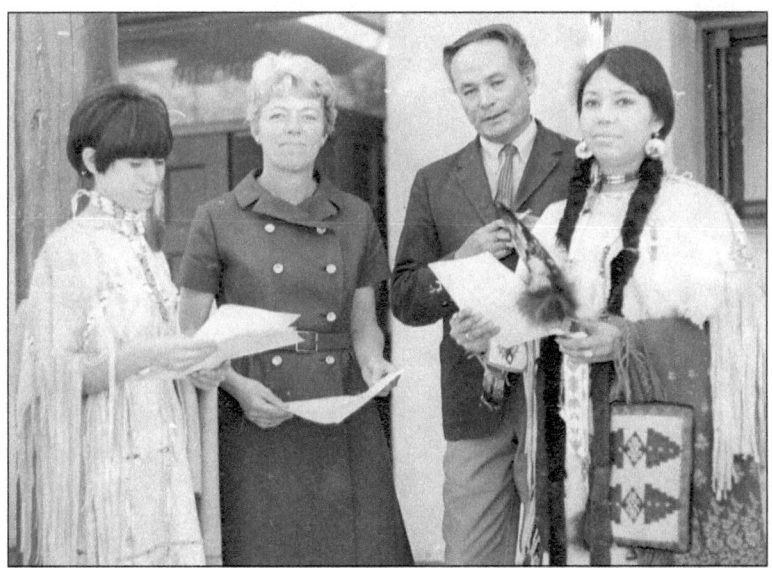

Lee Udall (center left) and Lloyd New (center right) with two IAIA students, c. 1966. (Courtesy of IAIA Archives, Santa Fe, New Mexico)

JM: I can't remember when I first met them. It could have been at an exhibit at the school. They liked the way we did our exhibits because we did them like environments. If we were doing a show on baskets, for instance, we would bring in bird nests and we'd put the bird nest as part of the exhibit. We'd get these huge tumbleweeds, put them on the walls and we'd put the bird nests in the tumbleweeds, or else we'd get a dead tree and put in a bird nest. Then, we would bring in the baskets and talk about how the birds taught early people how to weave and how to make things. We brought in turkeys and had a little cage built in the gallery with the turkey, and the kids would have to take the turkey out a couple times a day to walk it. So we really made these exhibits like [living] environments.

Well, Mrs. Udall found a whole wing that was a gallery on the top floor of the interior building. When they built the building [it was included], but it was [being used as] a storage area, so she wanted to open it up because she was so supportive of Indian art. [For that opening] she called on us to do the exhibits, so I would go with the students back there to set up and [later] to create [other] exhibits. Once in a while she would give us some money to do special exhibits on the campus . . .

I would say that they were *so supportive* of what we were doing and wanted to show it off in Washington to congressmen and to people who had *influence* on Indian welfare, Indian schools, and Indian education—to see what could be done, can be done, and what is being done. They were right there for us, encouraging us to come back and do projects and activities there.

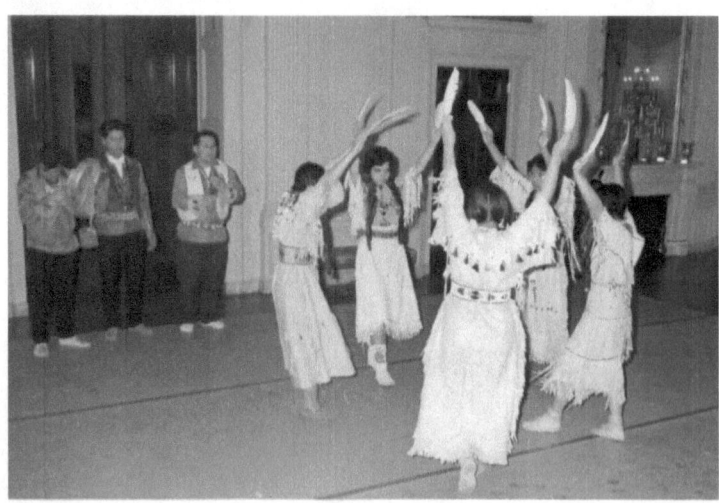

IAIA students performing at the White House, 1965. (Courtesy of IAIA Archives, Santa Fe, New Mexico) (rg03box18f33i01)

One time, President Yaméogo of Upper Volta came to America to visit the White House and he wanted to see Indian dances. Well, [Secretary Udall] didn't have much time, so he called the school and asked, "Could we have some Indian dancers come to the White House?" The reply was, "Well, I suppose we could." So they said, "McGrath, get some Indian dancers"—so I had to do this. Otellie got the Pueblo group together, and Josephine got another group together and somebody else got the Apache kids together. Then we went back and danced in the East Room of the White House . . . But out of that came some really interesting times—but the Udalls were always there—supporting the school . . .

RD: How do you think it was a benefit locally? On a national level and international, that's one thing, but locally?

JM: I think there was some resentment that we had an "in" so to speak. In fact, I'm quite sure there probably was. Even later on when I came back as dean I still heard some rumblings about that. But I tell you, it made a difference in people's lives. That's all there was to it. It really made a big difference in people's lives.

RD: Now, of all of the relationships that were established for the Institute here in Santa Fe . . . who or what was a local support for the school?

JM: I think Dr. Boyce really knew how important that was. I think the main supports that I recall . . . for instance, he allowed the art staff to have a gallery on Canyon Road—*Guild 7*. There were seven of us in it—art people—and we had our artwork there. Louis had his (music) tapes, I had my paintings, Otellie had her sculpture, Charles had his jewelry, and Lloyd had his textiles. It lasted for about a year and we ran it ourselves, but it didn't work out because we were too busy doing other things. It was right next to *Geronimo's*, in a little spot in there.

Another thing I know he did was [getting] particularly staff and students to go speak at luncheons [and other groups]. I can't remember which ones they were, except it could have been Lions, Kiwanis . . . maybe the Chamber of Commerce.

RD: So civic organizations?

JM: Civic things—yes, we did that. We had complete access to the collections at the Laboratory of Anthropology and the Folk Art [Museum]. They were always willing to loan us items for exhibit or take students on field trips to their collections and exhibits.

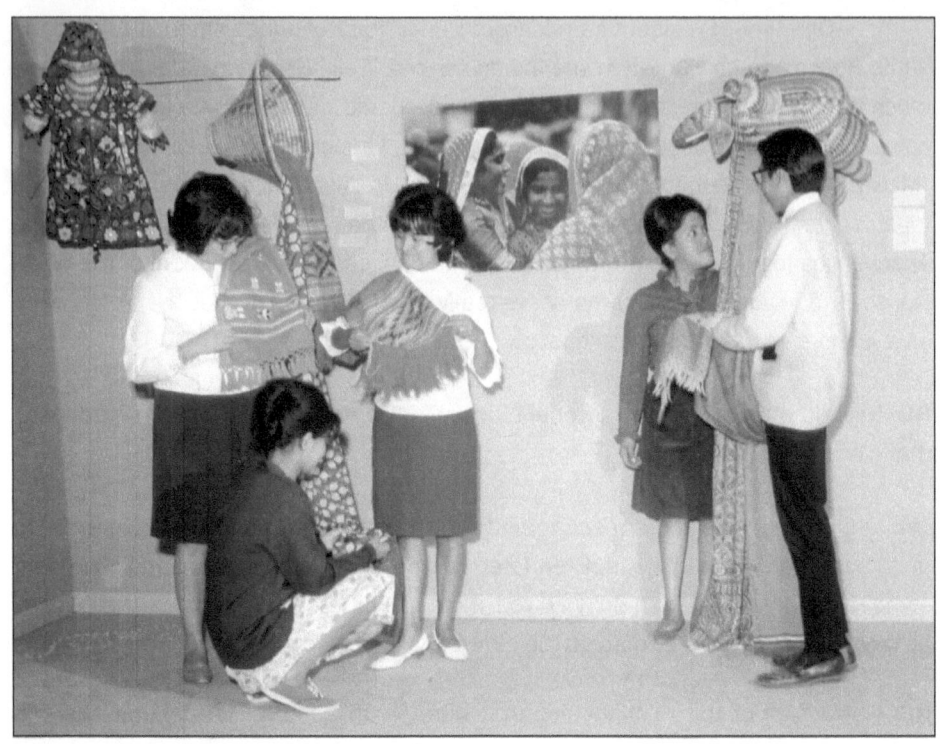

IAIA students installing "Indians East and Indians West," 1966. (Courtesy of IAIA Archives, Santa Fe, New Mexico) (rg03box18f13i06)

One time we did a show called "Indians East and Indians West," comparing *India* arts and crafts to *American Indian* arts and crafts. That came out of a time when we were in Washington and the New York World's Fair was going on. There was a big India pavilion, and Lee said, "Well why don't I work it out and we can get you some materials from the India pavilion after the fair is over?" So we got some clay sculptures, weavings, fabrics, and some photographs and had them shipped out here. Then, in turn, we added Native local pottery, textiles and such things.

RD: Always a learning experience.

JM: Always learning, but the point of that is that we were able . . . to borrow things from museums. They were very supportive here in town of that type of thing. So that was part of our local outreach.

Also, when we did have our *Indian Foods Day* some of the families would come and bring food and support us. I think it was the San Juan group that may have taken the boys out deer hunting. It could have been them or Taos—I can't remember what village [specifically]. So there was support *locally*—but not 100% . . . We were very fortunate, *very fortunate*.

RD: I'd like to go back to some of the partnerships or relationships that [developed among] staff . . . faculty . . . administrators? How Dr. Boyce and Lloyd New compliment each other . . . or not?

JM: Yeah, they were like complimentary colors—red and green, blue and orange. They were there and there was a balance . . . but it was a little unbalanced, I think as well. I think Lloyd was *definitely* not very conservative—he was in a way—but not maybe educationally. I mean, he was really out there [open] to new, new things, and—so, I know there were conflicts . . . I don't think Dr. Boyce [after his retirement] was happy when Lloyd became the director . . . I don't know who he wanted in there, but I don't think he wanted Lloyd to be the director—but it worked out that way . . . I think they both respected each other deeply for what they did.

RD: It would seem that Lloyd, coming out of the University of Arizona Rockefeller program . . . did his connections remain with ones he had made through that program?

JM: I know some of the students that were [in Tucson] still came. Not all of them came to the Institute but some did—George Burdeau and Roger Tsabetsaye were two for sure—that I remember.

RD: I was just curious about any further foundation support?

JM: Well, we had Ford Foundation support . . . I don't remember Rockefeller. I don't know that we needed very much those first years. I think we had so much available to us through the Bureau—through what Stewart could maintain—that I don't think we needed very much.

RD: What was the Ford Foundation grant relationship?

JM: I'm trying to think. I wonder if that was part of the traveling vans . . . The idea was to develop some traveling vans that went into schools—that brought *our* philosophy, examples of work, and teaching examples into these schools. I think some of that grant money could have come from Ford. I think some of the publications, like *Art and Indian Children, My Music Reaches the Sky: Native American Musical Instruments, and Dancing with Indian Children*—[all were] BIA curriculum bulletins.[24]

I think some of that money came from the ESEA Title I Project with the BIA as well as the Ford Foundation, and so the vans were developed and went into some of the schools . . . I think that idea caught on. I think there were others developed, but I don't know what happened to them . . .

RD: . . . you came back in 1988.

JM: I came back, yeah. That was a time when it was going from the BIA into whatever it's called (Institute of American Indian and Alaskan Native Arts and Culture Development) . . . it hadn't left BIA—and it hadn't quite got to that.[25] So it was that transition year and the board chairman . . . Bill Johnson.[26] He was there already. I hadn't met him prior to that, but I think he talked to Lloyd and then Lloyd talked to me and we thought, "Oh, we'll make a big difference"—ha, ha, ha. So we did come back for a year, and that was when we were doing the North Central [Accreditation] things[27] . . . But it was important, because it was a transition time . . . and it was very, very important that we did those things. There were major, major changes, and boy, I tell you, belief systems really came out to the fore.

RD: We talked a little bit about it but . . . here we have a stable faculty with all of the people that we've talked about. When you began to add new faculty, what was the vetting process for that?

JM: Well, we kind of talked among ourselves—who do you know that might be good to come in, say, as a painting teacher? Who do you think might be good to come in when (Charles) Loloma left as a new jewelry teacher?

Some of it was through advertisements. I'm not sure how it was advertised when I think about it, but we usually found people either by word of mouth or through somebody that knew somebody else. Some of them only lasted a year and some stayed on for more than that time. You know, here's a new person coming into a situation that is very unusual, very dynamic, and [with] lots going on. If you *didn't* have that kind of a system—it would be a struggle . . . there were some that didn't stay very long and there others that did. We also looked at [other] institutions. I remember we got a couple [of names] from the San Francisco Art Institute where the students went after they left here—Kevin Red Star, Hank Gobin, and Carol Frazier and few of others that went there, and were successful. So, we knew that their teaching situation sort of reflected our philosophy. I think we had a couple people that came from there, but they only stayed a year or so. When you come from San Francisco—with that environment—into Santa Fe (even as low keyed as it was), it doesn't always work that way.

RD: I know we've talked some, and you've mentioned just now, the model programs that you took from to develop the IAIA program—the San Francisco Arts Institute, the Chicago School, the California School in Oakland, and the Kansas City Art Institute.

What do you think were the most important parts of *those* programs in putting your program together?

JM: We really didn't model our curriculum from those other institutions. Probably accepting the differences and the uniqueness of the students. Those institutions knew who the students were because we sent portfolios . . . of their work and letters from the [students], letters of introduction, letters from other people supporting them, tests, and what they wanted to get out of a school. Some [programs] were very *avant-garde*—like the San Francisco one compared to Oakland, compared to Kansas City, compared to Chicago.

As advisors we were a little careful on which ones we would recommend to people knowing that they could handle it or they couldn't handle it. I think there were some judgments made from the staff more than there were from the students in some of these situations.

RD: Now did you visit those programs? Did you have any relationships with them prior to sending [students]?

JM: I knew about a couple of them. Lloyd knew Chicago because he'd been there. I knew San Francisco, because I had other students that had gone there. Oakland I had known about . . . We kept in contact with them to see how people were doing. There was a real follow-up type of thing.

RD: Oh, that's good, because the students didn't lose their family here. In a way they kept that relationship.

JM: Yeah, but probably not as strong. We didn't want to coddle all the time, but we wanted to give them support at least.

RD: Well, support in terms of getting them there was a big push.

JM: Yeah, but I think these were what we would call "supportive" types of institutions that would allow them to develop as themselves—not to have something imposed on them. Some of them had their academic courses integrated with the arts, which we knew [within] our philosophy that it was important. I wish we could have done that more here (at IAIA), but we just weren't able to do it as much as we would like to have.

RD: When you came back in 1988 did you find a difference . . . the academic programs [for example]?

JM: Well, they were with the college. They weren't in the Institute then—they were all right there in the College of Santa Fe.[28] I don't know how much success there was. I really don't know, because it was a college level, number one; and I don't know how supportive it was for the students themselves–that I don't know.

RD: By 1968, IAIA is established within an international forum through your participation in lots of activities [and travel]—the Edinburgh Festival, Berlin, the Alaska Centennial . . . Turkey . . . South America, the 1968 Olympics [in Mexico City], and then the connections with Washington, DC.[29] How were students chosen to participate in those activities?

JM: Primarily they were exhibits, so they often were *my students*, and then there were [additional] students. If it was a music program—it would be Ballard's students [and] for a theatre group it would be either (Rolland) Meinholtz, or else Josephine (Wapp) and Otellie's (Loloma) dance groups. So they were usually chosen depending on what the formats were. If there were exhibits . . . it was that group, for theater it was this group, for music it was that group—that is basically was how it was.

RD: So would students from all levels . . . from freshmen through seniors would participate.

JM: Exactly, yeah. And it would also be multi-tribal . . .

RD: Well, I'm interested in the changes that you saw in people through these experiences and the exposure to these cultures and [to] new things.

JM: Well, in fact it was as if more life came to them. There was something about how they were just more present—more alive! You could almost feel that something was going on—that there was some learning. There was some feeling of worthwhileness—something that just wasn't there at the beginning. It was wonderful . . . just something very, very special . . . I think that is a lot of the self-assurance of people like Kevin (Red Star) now—and other people who came through some of that. I think that what they learned in a way—is to be more themselves—more outgoing, more listening, more there, and more present.

RD: Well, to wrap this up. What challenges did you think were the most profound for the Institute in all of your years connected to it?

JM: Probably the curriculum and . . . the real willingness and risk-taking to do some of the things that we did. I don't think they were always something that we did a lot of *research* about. I think it was a lot of *intuitive* things that we did that we felt were important for students, important for creativity, and to the spirit of being a creative person. [It was less] about having a lot of models. Some of us had some experience, but we didn't have all that—I think those were probably the important things.

Also, the living conditions were important—the dormitory life, how people got together—especially because it was just a boarding school basically. That was very important—the environment and how that could be—how that could be set up so it could be joyous, it could be family, it could be trusting. It could be all the things that we know is important to live together . . . There were still some animosities and things . . . but it sounded more playful at the same time.

But I think the living thing—the curriculum, the staff, and the student rapports—are probably three of the main [important] things. And, underlying that is all the financial and the institution itself—so it does blend together.

RD: What do you hope for the next fifty-years for the institute?

JM: Well, I was concerned about how students were selected—with the grades and things like that. Knowing when I go to the reservation or go places—that I meet young people who just are struggling. They are struggling to learn, to read, to do things—and I keep thinking—"you're not going to be able to go to the Institute. You just are not going to get the grades, and I wish you could." I would like to see a whole different approach to who the student body is. That's probably my number one thing.

Staff-wise, it's exciting to see . . . I don't know whether it's balanced or not . . . but to see both Native and non-Native people in there. Again, I would *love* to see teachers in there with no degrees but who really *know* their craft and really know what it is to be who they are. They're the ones [in the past] I saw getting to the students *so much quicker* and [that brought] so much depth as compared to the others. So those are a couple things. And I would like an arts education degree component—teach teachers, teach students who want to be teachers to carry on the IAIA philosophy . . .

RF: The museum always has seemed to be a good support system for the students. Can you talk a little bit about how the museum started and how the collection was started?

JM: Oh, definitely. Well, we needed material. We needed to have baskets and pottery. We needed to have objects that the students may have lived with or at least that families may have. Even though they may be coming from San Francisco they may not have had them, but I think they would like to know about them. We couldn't go around buying all of this because it was expensive. We didn't know how to do it, but we had a building that we blocked the windows [out] and covered the walls with burlap and put in a grid for lights—and that was our gallery.

It started out as an exhibition gallery, because we borrowed stuff from museums to have that as a source for them to see their things. This was out of the training on how to take care of [objects], how to make labels, how to [produce] a catalog . . . how to do the things that would support the information. Sometimes they were just typed up and mimeographed, but some were also printed when we got more money. [All of that] expanded into some major exhibits (as I mentioned earlier)—Maria and her pottery, the Gilpin photographs, John Hoover's collection of Alaska materials.

We were able to call upon galleries and private individuals to bring things in, and out of that came the *training* on how to set things up and to do it in different ways. It was always *rooted* in Indian cultural ideas and visual things. So that's how it started and when I left it, Chuck Dailey[30] was hired. His philosophy was different from mine . . . more academically oriented for a *museum person*, which was fine—they're needed. That was important, but we did have a little different philosophy on it. That's kind of how it started and evolved.

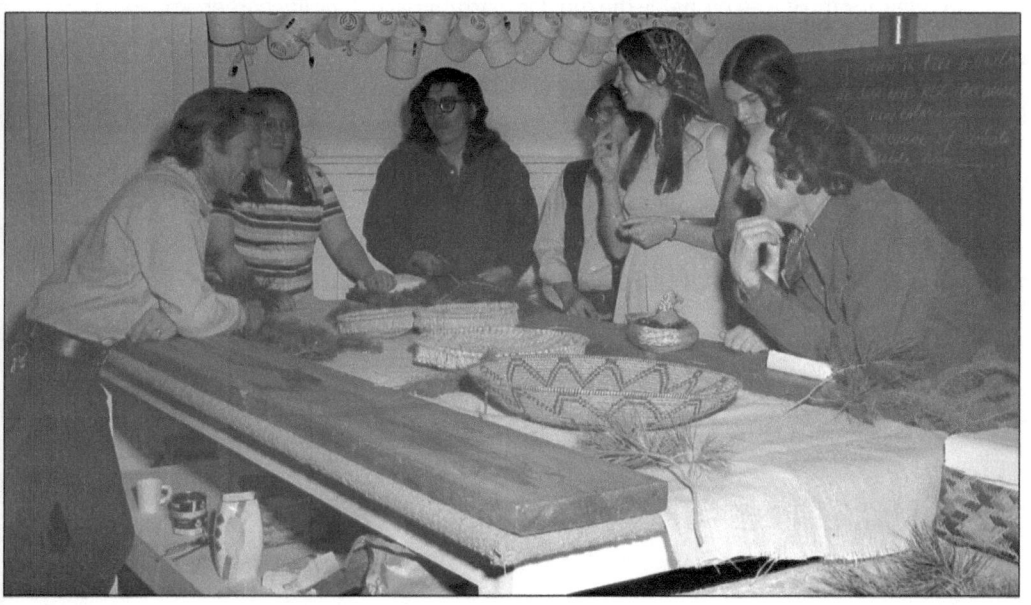

Charles Dailey (left) and James McGrath (right) with museum studies students, c. 1971. Photograph by Kay V. Wiest. (Courtesy of IAIA Archives, Santa Fe, New Mexico) (ms10.box10.05)

It is now a resource—a national resource of materials. To get the collection [going] we noted the San Francisco Art Institute's philosophy was that they could have a piece of student work from every student during each year and [that's how they] developed their collection. So that [became] our philosophy and for several years—that's what we did. We *took* from the students saying we would like to have that for our *Honors Collection*[31]—to give us a collection that showed their progress as artists and the progress of the Institute and what was going on [here]. Early on that's how that collection started and then later on—in the '70s—the students said they did not like that. "We don't like you taking our artwork. Either buy it or . . . " There were always a few at that period who were very vocal that way. The rest of them they said, "Oh have it—take it, take it." So [the collecting] changed. But, that's how it started, and how the base collection [came about].

RD: Is there anything that we haven't asked you that you'd like to add . . . or anything that came to mind while we were talking?

JM: Well, for me it was probably the most important part of my life career—my vocation. It made a *big difference* for me, and I'm still living it and it's still important. I don't do much there . . . even though I keep my ears open . . .

RD: Well, Ryan and I would like to thank you so much for doing this interview and helping us set a foundation for the interviews to come.

JM: Well, I'm thrilled that we're doing this too.

RD: Thank you.

JM: We'll make a difference. We've made the difference and we'll continue making it.

5

Photo Essay: IAIA at The College of Santa Fe

n 1999, not long before IAIA opened its new campus in Rancho Viejo, IAIA director of communications, Merritt Edson Youngdeer documented the IAIA facilities at the College of Santa Fe (CSF). Between 1981 and 2000, IAIA rented space from CSF after the BIA displaced the college program from the Santa Fe Indian School campus in 1980. Many superb students and artists graduated from IAIA during the CSF years, but many would agree that the facilities were less than optimal.

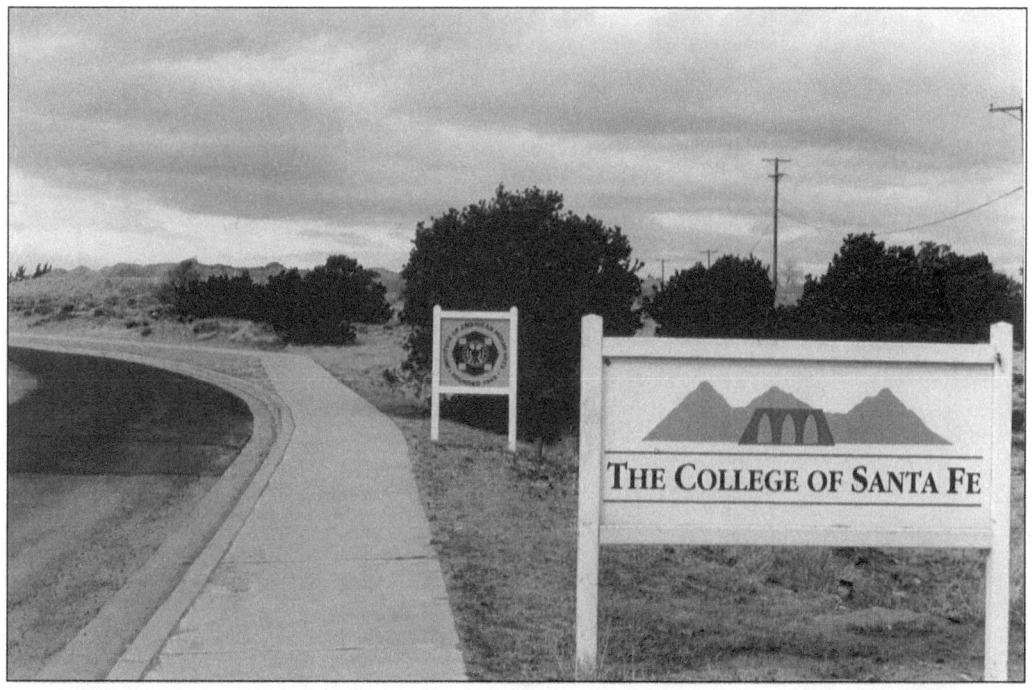

CSF/IAIA entrance. Following a congressional decision to reestablish the Santa Fe Indian School, IAIA relocated to the campus of College of Santa Fe in 1981. Photograph by Merritt Edson Youngdeer. (Courtesy of IAIA Archives, Santa Fe, New Mexico) (rg03box24f15i3a)

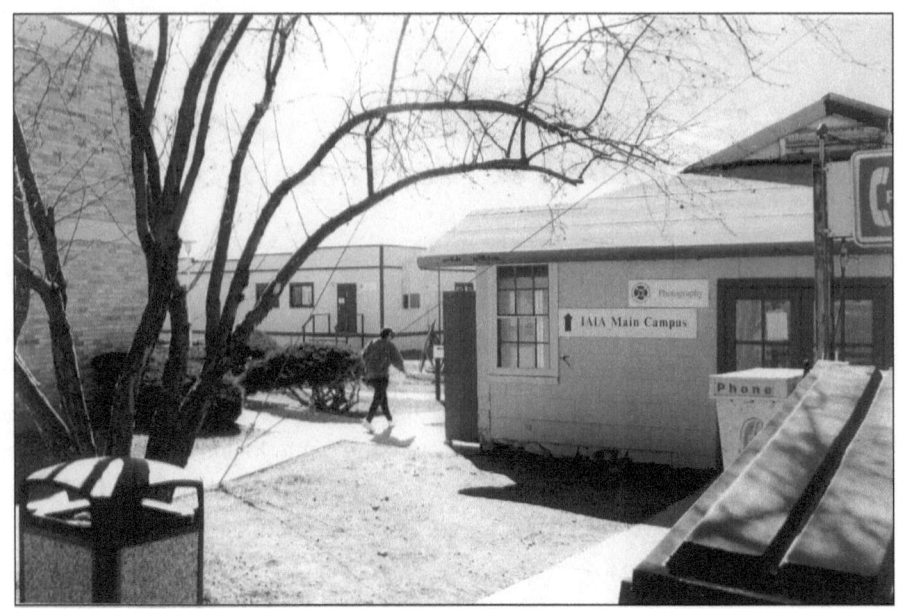

IAIA Main Campus. While most of the IAIA college operations moved to CSF, the BIA allowed IAIA to keep the museum and a few other buildings at the SFIS, known as 'North Campus.' Photograph by Merritt Edson Youngdeer. (Courtesy of IAIA Archives, Santa Fe, New Mexico) (rg03box24f15i3b)

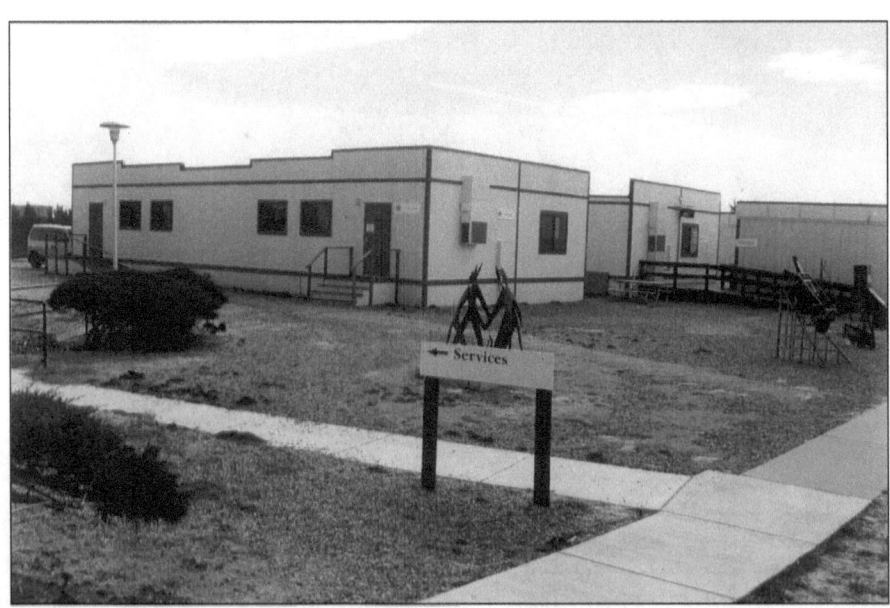

Studio buildings. Many of the classrooms and studios were held in portable trailers. Photograph by Merrit Edson Youngdeer. (Courtesy of IAIA Archives, Santa Fe, New Mexico) (rg03box24f15i3c)

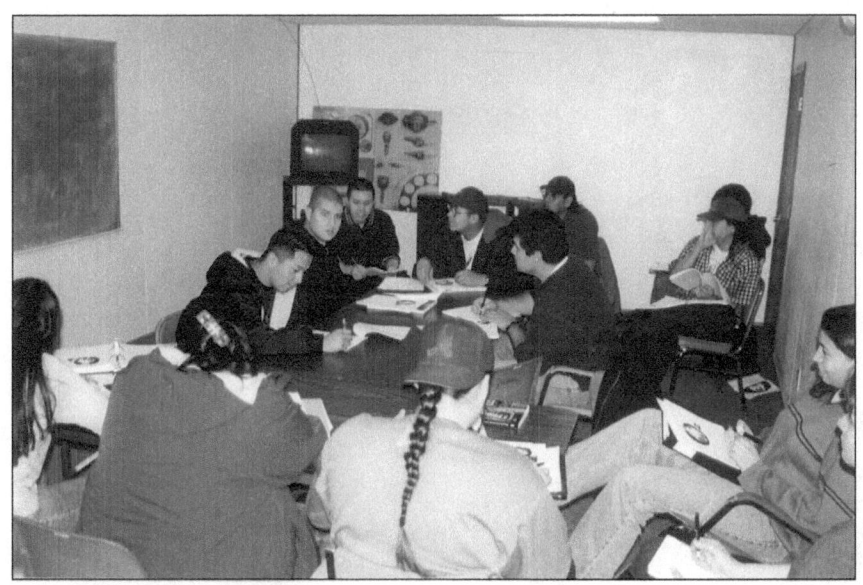

IAIA students. Inside the portables, the lack of workspace was an ongoing problem. Photograph by Merrit Edson Youngdeer. (Courtesy of IAIA Archives, Santa Fe, New Mexico) (rg03box24f15i3g)

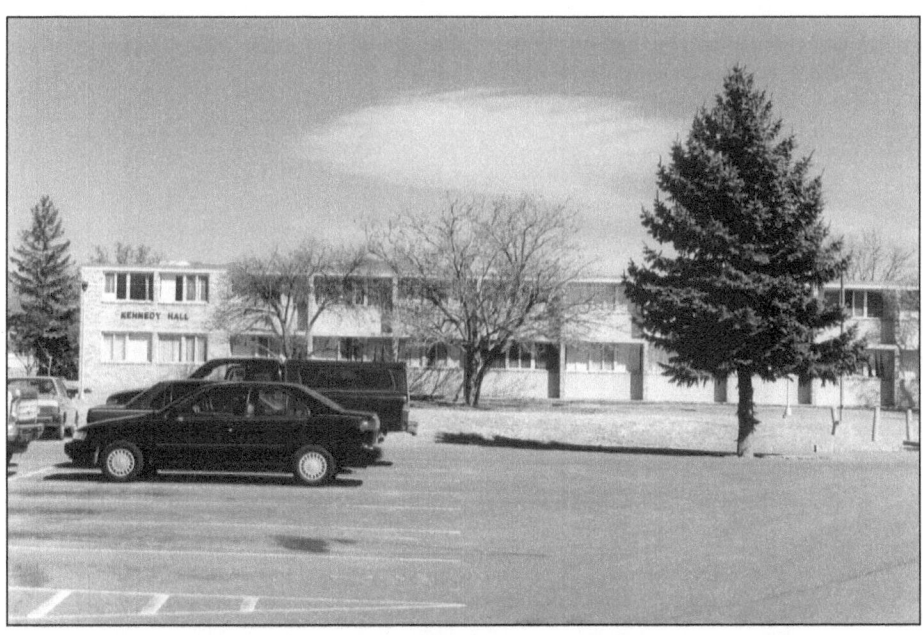

Kennedy Hall. Kennedy Hall was one of the dormitories used by IAIA during the CSF years. Photograph by Merrit Edson Youngdeer. (Courtesy of IAIA Archives, Santa Fe, New Mexico) (rg03box24f15i3i)

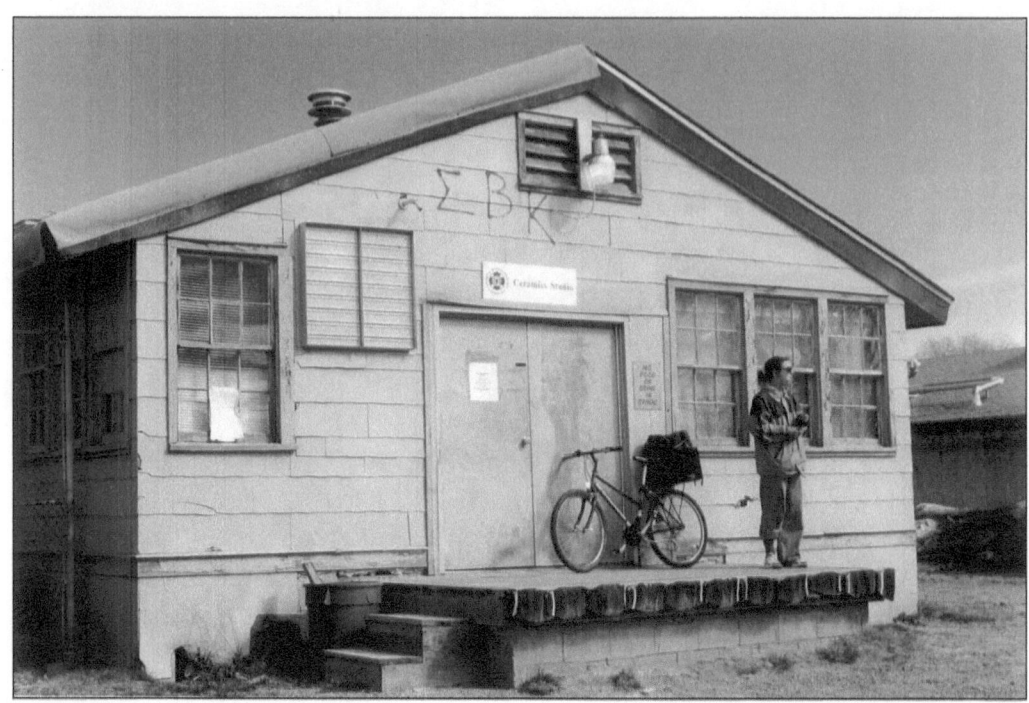

Ceramics studio. The portables made up the majority of classroom and studio space, but other buildings were used as well, like this repurposed World War II era Army barrack. Photograph by Merrit Edson Youngdeer. (Courtesy of IAIA Archives, Santa Fe, New Mexico) (rg03box24f15i3m)

Dreams, Landscapes, and Sacredness at The Institute of American Indian Arts

by
Rina Swentzell, PhD
Photographs by Bill McIntire

A ustralian aborigines describe the earth's power as the "dreaming" of a place, because anything that occurs in a particular location leaves "seeds, myths or images, unseen vibrations that provoked the place into being in the first place."[1]

—A.T. Mann

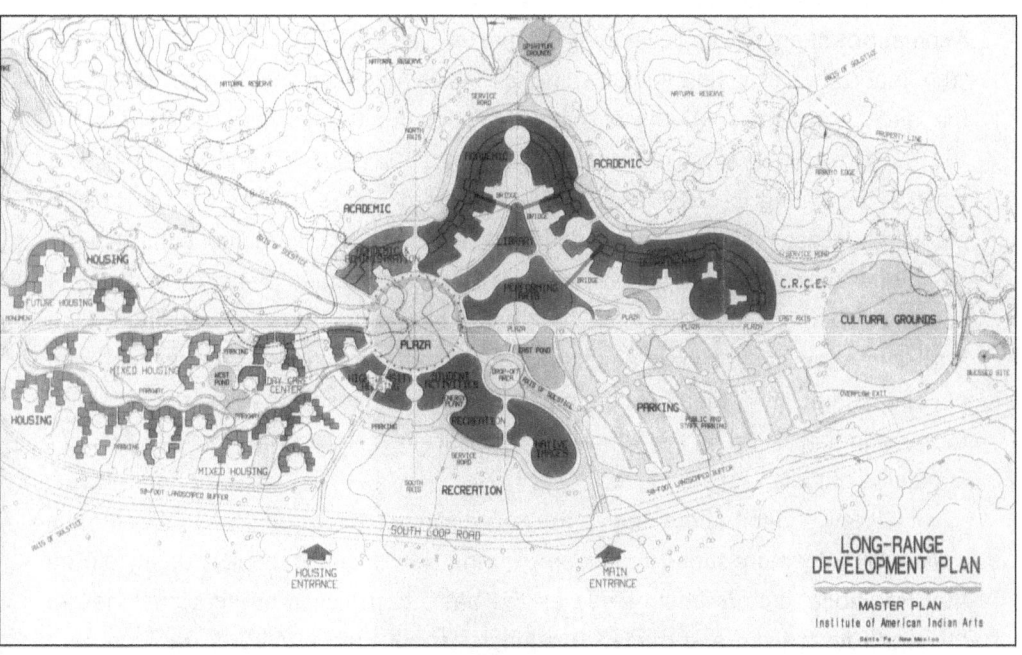

The "Long Range Development Plan" map was part of the IAIA campus master plan report to Congress, developed by Douglas J. Cardinal Architects in 1993. (Courtesy of IAIA Archives, Santa Fe, New Mexico) (master_plan)

A prayer and song were offered when the Institute of American Indian Arts (IAIA) prepared for the relocation of its campus to its present site in the early 1990s. The prayer and song asked for wisdom, knowledge, and love to follow the sacred path of life by watching "over every plant, every tree, every animal, every rock, every winding stream, every lake, the sacred fire and the clearness of the sky." The song also acknowledged the encircling mountains and healing winds.

Here, within these circling mountains—a cradle of learning—our artist-scholars will examine these truths, reawakening within us all, a great love . . . singing truthful songs held in the old hearts of these gnarled trees of this land which have sheltered others for infinity. "In this circle of mountains, we hold these visions to be self-evident."[2]

These self-evident visions led to the creation of a gathering place where clans, tribes, elder leaders, and teachers would renew and honor the wholeness of the family, the sanctity of all living things, the earth, and the sky. It is a place of rediscovery and cultural enrichment through fostering and nurturing cultural traditions and teachings, which would be reexamined, rediscovered, and reaffirmed. A committee charged with developing the master plan for the new campus determined "the importance of maintaining traditional Native American values: the respect for the land . . . and the continuity of our tribal codes into the next generation."[3]

Lloyd H. New, art director of IAIA from 1962 to 1967, and director of the Institute beginning in 1967 until 1978, reiterated before and during the master planning process that the Institute needed to reaffirm cultural traditions through the plan. But New insisted that cultural awareness was only a means—not an end—to the educational experience at the Institute. It was to be a springboard to creativity, "Indian art lies in an ability to evolve, adjust and adapt to the demands of the present, and not upon the ability to manipulate the past. Art is a manifestation of the times."[4] "The future of Indian art lies in the future, not the past—let's stop looking backward for our standards of Indian art production."[5]

New's ideas about Native art education predated the 1993 IAIA campus master plan by more than thirty years. During New's career, he repeatedly stated that traditional culture could serve as the basis from which an individual viewed the world for artistic and human meanings. By his theory, culture, tradition, and the past were optional for the contemporary student; but New understood that by knowing one's past and self, an artist could value and determine the place of art in society. New also wanted Indian art to contribute to the general cultural stream, "Our first responsibility is to fit Indian artists into the world of art in general," yet at the same time worried about hastening the assimilation of Indians into the American mainstream.[6]

New believed that beauty was universal and beyond cultural continuums. He argued that the beauty of a shape and the skill of execution alone were qualifications for artistic expression, but that beauty was an absolute and abstract quality that could be assigned by the individual artist. Hence, the artist could contribute to the beauty of the environment.[7] New implied that the environment was also abstract and separate from human existence; it was "something out there." By his line of thinking, the artist could include the Native cultural focus on the environment in their work, but was not required to do so. His primary concern was to create an institutional atmosphere of freedom that encouraged individual expression addressing human and societal issues. For New, Indian art was about "the universal forces of creativity, contemporary demands—and respect for cultural differences."[8]

A major component of the traditionalist vision statement of the IAIA campus plan was the concept of sacredness and oneness with nature. There was an assumption that beauty and creativity exists within the natural world from which the human soul can learn and emulate. This concept reflects upon traditional Native American values of respect for the environment and culture, which includes a communal way of life. Respect for the "old ways" meant respect for traditional arts and cultures, and that respect would best provide identity and personal enrichment for the individual. Creative expression is dependent on the continuum of known cultural traditions and Native art is a result of traditional thoughts and practices held within the human community that are assumed to be within the natural world.

These concepts—beauty, sacredness, and oneness with nature—run concurrently within the landscaped spaces of the IAIA campus. If human-made structures and landscaped spaces are reflections of philosophical thought, as is believed by many architects, both abstraction from and communion with the natural world are expressed in the buildings and outdoor spaces on the campus. The "sacred spaces" of the campus are focused primarily on the exterior spaces and less on the built forms that are mostly in the "form follows function" model of architecture. The campus buildings align with Lloyd New's sense of art as being individualistic and meeting contemporary demands without disturbing the conscious relationship to the natural context. Each building is inwardly focused, including structures encircling the central plaza area. They are essentially self-contained with high-powered technologies of our present times; they are contemporary buildings. And once inside any of the buildings on the main campus, the natural world is mostly forgotten. The buildings serve the needs of individuals working and living within modern society.

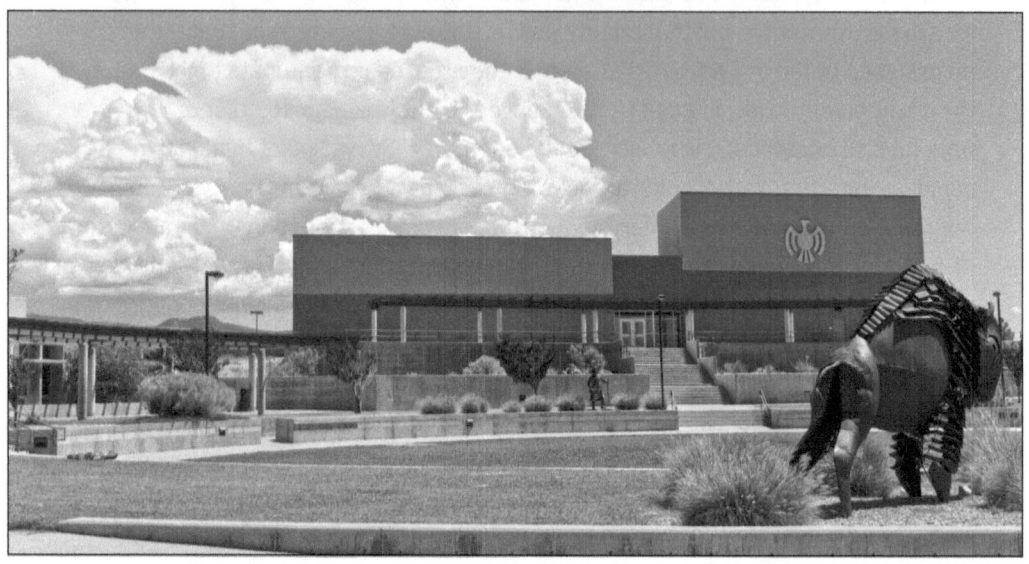

Looking east across the central plaza towards the Science and Technology Building, IAIA Campus. Photograph by Bill McIntire. (Courtesy of IAIA) (sc_bldg1)

The central plaza is culturally significant and symbolically gathers, embraces, and connects the campus. Sidewalks and plaza-like spaces were designed around the buildings to connect neighboring structures. The modern environment, however, is harsh in its concrete surface and feels alien to human use or plant life. Yet despite the modern harshness of the environment, the campus master plan calls for a harmonious relationship between the buildings and natural elements such as earth, plants, and the sky, "in keeping with the wholistic (sic) nature of American Indian traditions, the landscape and architectural design concepts for the campus master plan will be developed in harmony with one another. The buildings will appear to grow out of the land, and the relationship between building and landscape will be harmonious; landscape and architecture will complement one another."[9]

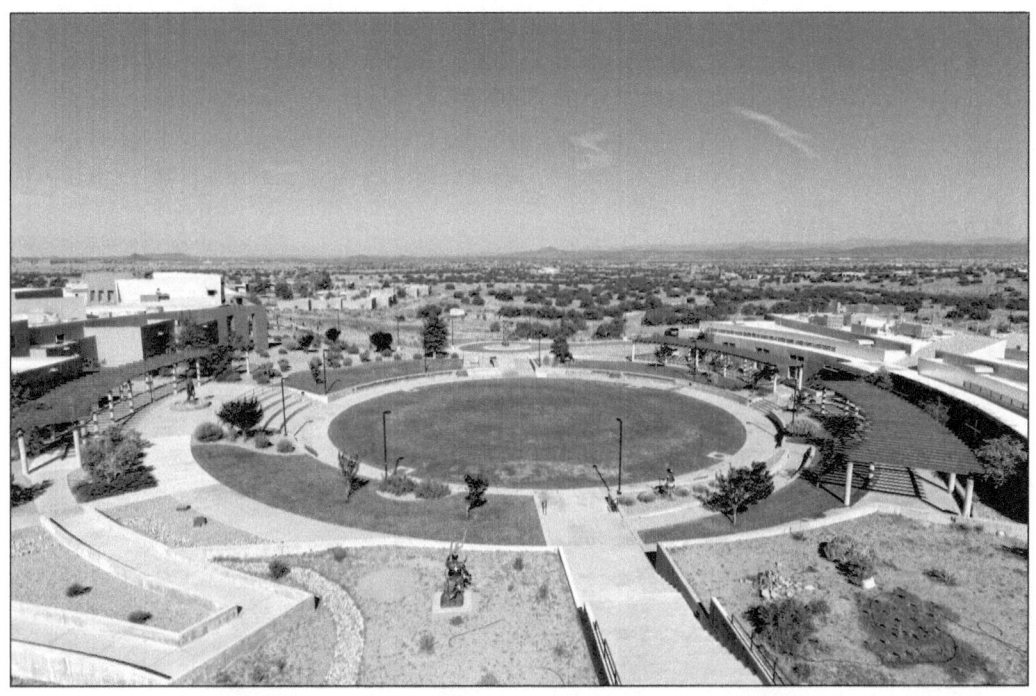

Looking west across the central plaza from atop the Science and Technology Building. On the right is the main Administration Building, containing office space and classrooms, and to the left is the Library and Technology Center. Photograph by Bill McIntire. (Courtesy of IAIA) (plaza2)

The chief characteristics of the landscape design in the master plan was inspired by Native philosophy and included statements supporting the philosophy:

The landscape development will reflect American Indian and native peoples' spiritual values related to the land and its use.

The landscape development will foster human interaction that creates a sense of communal connection, fundamental to American and native cultures.

The landscape development will sustain and enhance the natural existing environment on the site, and provide appropriate areas where humans and human activities can relate and coexist within that environment.[10]

Accordingly, the physical design elements of the master plan included sightlines to distant places and mountains, cardinal directions, solar equinoxes, solstices, circles, wind, water, animal lifelines, and native plants. These natural elements assured that the IAIA campus honored the relationship with and between "the Natural World, the Animal World, the Spirit World and the Human World" thereby creating sacred spaces.[11]

The landscape of the IAIA campus was designed to create spaces that connected the human world to larger energies and powers of the universe. For traditional cultures across the world, the entire earth is sacred. Tribes throughout the Americas consider the sky, the earth, rivers, ocean, mountains, valleys, trees, rocks, and animals to have special powers. All domains and species are part of the divine. All are sacred.

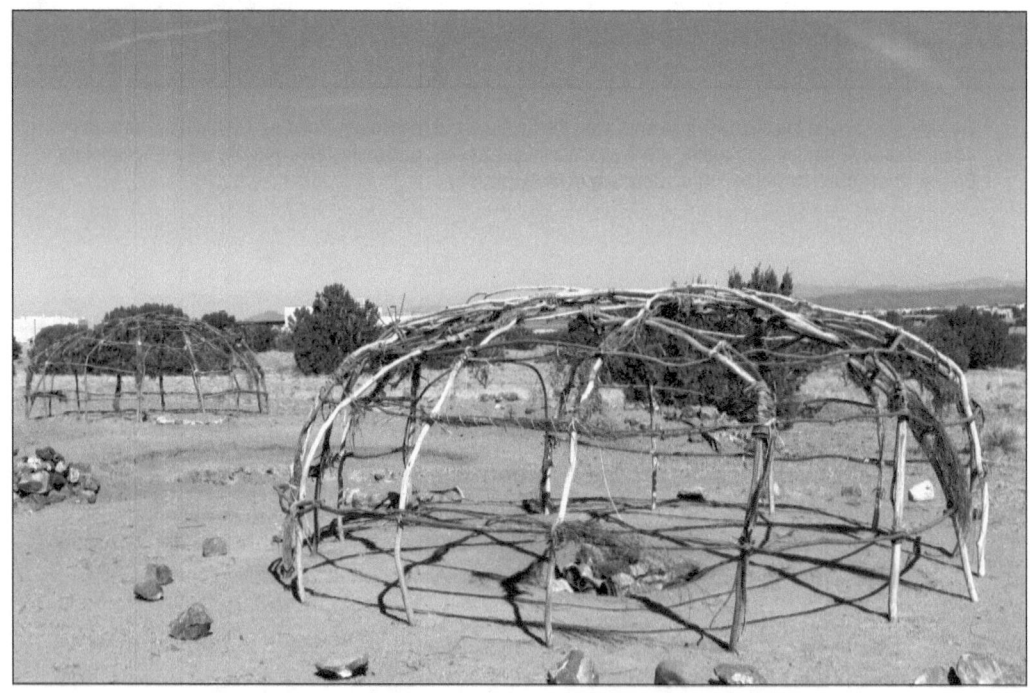

On the eastern edge of campus sets the cultural grounds, where sweat lodge ceremonies are regularly held for the IAIA community. Photograph by Bill McIntire. (Courtesy of IAIA) (sweatlodge4)

How did the Institute of American Arts acknowledge and honor this sacredness? The campus master plan clearly described how the natural elements (sun, moon, wind, animals, and plants) were to be incorporated into the buildings and landscape. The movements of the sky, namely the summer solstice and winter equinox, determined the layout of the campus. In reality, there is only a vague reminder of the cardinal directions with an east/west concrete walkway that leads from the main plaza to one of the living areas. The walkway serves as an abstract linear component in contrast to the circle of the plaza making it a line imposed on the land with the pure function of getting from one place to another in the straightest way possible without interruption by land form or plant life. In the master plan, texture, materials, and form of the buildings were to reinforce the human connection with the earth and landforms. Such ideas find vague identification in the actual place. The layout of the campus does not correspond with where the sun comes up or goes down and between the sharp edged buildings, there are glimpses of the far mountains as if they can't be ignored.

"The focus of the campus development is the central plaza. The plaza symbolizes the concept of fostering communal connections and human interaction, that are a strong part of native cultures."[12] For Pueblo peoples, who claim ancestry to the land where IAIA is located, the plazas in their villages are sacred places where humans interact and connect with the energies of the sky and the earth. The breath of the earth flows through an opening in the ground of the plaza, and through the community of dancers who wear cloud and mountain headdresses, it invites the sky to meet the earth. Human feet touch the dirt of the earth and heads acknowledge the sky. Humans become crucial elements in the flow of energy through this sacred space. They are conduits of cosmic energy flow.

At IAIA there are several circles defined as plazas. The central plaza, sometimes called the dance circle, is beautiful in its pure form. During any normal day, one can contemplate its perfection and wonder if ancestral spirits dwell there and if the circle's healing powers facilitate personal transformation through communication with forces beyond human reality. On a platform alongside and above the central plaza, an adjoining circle is about fire. For safety reasons the fire is well contained in a concrete space, but there is no earth to stomp, dance, or sit on to contemplate fire and sky. It, again, is a perfectly inscribed circle that holds the possibility of social and celestial interaction.

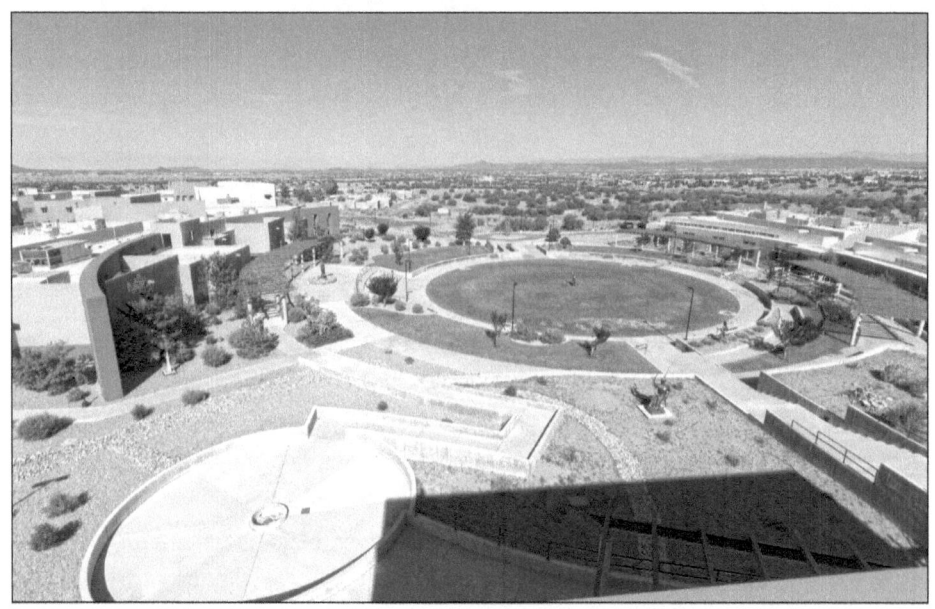

The fire circle (bottom left corner) is southeast of the central plaza. Photograph by Bill McIntire. (Courtesy of IAIA) (firecircle1)

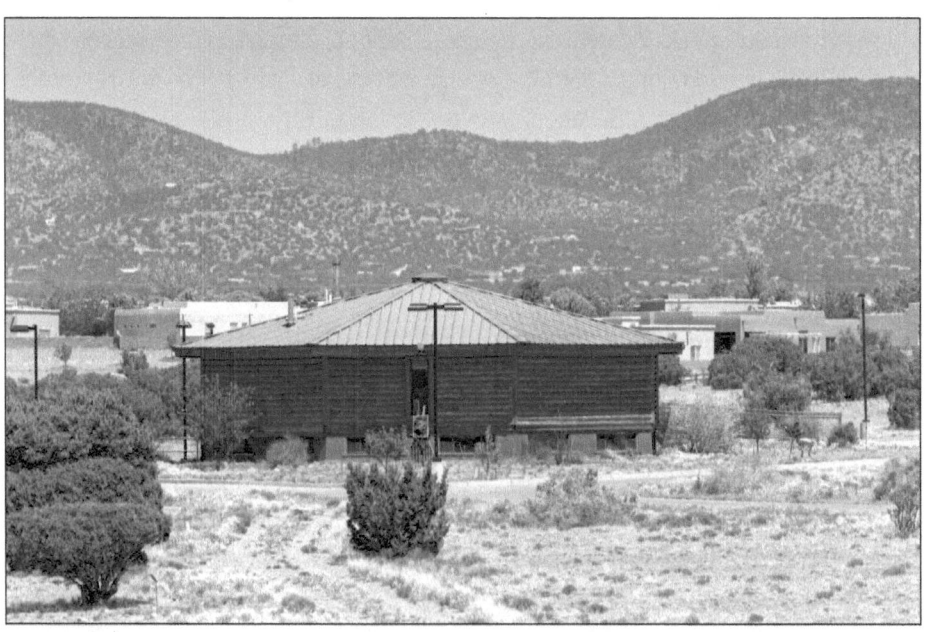

The hogan was the first building constructed on the campus. Photograph by Bill McIntire. (Courtesy of IAIA) (hogan3).

Some distance from the main campus is an isolated octagonal hogan. This structure is set in place with wooden walls that resonate with the surrounding pinon trees and chamisa bushes. It sets on a low hill among native plants and invites the presence of the far mountains. The main door opens to the east power center—the direction of the rising sun. Once inside the hogan, the atmosphere is conducive to gathering, contemplation, and renewal, reinforcing the incorporation of spiritual values outlined in the master plan:

Understand the symbolic and spiritual context
Incorporate important plants
Orient designs to symbolic power centers
Dedicate areas for spiritual renewal[13]

Other areas of the campus incorporate similar qualities of spiritual renewal through connection with the natural world. Unpaved walkways and potential mediation areas located away from the main, developed campus provide places of communion with nature. The terraced garden area along the linear east/west concrete walkway sits beautifully within a wide natural drainage. It is an area where "the landscape development sustains and enhances the natural existing environment on the site and provides appropriate space where humans and human activities can relate and coexist."[14] On the asymmetrical terraces are corn stalks, squash plants, and weeds—all needing human interaction. The area could easily be dismissed as "something out there" and not as significant. The terraces, however, hold the essence of the stated landscape dream for IAIA; a place on campus where human activities intersect with nature.

In conclusion and true to its tradition, IAIA is a place where big ideas are growing and big things are happening. It is a transforming place where tensions exist and thoughts are provoked. The tension in the landscape environment of IAIA seems to flow out of the stated philosophic dreams for the Institute, which struggle between pure art concerned with general societal issues and art that considers cultural, traditional, or natural contexts as solid foundations. Essentially, the tension is between a focus on nature and a focus on individual and social concerns.

The campus landscape reflects those tensions. Abstraction and a desire for communion are both apparent in the physical place. The abstracted circles and lines are pure forms yet suggest the possibility of connection with other humans and with spiritual and cosmic energies. There are native plants that soften the hard concrete surfaces and places where one can see and feel the mountains, clouds, and rising or setting sun even if they are not created for that purpose.

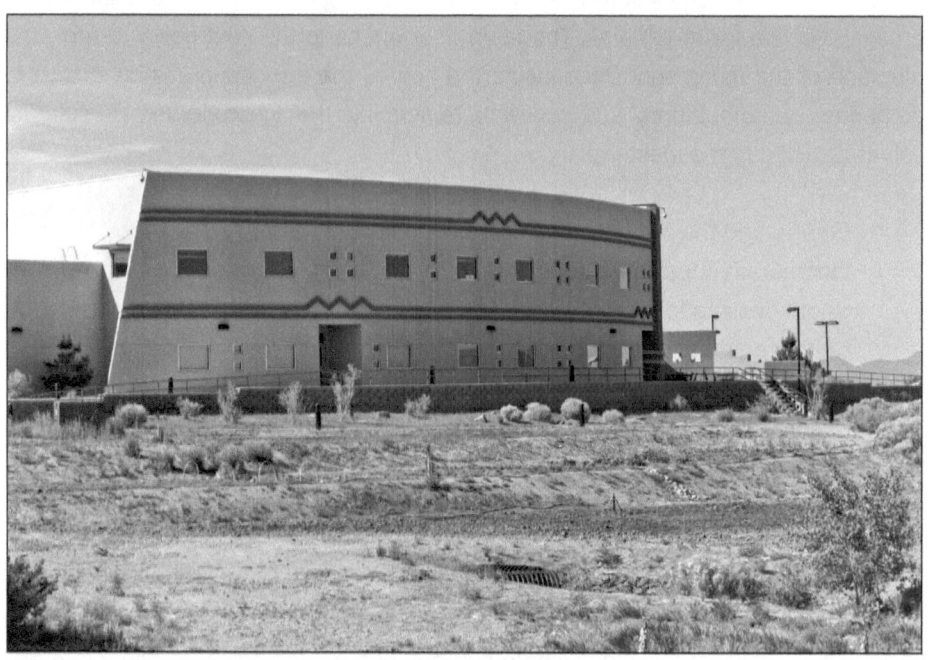

The terraced gardens of IAIA sit at the foot of the Center for Lifelong Education. Photograph by Bill McIntire. (Courtesy of IAIA) (garden1)

The Institute's campus is in a beautiful location. The beauty of the surrounding landscape contains the place, yet grey concrete surfaces embrace inward-looking activities seeking to uncover universal meanings attempting to make spiritual connections. Tensions and disaccord are evident, but so are intentions to keep growing, to keep moving, and to become something more than the disparate parts. Is this not what Native philosophies consider? Certainly, Pueblo thought acknowledges and honors the dualities of nature and human existence: summer and winter, male and female, dark and light, hot and cold. They are opposites but are also complementary qualities inherent in nature and society.

In this way of thinking, striving to acknowledge "the other" is a goal of a worthwhile life. It is not about "this or the other"; it is about both. Together they form a continuum of thought, experiences, and tradition. In Pueblo thought, harmony is desired while dualistic forces are honored. In doing so, past and present are brought together. Lloyd New once stated, "to be concerned about the future does not mean to forsake the past, for it is the well from which we draw the strength that serves the present."[15] In his words we find a personal continuum of thought that was developing around the core idea of freedom of individual artistic expression and the need for community and tradition.

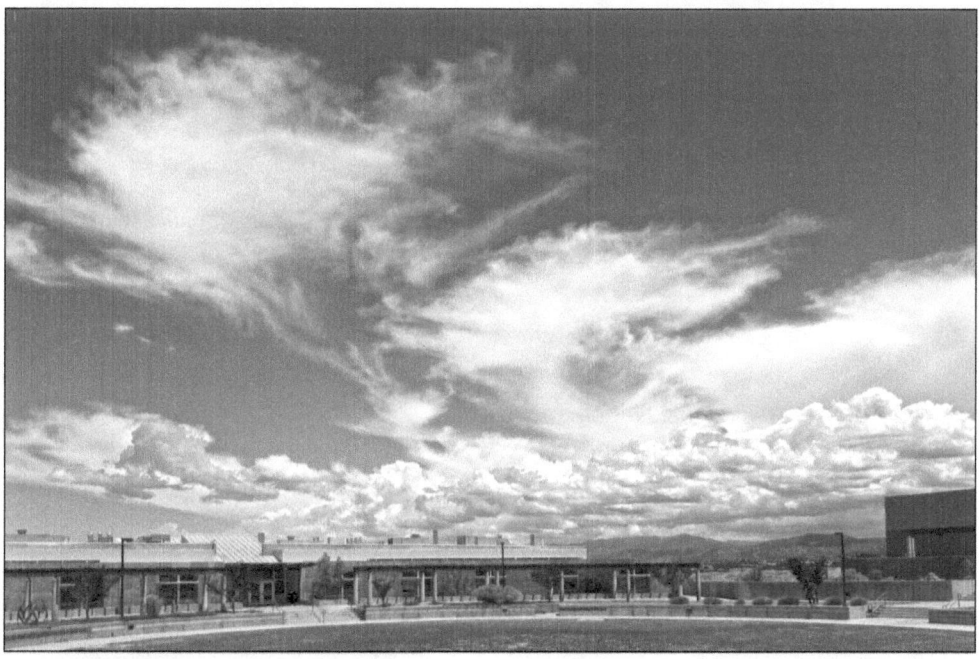

The IAIA campus looking towards the Sangre de Cristo Mountains northeast of Santa Fe. Photograph by Bill McIntire. (Courtesy of IAIA) (adminbldg1)

In the end, community and tradition need individuals and vice-versa. In a similar fashion, art needs nature. The human-created landscape of the Institute will grow and change to reconcile with the surrounding natural environment. It is a created space that has the possibility of nurturing communication with wind, clouds, and mountains. The earth's power, the dreaming—which brought the place into being— is strong. Vibrations rise from the land and are there for the taking to give spiritual meaning to the people living and working at IAIA—which remains an inspiring work in progress.

7

Just Another Day in Raven's Lifetime
IAIA as the Future of Education
by
Theodore (Ted) Jojola, PhD

"The end result will be as Indian as the Indian."[1]
—"A Proposal for an Exploratory Workshop in Art for Talented Younger Indians"

n a moment of frustration, a contemplative Lloyd H. "Kiva" New penned the following comment as he reflected on the success of the first of two Rockefeller Foundation workshops for American Indian artists:

> Helen Hardin [among three others] profited less than most of the students; if talented, not seriously interested in art as manifested by their lack of application. Helen wants to become an airline hostess before becoming a nun . . . And while not many people at this age know what they want to do, the least we could do in our selections would be to choose those who *think* they are interested in art in a fairly serious way.[2]

The irony of this comment is that Hardin, a Santa Clara daughter who publicly admitted to being suffocated by the reputation of her famous artistic mother, Pablita Velarde, went on to become a premier artist of her own right.[3] Her life, cut short by cancer in 1984 at the young age of forty-one, was one of several dozen students who had been part of a program for spring-boarding young people into a career in Indian art.

Funded by the Rockefeller Foundation, the first of two summer art programs began in 1960 at the University of Arizona. These summer workshops were not only designed to bring together talent-in-the-raw, but also assembled luminary mentors of the Indian art gallery scene including artistic pioneers Lloyd "Kiva"

New and Hopi artist Charles Loloma. It is unclear whether New and his assembly anticipated that this seed effort would grow into the vital and vibrant Institute of American Indian Arts (IAIA). What they did admit was that architect Frank Lloyd Wright, who must have told them to quit whining and take charge, had egged them on:

> The Hopi, Charles Loloma and the Cherokee, Lloyd Kiva New were Co-directors of that program. Loloma had been a student of New's at the Phoenix Indian School. Together they had befriended Frank Lloyd Wright (then in Scottsdale); and the three of them, Loloma remembers, spent many hours discussing Lloyd New's dream of an Indian arts academy.[4]

In short order they began to cast their collective lot as rogue architects reasserting themselves in time and place:

> Few may think of you, Indian Child, as a future architect. Indian architects? Why not? Some of the finest buildings ever erected on this continent were designed and built long before the coming of the white man. Indians had a great tradition as architects . . . Unfortunately, your rich tradition in architecture was stopped dead without opportunity for your acquiring knowledge of steel and glass and new functions like churches, schools, hospitals, banks and offices.[5]

That challenge became the embodiment of a broad new vision of the future. By the end of the second summer arts project, Lloyd New drew from the experiences of not simply training new artists in new techniques, but enriching them through knowledge and ideas. It became the underpinning of a fledgling Institute:

> Teach them the secrets of creative expression based upon a thorough knowledge of the universal principles of art (these are common to Indian art, also). Encourage them to use this knowledge of cultural tradition as a springboard for personal creative artistic expression. If a youngster is a product of a living tribal culture, and he identifies with that culture, then I would expect his art to be less creative and more within the style of that group. With the purely creative-minded Indian youngster, I would hope for reflections of his heritage.[6]

In order to grow IAIA, it first required dusting off the carcass of a quaint traditional artistic idiom and rejuvenating it into a vibrant image staged by curriculum and innovation. That opportunity came in short order. The Rockefeller art program influenced a 1960 recommendation by the Indian Arts and Crafts Board of the US Department of Interior to create an arts program for Indian people. In 1962, the Bureau of Indian Affairs (BIA) founded IAIA. At the helm of its arts department was Lloyd "Kiva" New.

IAIA was created as an arts-related vocational institution whose student body initially ranged in age from fifteen to twenty-two.[7] One hundred and forty "carefully recruited students" were admitted for grades ten through twelve.[8] Among the inaugural class was Hopi-Choctaw visual artist Linda Lomahaftewa. Barely a teenager when she enrolled in IAIA's inaugural class, she went on to get her master's in art at the prestigious San Francisco Art Institute. In 1976 she returned to teach at IAIA and has been a faculty member in the Studio Arts program ever since. She described her early experience:

> I was going to the Phoenix Indian school for high school and my mother had read an article in the paper about this new Indian arts school that was opening in Santa Fe. She knew I had always been in the arts, always called myself an artist, so she called me and asked if I was interested in going. So I said "yes" and we worked on the paperwork over the summer. You had to be accepted in the school . . . Yes, I had to be interviewed. My mother calls it to this day, an "FBI check on the family." I was only fourteen years old; I had no idea what was going on. They actually came out to Hopi and visited with the family out there.[9]

The Institute began on the hopeful note that it would elevate students to a higher plane of expression; one beyond tradition. IAIA assumed the foundation of that beginning was identity. Those students who came to IAIA were raised by and invested in their own culture. It informed their worldview, and combined with the newly designed studies would allow them to fly towards the fine arts stratosphere of creativity and innovation. This assumption was doggedly pursued to a fault. As Linda Lomahaftewa recalls:

> It was kinda' negative when they talked about the traditional arts. They didn't say, "don't do it," but they said we want to move on from that. The whole time I kept thinking, "but that's where I come from." I like Fred Kabotie's work and I like looking at the old style traditional paintings. These are key for me, this is

who I am. It felt kinda' weird that they kept on saying in a negative way that that wasn't good art, but—just trying to push us away from that, I guess. These are just thoughts I had for myself. I don't remember talking about it to anybody.[10]

It was also implied that the contemporizing of Indian art should transcend the mundane and rejuvenate itself as a profession. The evolution of Indian art as staged by Indian artists seems mainstay now, but at that time the concept was decidedly radical. It was a call to the times:

> Gentlemen, we submit that there is a positive solution to the Indian "problem"; that the Indian is educable in the fullest sense of the word; and that the implementation of a program along the lines of this presentation would result in immense benefits to the American Indian and to the Nation.[11]

When IAIA was first established, it existed as a high school enrichment program with a couple of years added on for the vocational component. Under the BIA's tutelage, IAIA was put under the weight of bureaucracy. It was a new initiative and was under the scrutiny of tribal leaders and politicians alike. The compass of events going on elsewhere often sapped its efforts. This included contentious ideological battles over identity and race.

Civil rights, red power, and the ilk coursed through the blood of fledgling decolonialists and enlivened it. Art as politic or what everyone seemed to infer when he or she drew the distinction between "contemporary" versus "traditional" art, became a legitimate idiom for describing the empowerment experience of collective assertion. At the same time it polarized both the campus and the community at large, between those who supported the American Indian Movement (AIM) and those who didn't.[12]

As a result of such turmoil, beginning in 1973, IAIA's existence was in jeopardy. The BIA and, more specifically, the U.S. Department of Interior came under more scrutiny in its efforts to improve Indian education. Attempts to reconsolidate its regional operations as an effort to save face inadvertently put IAIA's mission and finances under the microscope.[13]

These efforts were pursued under the pretense that programs could be reduced and consolidated. In one of these proposals, the Institute was nearly subsumed through the discontinuation of the Albuquerque Indian Boarding School. With support and resources locked down, and in the words of one witness, "IAIA has been forced to feed off itself."[14] This disquiet spurred New to make a last-minute attempt to recast IAIA into a larger global light:

[C]reate self-generative cultural scholars and technicians;

[R]ecognize and assist in the interpretation of the full meaning of native American culture to the world at large through the development of exponents of Indian culture such as writers, playwrights, performing artists, fine artists and craftsmen, teachers (cultural specialists), designers, vernacular architects, community planners, museum specialists and other professionals in fields related to the arts; [and]

[S]erve the Indian community as a focus for cultural self-recognition and pride and promote the growth of satellite cultural institutions throughout the Indian world[15]

By 1979 IAIA began to forward its candidacy for the Association of Schools of Art and Design (NASAD) and the Higher Learning Commission of the North Central Association (NCA). In its verve to keep it from capsizing, accreditation became a means to keep it afloat. It was not until 1984, however, that it was finally granted accreditation.[16]

◊◊◊

By the eve of its twentieth anniversary, IAIA had regained its footing. The campus was now split between the Cerrillos Road campus and the College of Santa Fe and its enrollment had doubled.[17] But no sooner had one set of political issues settled, another arose. It was the contentious on-again, off-again relationship with the All Indian Pueblo Council who by this time had negotiated a PL-638 contract to reestablish the Santa Fe Indian School.

The traditionally conservative attitudes of some Pueblo leaders were often at odds with ideologically progressive IAIA, something that caught IAIA students and staff in the middle. As described by Linda Lomahaftewa:

There were ill feelings and I didn't like that. I couldn't understand why certain people couldn't get along. You would hear different mumblings from different groups of staff. It was like, "blame the Pueblos." I didn't like that because I'm half Hopi and half Choctaw and that's part of my background too. It's like turning against your own people.[18]

This divide was summarily described as "treading a thin line between tribally accepted modes of expression and individual expression."[19] This viewpoint was historically rooted. It had already emerged in the directives ushered from the 1934 Reorganization Act when the solution to repositioning Indian art as a commodity meant commercializing traditional art in a manner that was decorative and authentic:

> Dorothy Dunn told me that if I was going to do things that are realistic, then you better go on out and take the next bus home. Well, some of the kids did just that . . . What Dunn did was this—and I can tell you because I was right here at the Studio when it was beginning. Everyone was encouraged to search their background for traditional things. That's all she permitted us to do . . . My only objection to Dorothy Dunn was this: she trained us all the same way. 'You either paint like this, Mr. [Allan] Houser, or it's not Indian art.' But what the hell, you have to have your own interpretation of things.[20]

So it is no surprise that another part of that contention were the economics of art. This topic always loomed in the background of the curriculum. An IAIA Studio Arts instructor Linda Lucero (Taos), quoted in 1982, stated it best:

> But the public is perpetuating this thing; the public doesn't want to just buy art for art's sake, it wants to buy it because it's *Indian* and may have some kind of investment value in the future.[21]

Reframed and restated some thirty years later, it is evident that this facet of IAIA's role has not gone away:

> Am I just going to be concerned about what someone at Indian Market will purchase, or am I going to do art that I'm interested in doing, that fulfills my vision as an artist? I think a number of people do both. Nocona Burgess, for example. He once told me, "Oh, this work here. I just do this for Indian Market. What I do for my collectors on the east coast is totally different." He does a series on rock artists, like Bob Dylan. You're not going to see that at Indian Market. When people go there they expect something else. Each of the artists has to struggle with that. People have this image stereotype of what Indian art is—all the beads and feathers stuff.[22]

IAIA's threshold year was 1986. At the cusp of its twenty-fifth anniversary, a "new" IAIA was constituted under the provisions of the Higher Education Act of 1986 (PL 99-498, Title XV). Among the new provisions was the inclusion of Native Alaskans and Hawaiians into its mandate. Under a section entitled "Art is a Way of Perception," the then-chair of the Academic Affairs Committee, Gregory Cajete, issued forth a new edict:

It is our thesis that all Native Americans have the right to know their own cultural histories so that they may come to understand the relationships that exist between themselves and their forbearers . . . The Institute must continue to search for *new* ways; ways of relating its activities to the artistic and cultural extension needs of Native American communities at large.[23]

The policy change allowed IAIA to reconsider major aspects of its organization and metamorphosed into a full-blown, post-secondary college:

One of the best things that happened here is that the legislation allowed the Institute to become independent of the Bureau. Although we still have some of that legacy and our culture, we're working on it . . . People here complain about the bureaucracy, but they should go to places like SIPI or Haskell if they want to deal with bureaucracy.[24]

By 1991, the trajectory towards becoming a post-secondary college included a wish list of new components necessary for achieving its new role. First and foremost, it entailed creating a new campus with new centers necessary for meeting the NASAD/NCA certification needs of a college.[25] The construction of a new campus on Avan Nu Po Road in the Rancho Viejo subdivision soon superseded any further doubt that IAIA had come of age.[26]

Tony Abeyta, he was our convocation speaker last year [2010]. He said, 'I came here and learned so much. We didn't have these kind of facilities. Now you got 'kick-ass' facilities, there's no excuse for you not going beyond what you would normally expect."[27]

Accreditation, however, carried a set of requirements that, some said, restricted the ability of IAIA to think out of the box. The only way IAIA could continue its founding integrity was to assure that its:

[F]aculty are working writers, performers, and artists, who seek to create a bridge between past and present, collaborating with students and employing, when possible, Indigenous forms of creativity and inquiry-based instruction.[28]

Ultimately, in late 2001 a slate of baccalaureate and associate programs were approved by NCA. This substantial change catapulted IAIA into its present mode. It also began to put to rest the art-for-art's sake Achilles heel that had long hobbled the Institute:

[So this tribal leader] asked, "Why should we send any of our students there. Art is part of our culture. You don't have to go to school for it." So I told him, "Well, we're more than studio arts. I think you can take that and expand your horizons, but we also have creative writing, we have museum studies, we have Indigenous liberal studies." That's part of increasing our profile, our visibility. Letting people know that we're famous for studio arts, but we now have more programs.[29]

◊◊◊

Walking into Stephen Wall's office, one was immediately swept up by its unsettled feeling. Empty Xerox boxes were strewn about the floor, occupying the precious little floor space where a nice-and-neat conference table should have been planted instead. Upon sitting down, I first had to overcome the feeling of being inspected by a penciled portrait of a pedantic Vine Deloria Jr., sitting on a stool with an impish rendition of a canary yellow Sponge Bob bestraddled atop his knee. "Some of these kids nowadays have no idea about how important he is, no respect," Steve mumbled. "But then again, that's they way they see it and it's okay."

Stephen is a professor and the chair of the Indigenous Liberal Studies Department (ILS) at IAIA. "I have this kind of pan-Indian existence," he minced. An enrolled member of the White Earth Chippewa, his grandfather was Iroquois from the New York, Cattaraugus Territory. He was born, however, on the Mescalero Apache reservation where he lived as a youth. The ILS represents a significant portion of the academic branch of IAIA and Wall's self-ascribed mission is to get students to reexamine things through the aperture of an Indigenous lens. Using his words, "We're in the business to create leaders and scholars based in Indigenous knowledge."

All institutions, large and small, are driven by their mission. From the get-go, IAIA's mission was ostensibly focused on the process of great art and the production of great artists. But these artists began to learn that practicing art without a basic academic foundation was shortchanging their ability to think outside the box:

> The mission when IAIA was created, the one that was created as part of the authorizing legislation, the Institute of American Indian and Alaska Native Arts & Culture. There's kind of long mission statement, probably five sentences long about arts and culture. It was already built into the scenario that there would be a strong academic component here. Just the way that certain departments are privileged in all institutions, there wasn't a focus on the academic stuff at all.[30]

The maturation of the Institute constantly weighed the juxtaposition of art as a process and liberal studies. It adjusted the fulcrum towards the center of what had been characterized as a lopsided relationship favoring the creative (artistic) over the mundane (scholarship):

> I'm dealing with students that have never been rewarded for thinking. So it's really hard to get them to think. And that may be something else in the future, that students come here not only prepared to express themselves but also to be able to think about what they are expressing and be articulate about the way they are talking.[31]

When IAIA's current president, Robert Martin, PhD assumed the helm in 2007, deconstructing and revising the Institute's mission became his number one priority. President Martin is Cherokee and married to Lucy Tapahonso, an accomplished Diné poet and writer. In addition, he is the consummate educational administrator, having been president of other tribal community colleges at Haskell, Tohono O'odham, and the Southwest Indian Polytechnic Institute (SIPI). He described his first duties as such:

> I knew about the major problems they had in the 90s. So we planned for the 2012 [mission]. I asked people, "do you know what the mission statement is?" I think one person, it was a new person, knew it. It was a convoluted long thing and no one knew what it was. Nobody knew what our core values were. We revised the vision statements and established our priorities.[32]

But when I asked a student, Daryl Lucero, what he knew about the mission statement, he gave it his best educated guess:

"To empower creativity through lifelong learning, community outreach, and something . . . " But I'm not sure yet, that's the question that will still reveal itself.[33]

Daryl is a 2012 graduate of IAIA, and majored in Studio Arts and Indigenous Liberal Studies. He hails from the Pueblo of Isleta and is amongst the throng of IAIA's best and brightest. His impromptu recollection of IAIA's mission was an excellent save! The actual words of the mission, though, are:

To empower creativity and leadership in Native arts and cultures through higher education, lifelong learning and outreach.

But that's the nature of mission statements. They're supposed to be fluid, dynamic, and somewhat unmemorable. Some would say that they might be as thorny as a desert cactus, and just as likely to prick. When President Martin first attempted to reach out and engage the larger community in conversations about clarifying and simplifying the mission, he felt the sting of its nettle:

Some of my colleagues tell me, "You're teaching arts and culture? They're no jobs on my reservation for those kinds of people! Why should any of our students come down there?" We have a history of training those artists, but we also have our graduates that are faculty, not only here but at other major universities across the country. We have some that are attorneys, and then we have people like George Rivera, a tribal leader [Pojoaque Pueblo]. He started here, went on to study elsewhere.[34]

Enter Hayes Lewis. Hayes is the former director of the Center for Lifelong Education (CLE), established in 2008. Born and raised in the Pueblo of Zuni, members of his family have been advocates of education over successive generations. His father, Robert Lewis, is considered to be one of the greatest Pueblo leaders of the twentieth century. In this role, Hayes had the task of broadening IAIA's reach beyond the hallowed academic halls and onto tribal communities:

When people first heard about the Center for Lifelong Education, and what we represented, they said, "I thought IAIA was an art school?! How can an art school be doing this?" "Well, it's a four-year tribal college. It's an institute of higher learning." And, so in building capacity, there's been tension both internally and externally.[35]

Outspoken, Hayes did not falter when he talked about the challenges that lay ahead for the CLE:

Some of our tribal leaders, as young as they are, are really getting jaded by the casino income. And they're forgetting that they are there to serve its people . . . There's conflict within families and clans that create unsafe community environments. There are challenges, but how do we get beyond that? [We need to] use community strengths to respond.[36]

In addition to challenges at the community level, there are new emerging challenges within the student body as well. Foremost is the fact that the Institute as a bona fide college now has open enrollment:

The other tension is the population of the students and who they represent. About ten percent of our students are non-Indian. It's an open college in that way . . . one student called it "the whitening of IAIA." I have to agree. What are we trying to do here; this is supposed to be an Indigenous college? Lets focus on Indigenous needs, issues, and priorities. Don't push us aside. If we're going to be more of an international school, then let's make sure everyone gets their needs attended to, just not one group or another. And the Indigenous part has to be reflected in the people we hire too. What if we have an all-white faculty? Where the hell is the Indian art in that? We want to encourage that dialogue.[37]

Indeed, the force of gravity has begun to tug downward in other ways as well. This is the case among a new generation of Native students who, for whatever reason, are not necessarily rooted in tribal tradition; rather circumstances may have grounded them in what is now being referred to as the "concrete rez." Growing up in urban environments, their experiences are decidedly different. They bring a new perspective to IAIA:

When people came here in 1962, the vast majority of them came just straight out of their tribal community and they all spoke their language. And now you've got these kids here in 2011 who are second-generation relocatees who can, maybe, find their reservation on the map. And maybe can remember some people back home or maybe have met some people back home who are passing through the city. They have a very limited tribal experience.[38]

The situation vaguely reminded me of the Bangles' 1986 hit tune, "Walk Like an Egyptian!" It was a song that was intended to be taken lightly, but when the 2011 Egyptian youth revolution was staged, it became purposeful. That's not meant to belittle the seriousness of this situation, but in the case of IAIA, attention to details is critical. Otherwise identity becomes brokered somewhere between pop-culture and pan-Indianism. That conversation is going to bring to light a new set of considerations as stated by Linda Lomahaftewa:

So a lot of them come here and they think they're coming here to learn who they are, like "tribally." I just tell them what I know, my life experience. But when they come in so young they don't always want to hear it. Because they come in so young, they don't know how to ask. I've heard from other faculty about the ones who come in not knowing who they are culturally or tribally. When you ask those questions in class they tend to get angry or negative towards you as a teacher.[39]

So clearly, IAIA now has other people sitting at the table; Native, urban Native and non-Native. As for a solution, perhaps Daryl's spin on the topic is the most introspective:

There is an interesting documentary [film] on Chaco Canyon. It holds its unique qualities as a place where Natives, at one point, had massive amounts of knowledge. They represented that in their architecture, through their paintings, and through their lifestyle. But there's also part of this documentary where this man says "something terrible really happened here. They knew too much. They were too in synch." I contrast IAIA with that because we have a school that has a huge diversity of students from across the whole American continent and beyond. What I see IAIA being is the balance that, maybe, Chaco Canyon couldn't have accomplished.[40]

◊◊◊

Outside the school cafeteria was a covey of ILS students. They sat around in clusters of small round tables—furniture that was more suited to having a casual latte and a quick read of the Wall Street Journal. Each jockeyed to be heard between bites of chicken chow-mien, the lunch special of the day. A few minutes earlier, President Martin had boasted to me that the kitchen had switched completely over to a healthier, smarter cuisine. "We don't even have a deep fryer in there," he quipped, "and we buy local if we can." Sure enough, next to the serving line was a blackboard; locales smooshed in colored chalk indicated where the menu's ingredients had been harvested.

The students were part of an anti-Columbus Day organizing committee and were in a spirited conversation about what they might do to drive the point home about the lessons of cultural genocide. One idea that was floated was to create a newspaper inset using the style of a DWI lineup. The mug shots would be of infamous colonialists and American leaders. It was clear that they were beginning to flex their post-colonial muscles.

Most of them want to go back to their community and make a difference. They also want to teach. We're thinking about creating an Indigenous education program here that's different than the UNM's of the world. [It's] grounded in cultural values, things that work. [Come up with] a better way to do it than what we've seen. They're like that, they're very creative, and they're a mix of—Indigenous Liberal Studies have minors in Studio Arts, Museum Studies, or Digital Media, or something. They don't mind getting up and talking or challenging; challenging the status quo. And that's good.[41]

For one of those students, that characterization fit like a glove:

I'm definitely going to be at home. Definitely going to live there the rest of my life, but I'm definitely going to travel for as long as I can. I don't see myself living outside permanently . . . I have a lot of responsibilities at home and I belong there mentally and physically. My family is there. My friends are there. My home is there. The animals I love to eat are there! There's no place like home. I can't go fishing the same way that I can at home, I can't go cockle digging or seal hunting or eat moose soup or hang out with my family or go to the potlatches that we have in our community. It just wouldn't be the same anywhere else in the world.[42]

That was a take from Crystal Kaakeeyáa Worl, a remarkable young Native Alaskan student. Tlingit and Athabascan, she is a transfer student from the University of Alaska at Anchorage and a 2012 IAIA graduate with a double major in Studio Arts and Moving Images. But getting to IAIA was not necessarily an easy journey or an easy choice for her. When I asked about her first experiences here, being removed from the verdant coasts of the Northwest, she responded:

The first semester I was here, I had such a hard time being away from home, I physically got really sick . . . I was on the very edge of deciding to go home. I was going to—and this was when I was pretty introverted at that time—make myself step outside of that comfort [zone] and go up to ten random people that go to IAIA. Ask them—whether I had talked to them before or not—to convince me to stay. And sure enough, after I talked to ten people, I was completely convinced that I had to stay. They talked about the things that it had to offer, which I wasn't aware of at the time. Because I had been so introverted I didn't bother to look beyond my own interests or what could possibly interest me. They really reached out to me. They reached out and comforted me. They said there is a place for me and "you do belong here!"[43]

In a paradoxical way, Worl represents both the uniqueness and, in the same breath, the sameness of her collective peers. In her role as an IAIA Ambassador, she amplified that she was just as fallible, just as curious, and just as artistically inclined as any other young person enrolled there:

My grandma, she'd known I was going to be an artist from when I could walk. She said as a child I would be running around all-hyper, just running around. She said when I saw something interesting to my eye—that had an interesting color or shape—I would just stop what I was doing. I would stop. I would observe it, I would look at it and then go back to running around! Driving her crazy. And that's when she knew I was going to be an artist.[44]

Her grandmother is Rosita Worl, PhD. Dr. Worl, a champion of the Sealaska Foundation, was the first Native Alaskan to graduate from Harvard University with a doctorate in anthropology. Crystal was the first to admit that her grandmother "set the bar high," and that failure wasn't an option. In circumspect, it was rather uncanny how it echoed the same recollections from Studio Arts professor Linda Lomahaftewa:

I had always been interested in the arts, even before I can remember. I liked to do painting and drawing, my family always called me "the artist." My whole family did art. I don't know why they called me that. I guess it's because I'm the only one that went on to art school.[45]

Linda went on to elaborate:

When my aunt was still alive, I would ask her what do you call yourself, just a basket maker? And to me that is a beautiful form of art. When you ask someone what do they do, like make baskets or painting, how do you describe them? She told me in Hopi how you say it. You don't call it art, but you call that a person who knows how to weave. You say it like that. It sounds so simple, but there is a lot of responsibility.[46]

So when I asked Daryl Lucero about the future and how he'd place his schooled vocation back at Isleta, he bounced the topic back to me with a litany of questions:

What is a "thinking artist" to do when they go back home? Do they still create the paintings or the lithographs, or these new forms and create a process that hasn't been thought of in a contemporary context? In a contemporary art context, how do they meet the community and how does the community respond?[47]

Later that day, during the opening of the "Art in the Raw" exhibit of student work at IAIA's *Primitive Edge Gallery*, Daryl gave me a double dose of existential expressionism. I stood by a videographer as he cautiously clicked open the door of his piece. On the literal level, it appeared to be nothing more than an old decrepit refrigerator. Inside were bowls and glasses filled with raw concoctions of multicolored jello. I dared the videographer to open the upper freezer compartment and he cautiously nudged it open with the edge of his camera. We were both unwilling to take the risk of looking into the unknown. More jello bowls and glasses. So I turned into my head and mused, "so what the heck is he thinking now?" I knew that if I asked him, he would simple retort, "well, what do you think?" And so, the unstated message now forced me to solidify my own explanation, wiggling at my brain just like jello, in a contemplative flash of time and space. It made me flashback to an earlier comment Daryl had made:

[T]hese conceptual forms of artwork, where they are talking about hidden meanings or multi-perspectives. That's where much of the youth are coming from now. Yes they have their communities, but in a sense a lot of those communities are no longer defined, definitive anymore. They're one, two or three experiences of what a community is now, or more. That's where IAIA is right now. That's the discussion. What kind of art are they creating? On a subconscious level, what kind of identity?[48]

As students bring their myriad of new experiences, many are clearly wrestling with the framework of traditionalism. The divide between tradition and modern may ultimately become even more blurred. For ILS Chair Stephen Wall, at least, its resolution remains a mountain yet to be climbed:

. . . We're still very new. We still haven't been able to articulate a full knowledge system. We can articulate bits and pieces, but we haven't seen how all these things relate. That has a lot to do with language. Perhaps language is where we ought to be looking at in the next few years . . . We can only hope that in the next thirty years, and including everything that is being done around the world will create the kind of movement where "depth" comes natural to us.[49]

But just as quickly, he retraced his thoughts. After an unsettled pause, he threw out the following lifeline:

We have, intrinsically, what major corporations spend millions of dollars in their branding efforts. It just exists here. I just hope we can maintain that as we move into the future.[50]

◊◊◊

In 1959, the IAIA ticking clock sprung to life when Lloyd "Kiva" New wound out the following passage:

Let's try to find challenging opportunities for the young Indian mind. Let us be more concerned with the evolution of artists rather than of art products. Let's see that the young Indian realizes the values of his great and wonderful traditions as the springboard for his own personal creative ideas. Indian art of the future will be in new forms, produced in new media and with new technological methods. The end result will be as Indian as the Indian.[51]

Great expressive ideas sometimes lead to unimagined results. In the beginning, New and his then contemporary, ragtag band of artistic colleagues took an uncalculated risk. They had fancied themselves as architects with ideas and expressive talent. They enlisted like-minded others and rode on the coat tails of bureaucracy. Success was not easy. Surviving the machinations of naysayers is never easy. They only had an inkling of its possibilities. They would have hesitated to think that it would one day become a major campus, replete with world-class Indian art and buildings designed by Indian architects.

The fact that this Institute exists has to do with post-modernist thought. The fact that Lloyd "Kiva" New's thoughts about education could be implemented in a heavily regimented program of education that the BIA was offering was a testament to post-modern thought. But I don't [mean to] say that Indian thought, Indian philosophies, Indian worldviews—regardless of what tribe— would have anything relative to post-modernism. We were post-modern, before post-modern was in.[52]

Its mission was drawn from the breath of artistic expression. Today it exhales towards its existential future. Identity remains IAIA's lifeblood and is firmly wedded in culture. Helen Hardin, in retrospect, couldn't have nailed it any better than Crystal:

I was studying philosophy and it was all focused on western philosophers like Aristotle and Plato talking about art as—art was created by man because they wanted to separate themselves apart from the animals, which I find totally invalid! Because when you see the way Native people live and the way we make our art, we make our art to make relations, ties, and bonds with the animals. Not to define us apart, but to bring us together, to keep that relationship! Before western contact, there was no such thing as art. The term art didn't exist. We did do weavings, textiles; we did do paintings, and forms of sculpture that would be considered art today. But then it wasn't a practice of art; it was a way of life. It was a way that we lived life. It was a way of being.[53]

So at the end of an auspicious day of engagement, I was physically wasted, exhausted, and bleary-eyed. Mentally, however, I found myself upbeat and optimistic. Daryl and Crystal, in particular, had disarmed any qualms that I might have had. They exuded from their intellectual essence, IAIA's deepest value sets. Deep down I intrinsically concluded that these children—one of the desert and one of the seas— were poised to renew the next generation of thinking artists.

All in all, I learned that the future of IAIA was just another day in Raven's lifetime.

> Raven, he taught us that that there is always a way. There's always a way. And Raven would always find a way whether it was being mischievous or using his magic powers. He would find a way to do it. And IAIA teaches us how to use those powers—find those powers within ourselves, to achieve whatever it is that we want to do.[54]

Appendix 1

"Using Cultural Difference as a Basis for Creative Expression"

by

Lloyd H. New

Institute of American Indian Arts
Department of the Interior
Bureau of Indian Affairs
Santa Fe, New Mexico

Editor's Note:

The following manuscript from the IAIA archives is the philosophical backbone of the Institute. Lloyd H. "Kiva" New first penned the monograph in 1964, expressing his vision and pedagogy for the new, experimental school. First published by the U.S. Department of Interior's Arts and Crafts Board in a 1968 serial publication "Native American Arts 1: Institute of American Indian Arts," "Cultural Difference as a Basis for Creative Expression" was the literary primer used to understand the premise of the unique institution. Over the years, the monograph was slightly altered for planning documents and legislative requests, but the primary text and message remained intact throughout the revisions. The version presented in this appendix is the 1968 revision.

The Institute of American Indian Arts is a new national school for Indian youth founded in the fall of 1962 by the Bureau of Indian Affairs, Department of the Interior, in Santa Fe, New Mexico. It offers an accredited high school program with arts electives, and a post-high vocational arts program as preparation for colleges and technical schools and employment in arts-related vocations.

In the beginning of its third school year, it now caters to the educational needs of approximately 350 young Indian people with 88 tribes represented in a student body consisting of members from 25 states, ranging geographically from Alaska to Florida.

By providing adequate tools, professional leadership, freedom for exploration in various fields of art, and freedom for artistic expression, our Government makes a unique contribution to the social and economic betterment of the Indian population of this country.

At the Institute, emphasis is given to Indian traditions as a basis for creative expressions in the fine arts, including sculpture, painting, the written arts, the performing arts such as drama, music and dance. It also offers learning opportunities in the metal crafts, jewelry and hollow ware, ceramics, and woven and printed textiles, and various traditional crafts.

The approach used, stressing cultural roots as a basis for individual creativity, is a unique development on the world scene and in our national dedication to the enhancement of minority contributions. As a result of this approach, students find new directions and gain self-confidence.

With rare exceptions, Indians in this country have clung steadfastly to Indian ways for over four hundred years, in spite of social pressures which negate the value of cultural difference. In spite of this tenacity to maintain their own cultural ways, the past few years have seen American Indians plunged into an economic, social and cultural chaos. Prior to this, centuries old cultural ways—however different—served Indian tribal groups adequately.

Since World War II, even the most conservative and self-sufficient tribes have not escaped cultural changes of a traumatic nature. These rapid changes in Indian patterns have produced a generation of confused and insecure youth.

Many Indians of today find themselves in a psychological no man's land as a result of this impact of the ways of the dominant culture on Indian values. Most young Indian people now share similar educational experiences with the typical teenager of today. They no longer wear the tribal costume, and they speak the common language. They, also, are victims of televisions and followers of the latest fad. They have all the problems common to the youth of the country, and in addition, the special problem of making satisfactory psychological reconciliations with the mores of two cultures.

Theirs is the task of utilizing all that is good in Indian heritage to strengthen their positions in contemporary society. This calls for assistance in recognizing the factors within their traditions which are to their favor and in seeing themselves as the proud residual of cultural greatness, however obscure it may be in their natural awareness.

To be Indian all too often connotes a grievously poor socio-economic status viewed in terms of today's standards. As the Indian youth contemplates his immediate position in time and conditions, he has difficulty finding anything about Indian ways of which to be proud. Because his life is so different than that of his parents, he is estranged from them and lacks the guidance and comfort afforded in normal family relationships. Stripped to selflessness, he stands a victim of the demoralization inherent in conditions of family and cultural breakdown.

Desolated, he mistakenly equates the results of cultural breakdown and confusion with the simple fact that he is Indian and erroneously concludes that he must justify himself in some overly defensive way.

Often he takes refuge in Indianism and lives in a segregated and chauvinistic atmosphere, savagely defending his difference and shutting his eyes to the faults, the limitations, and the deteriorated forms of the "good old ways". He clings fetishly to the old, and the natural dynamism innate in a healthy culture comes to a stop. An anomalous situation results in which progress of the most beneficial type comes to an end; both individuals and whole tribes cease to adjust to the realism of the times. A vicious cycle begins whereby suspicion, distrust, and reactionary behavior compounds itself, resulting in all manner of human problems. Thereupon, epithets arise: Indians are lazy, unaggressive, resentful, uncooperative, withdrawn, ungrateful, aimless; and very often they are all of these, but for good reason.

However understandable the causes for such cultural disorder, there exist many Indian people who find themselves smothering under a blanket woven of despair and hopelessness. For some, this despair results in utter resignation: IF THIS IS MY PLIGHT, THEN SO WILL I LIVE IT. Many who counsel with Indians are familiar with the self-dubbed phrase, "I'M JUST AN INDIAN", meaning "WHAT'S THE USE". With such afflictions ever at hand, it is small wonder that the Indian often resorts to alcoholism and myriads of other escape devices to rind release, at least momentarily from the ill effects imposed upon him by an environment inimical to his Indianness. But these escape mechanisms stand as problems in themselves—new problems for the Indian to solve; and the price he pays for his short lived respite from reality is deeper despair.

It should be emphasized that the foregoing description applies only to the Indian in conflict; but, sadly, he appears throughout Indian history and in almost every group. In some instances, entire tribal regions are afflicted, resulting in serious social traumas. It is fortunate that these gloomy aspects are not predominant in the lives of all Indians and that there are groups who still maintain Indian ways within which a stable background for youth development is provided. In these cases, acculturation proceeds with basic sureness.

While the Institute does not label itself a psychotherapy center, it does core its program around the special psychological position of the individual and his identification with Indian culture. The basic task of the school is to develop specialized techniques for assisting a heretofore neglected group to enter contemporary society with poise and confidence. The ultimate importance of this approach lies in finding methods for structuring sound educational procedures upon the values of minority cultures.

The Institute believes that cultural differences are good. By linking the best in Indian culture to contemporary life, young Indian people find new levels of pride in their own heritage.

To the extent that these ends are accomplished, the program at the Institute may well become the prototype of a practical vehicle for superior approaches to cultural integration, within the nation—or between nations.

All students at the Institute are exposed to the beauties of Indian art, historically and of the present. They view exhibitions of the choicest collections of fine Indian art pieces, listen to lectures on the archaeology and ethnology of Indian cultures, and engage in studies of the accomplishments of contemporary groups. They are encouraged to identify with their total heritage, harking back to the classical periods of the South and Central American cultures—heydays of artistic prowess in the new world.

To be aware of himself as a member of a race tremendously rich in architecture, the fine arts, music, pageantry, and the humanities, gives the young Indian identification with cultural accomplishments of the highest order. It is gratifying, indeed, to witness the first glow of pure pride felt by an Indian youth who has accepted his identification.

Given the opportunity to draw on his own tradition, the Indian artist evolves art forms which are new to the cultural scene, thereby contributing uniquely to the society general. Through such accomplishments, he gains an awareness of the place of the creative artist as an important influence in the fundamentals of human interaction. He senses the need for contributing to the beauty of environment and realizes a responsibility to bring forth flavors innate in Indian ways. He learns to live up the best of himself in his role of the creative artist, evolving personal criteria for his conduct in the realm of the art world. He learns to stand on his own feet, avoiding stultifying clichés applied to Indian art by the purist who sometimes unwittingly resents evolution in Indian art forms, techniques and technology.

It should be made clear that the Institute does not ram anyone's culture down his own throat; but it does acquaint its young Indian students with an appreciation of his own traditions, to be used as a springboard for personal creative action. The Institute does not believe it possible for anyone to live realistically in outmoded tradition, but does believe it to be the business of the artist, especially, to create new and worthy actions leading to new traditions. The Institute assumes that the future of Indian art lies in the Indian's ability to evolve, adjust, and adapt to the demands of the present, and not upon the ability to remanipulate the past.

These ideals are happily justified in a look at the progress to date. Art critics of stature are excited by the quantity and quality of work coming out of the school in all areas, even at this early period of development. The quality of design and craftsmanship reflective of the classic standards of the finest traditional approaches is easily discernible in the sculpture, painting, and the various crafts being produced. Poetry and prose reflect a new source for richness and beauty in the written arts. Early developments in drama and music are gratifying.

Impressive as are these results in terms of the level of artistic accomplishments, the real value of the program lies in the general personal growth on the part of the student, himself, and in his recognition of the fact that such growth has taken place.

The student body is made up of youths ranging in age from 16 to 22. Most of them are insecure about their place in a bi-cultural world and are beset with misunderstandings regarding color, race, and suffer the stigma of a comparatively low socioeconomic position in which many find themselves circumstantially.

These are the young, who find themselves lost in a labyrinth of identity search, disoriented in a maelstrom of cultural and social conflict; these are, also, the revolutionists, the nonconformists, and the unacademiccaly minded who find no satisfaction in the common goals set for them in the typical school program. They are typical of the creative person to be found in that percentage of all cultural groups which seeks new ways for saying and doing things, those who are bent on searching out a very personal and creative approach to problem solving. Holding standards common to the artistically inclined, this is the youth who rejects and is rejected by the common school program which is tailored for the production of the scholar, the scientist, and the tradesman.

Without the opportunity to attend a school catering to this peculiar drives, he is more than likely slated to join ranks with the growing number of dropouts, who represent one of today's national problems. As proven historically in surveys of the creatively endowed, these so-called misfits, when measured by their future contributions to humanity, may stand in indictment of a system with excluded them—categorically.

In summary, the Institute of American Indian Arts is embarked upon a program, with many steps yet to be taken, the early outcomes of which are indicative of significant discoveries in education. The Indian student is being inspired to new personal strengths in dimensions heretofore unrealized. He can be oriented to his own cultural background, enabling him to function constructively in tune with the demands of today's culture, without sacrificing his cultural self on the alter of assimilation, as so often is the case.

Appendix 2

"The Role of the Institute of American Indian Arts in The Development of Indian Education and Its Potential as a Major Cultural Institution"

by

Lloyd H. New

Editor's Note:

On December 28, 1968 Adrian L. Parameter, staff director for the Special U.S. Senate Subcommittee on Indian Education wrote Lloyd New asking for "complete information about the Institute of American Indian Arts."[1] The subcommittee was interested in the uniqueness of the school and the role it plays within the BIA boarding school system. New responded to Parameter on January 21, 1969 with the "Report on the Accomplishments and Potentials of the Institute of American Indian Arts in Santa Fe, New Mexico." The report "covers the present school program, its accomplishments to date, its weaknesses, and its plans for the future."[2] The following manuscript from the IAIA archives was included in New's report.

Submitted to the Special Sub-committee on Indian Education
Unites States Senate
Committee on Labor and Public Welfare
February 1969

Lloyd H. New, Director, Institute of American Indian Arts
Santa Fe, New Mexico

In Pursuit of Indian Education
The Role of the Institute of American Indian Arts

For almost five centuries the American Indian has been subjected to a process of relentless attrition which has slowly but surely eroded the roots of his cultural existence. His physical existence has been completely obliterated in many areas and, presently, his spiritual existence is in extreme jeopardy.

The many and varied attempts that have been made to "help" him, and particularly to "educate" him, have been largely unsuccessful.

This lack of success is due, at least in part, to the fact that Indian education, from its beginning, was based on a policy of coercive acculturation: the premise being that the sooner the Indian was conditioned to abandon his ways and join the melting pot, the better off he would be. But he has displayed unique resistance to this idea, possibly because his psychological relationship to the land was different from that of the immigrant groups who eventually surrounded him. From the time of defeat, life in the Indian world has been colored by an underlying Anglo-focused enmity stemming from the Indian's feeling that his land-rights had been unfairly usurped. Another deterrent to the success of the melting pot concept of education is that its goals lie largely outside the Indian philosophical frame of reference. The American Indian has always been devoted to a philosophy which holds that ones existence should blend into the comparatively passive rhythms of nature, as opposed to the dominant society's quest for control of nature through scientific manipulation of its elements. In the main, all direct attempts to switch the Indian population from its philosophical position have failed, much to the consternation of those who have tried.

On the surface, the Indian evidences acceptance of his diminished role with little or no overt manifestations of rancor. He cooperates submissively, accepting the goods and services that are offered to him. But, in various subtle ways, he manages to subvert the intended outcome of these overtures. No longer in a position to make war with the opposition, the Indian has adopted a general tendency to withdraw and lie quietly in the remnants of his old world, only half-heartedly picking at the offerings made to him by his would-be benefactors.

Failure on the part of those who have dealt with the Indian to understand the deep-lying psychological and philosophical bases of his tenacious observance of his own cultural mores has resulted in the abortion of almost every attempt made to assist him. Even now, various kids of human salvage operations, such as urban relocation, employment assistance, on-the-job training, and other essential rehabilitative efforts, ultimately function only as stop-gap measures which temporarily help to meet his physical needs, while failing miserably to provide the cultural and emotional substance required to put his life in balance.

In the past, public apathy and disinterest permitted the Indian to protect his way of life, at least to some degree; but in recent times, he has been forced into the public struggle for economic survival, due to the lack of an environment supportive of his old and cherished ways. With limited land holdings and the inevitable encroachments of the dominant society, the American Indian is hard pressed to support his viewpoint while adjusting to the exigencies of a modern world.

Poverty, poor health, unemployment, and a growing rate of alcoholism among Indian adults; a shocking prevalence of suicide, drop-outs, and delinquency among Indian youth; all attest to the abysmal failure of our dealings with the Indian minority. We face the awful truth that we have never provided the American Indian with the kind of education required to promote constructive and meaningful social interaction.

The result is that the American Indian suffers severe psychological trauma and, by now, we must surely have gathered sufficient proof of the fact that the cure does not lie in dosing him doubly with the same old medicine, however first rate we hold it to be or however costly it may be. Simply enough, it is the wrong medicine for the Indian patient.

We need to jolt ourselves out of our comfortable line of patterned thinking in order to make room for new concepts and the definition of new goals.

Our primary, long range goal should be to find and apply such measures as will heal long-festering ills and provide an environment conducive to the growth of the American Indian so that, ultimately, he will contribute richly to the assembly of world cultures and take his place as an honored member of world society.

Neither the goals nor the means for achieving them are esoterically shrouded; mostly, they fall easily into the category of common sense. In order to give the American Indian solid ground on which to stand, steps must be taken which will free him from patterns of hostility, apathy, and other negative manifestations which are inherent in the paternalistic-dependency syndrome evoked by the untenable position into which he has been led. The honor attendant to this racial heritage must be renewed in his mind and he must be taught how to turn his cultural wealth into negotiable assets. He must be encouraged to retain his Indian identity and be shown how to relate it in a constructive and productive way to the modern world. The accomplishment of these acts will be as much to the benefit of the general American society as to that of the Indian population.

In fairness to the present institutional provisions made in behalf of the American Indian, it must be noted here that many of today's Indians are showing an increased inclination to independence and are managing to function with fair success both within the framework of their own culture and outside of it. It seems to be not so much a question of whether any progress is being made but, rather, a question of how wide a front is covered and whether or not this coverage will be sufficient and will occur in time to prevent continued mass casualties.

At the Institute of American Indian Arts in Santa Fe, New Mexico, we are painfully aware of the fact that we cover a very short front. But what is most important is the fact that we believe we have made significant strides in learning how to alleviate some of the problems that beset Indian people, especially the young. While it is too early to obtain statistical evidence reflecting the eventual progress of our students as they take their places in society, we are proud, indeed, of the immediate successes which can be measured in terms of the unusual number of students who seem to find personal identity at the Institute and then move on into programs of advanced education or some other form of personal development.

The underlying philosophy of the program at the Institute is that unique cultural traditions can be honored and can be used creatively as a springboard to a meaningful and productive contemporary life. We hold that cultural differences are a rich wellspring from which may be drawn new creative forces relevant to contemporary conditions and environments. We believe that, ultimately, by learning to link the best in Indian culture to contemporary life, the young Indian will be able to solve his own problems and enrich the world scene in the process.

Most of our students have suffered the consequences of cultural conflict and economic deprivation. They are beset with misunderstandings regarding race, color, and religion. They are sorely stung by discriminatory experiences. Our group includes the revolutionists, the non-conformists, and the unacademically-minded who find no satisfaction in the common goals set by typical school programs. Holding standards which are at odds with the majority, they reject and are rejected by the traditional American school system. Without the opportunity for special education relevant to their needs, such students are likely candidates for failure in life as well as in school, and will live only to perpetuate all the aforementioned negative aspects of contemporary Indian life.

Our goal at the Institute is to interrupt this cycle and we begin by honoring each student for what he is, recognizing his cultural ways and showing respect for them.

The young Indian takes pride in speaking his own language with his peers, or when he converses with an Indian administrator, or laughs at an Indian joke. We deliberately provide opportunities for him to tell the legends and perform the dances of his tribe. Through assigned research projects and field trips, as well as by audio-visual experiences, he cannot escape a growing familiarity with and respect for the history of his ancestors and the honored place they occupied in the beginning of this country.

It has been our experience that when we can successfully relate learning experiences to the student's own Indian frame of reference we are usually able to move him on toward tackling problems which are new and strange to him, and more challenging. Once a student recognizes the validity of his own cultural existence, he is able to shake free from previous feelings of inferiority and begin to function as a healthy, participating member of society, making neither too much of his cultural difference nor attempting to deny it. Once the student has been fully exposed to Indianism, he is free to choose his own course; no one demands that he be more Indian than he wishes to be.

Students who come to us, either from public or B.I.A. schools, are woefully poor in academic achievement and, at first, it would be extremely difficult, if not impossible, for them to experience any taste of success though academic subjects. In order to ensure the student a successful experience of some kind, we turn to the field of art where we offer a wide array of media including drama, music, dance, creative writing, painting, sculpture, and the crafts which include traditional Indian techniques. With few exceptions, every human being who is properly and sufficiently exposed to creative thinking is capable of doing something in one of these fields and doing it well enough to experience the joy of doing and to feel personal satisfaction in his accomplishment. Sooner or later, with a great deal of sensitive cooperation on the part of the faculty, a field is found in which a student can perform creditably. His first successful fabric design, ceramic bowl, sculptured object, or performance on stage may be his very first experience in the ecstasy of personal accomplishment. His reaction is one of justifiable pride and sometimes a shade of disbelief at having produced something of worth, and he equates this with his own personal worth. For him, this is a great discovery. It is, also, a most potent form of motivation toward personal growth.

In all cases, the Institute's primary goal is to give the student a basis for the attainment of genuine pride and self-acceptance. Without this foundation, it is doubtful that a productive aura for learning could be established.

Creation of the Institute was recommended in 1960 by the Indian Arts and Crafts Board of the United States Department of the Interior. Founded in 1962 by the Bureau of Indian Affairs, USDI, the school is administered by the Bureau's Division of Education. The Indian Arts and Crafts Board continues to serve as advisors for the development of the Institute.

The school offers an accredited high school program with emphasis on the arts, and a post-high vocational arts program as preparation for college, technical schools, and employment in arts-related vocations. The age range of the student body is from 15 to 22.

Statistics covering the past three years pertaining to the students' performance at the Institute are impressive. Dropouts (those who leave school and do not enroll elsewhere immediately) amount to 11.9% compared to a general Indian dropout figure of 38% to 60%, varying from area to area. 88.3% of the students leaving the Institute from the 12th, 13th, and 14th grades have continued in some kind of formal training program beyond the high school level; 41.6% of these went into vocational schools, 36% into universities or college level art schools, and the balance returned to the Institute for further work. Significantly, graduating students from the 14th year program show a college entrance rate of 43% as opposed to only 10.3% from the 12th year program (indicating the possibility that Indian students may need 14 years of secondary schooling in order to ready themselves for higher education instead of the 12 years required for less disadvantaged individuals). Of interest is the fact that of the first group of 16 Institute graduates who entered college prior to 1966, 12 have completed their college work, and two have received Master's degrees. The retention rate for all who have entered college during the past three years is 59%.

In the course of its relatively short existence, the Institute has caught the attention of educators and artists of national and international reputation who are often astonished at the quality and quantity of artistic production that occurs in all the art areas.

The Institute has enjoyed recognition from numerous publications and periodicals in the light of its being an important break-through in education for the American Indian. Reports on the school have been featured in *The New York Times*, *The New Yorker*, *Life Magazine*, *Craft Horizons*, *Education News*, *Think* (the house organ of I.B.M.) and on a recent Roger Mudd CBS television news presentation.

International exhibits of student work have been featured at the Edinburgh

Festival of the Arts, the Berlin Festival, and the Alaska Centennial; in Turkey, Argentina, and Chile; and in the Cultural Division of the 1968 Olympics in Mexico City. Students in Performing Arts Department have appeared in two major productions in Washington, D.C., and in a program of traditional dance at the Mexico City Olympics. Student work in creative writing has been published for textbook use and a full-scale novel has been published by the University of Oklahoma Press. We are presently negotiating with Doubleday and Company on a contract for the publication of an anthology of poetry and prose.

As impressive as these results are in terms of artistic accomplishments, the real value of the program lies in the general personal growth of the student and in his discovery of latent strengths and the carry-over of these into his academic efforts and social behavior.

Through the special emphasis placed upon his own cultural base, we imbue him with self-pride so that his tendency to view himself as a second-rate citizen is nullified. Out of this new position of personal security and confidence, comes a new personality endued with new and extended capabilities.

We, at the Institute, are proud of our achievements to date which, in large part, were made possible through the special and, indeed, preferential support received from the Bureau of Indian Affairs and the Department of the Interior. We enjoy unusual autonomy, funding, and freedom that allows for innovation, without which we could not function successfully.

Needless to say, none of our accomplishments would have been possible without the presence of a dedicated, skillful, creative-minded, and innovative staff.

The cost of special education is high; the cost of effective education is even higher. At the Institute, our cost runs $2,600.00 per student. In this respect and for the sake of maintaining correct perspective, there are two factors that should be noted:

1. The cost of providing effective education for the American Indian will be far less, in the long run, than the cost of not providing it, if only in terms of taxpayers' dollars that will be required for interminable support programs of various kinds—including those which produce little in the way of constructive results.

2. The errant expectation that the American Indian by some magic power, and without reference to his own cultural base, will move into an era of productivity and self-sufficiency is likely to result in future generations of this minority group being confused and is oriented beyond anything we have yet seen in our history. Indeed, failure on the part of our dominant society to devise the means to reverse the destructive direction of present policies, will result in cultural genocide for the American Indian, an event which would surely stand hauntingly in history as a monstrous embarrassment to this nation.

While billions of American tax dollars have been spent for the purpose of solving the Indian problem, perhaps not so much as a single million has been especially earmarked to further public recognition of the cultural wealth of the American Indian and to show him how to use these assets as a means of gaining financial independence and the dignity of self-sufficiency.

General Cultural Service

The Institute needs to be evaluated not only in terms of its potential role as an educational laboratory and pilot institution (and supported accordingly), but also in terms of its being expanded into a major cultural institution serving the over-all cause of the general Indian population.

The American Indian should take his place along with the culturally great on the world scene and the Institute should become a major vehicle for interpreting this culture throughout the world. In the few years of its existence, the Institute has been able to gain recognition for Indian cultural accomplishments at levels new to the traditionally anonymous position of the American Indian. Through further professional development of performing artists, poets, writers, musicians, and modern artist-craftsmen, the image of the American Indian could be given the substance of significant accomplishment, which might help to abate the popular inclination to immortalize the Indian as a scalping savage or an enchanting little basketmaker

Gentlemen, we submit that there is a positive solution to the Indian "problem"; that the Indian is educable in the fullest sense of the word; and that the implementation of a program along the lines of this presentation would result in immense benefits to the American Indian and to the Nation.

Appendix 3

"The Institute of American Indian Arts: Some of its Goals, Problems, and Successes"

by

Lloyd H. New

Spring, 1979

Editor's Note:

On the heels of his retirement as president of IAIA in 1978, Lloyd H. New wrote the following piece in the spring of 1979. High per capita cost, federal budget cuts, a revolving door of administrative oversight, and the subsequent elimination of educational programming pushed IAIA to the brink of extinction and culminated in the removal of IAIA from the campus of the Santa Fe Indian School in 1981.

The Institute of American Indian Arts (IAIA) came into being 17 years ago in response to suggestion made by Commissioners of the Indian Arts and Crafts Board to BIA authorities that something should be done to reverse a long standing neglect in the educational division's offerings in the field of the arts.

Largely due to the sympathetic interest of a few individuals, within the Bureau, (mainly, Hildegarde Thompson, the Director of Indian Education), a modest allocation of funds was made for the partial modification of the 70 year old Santa Fe Indian Board School plant for use as a national service school for young aspiring Indian artists. The plant was being considered for abandonment by the BIA, in keeping with a policy shift away from the boarding school concept, and Indian parents' wishes to have their children attend schools closer to their homes. Students in the program at the time of change-over were those who came mainly from the Apache, Navajo, and Ute Reservations—hardship cases of one kind or another—and some 60 Pueblos.

The initial funding allowed for the dismantling of the condemned buildings, the remodeling of the dormitories, one 1890 classroom building, and the construction of a small canteen, an attractive Academic classroom building, and an Administration complex. Funds being short, two "temporary" metal Quonset-type buildings were moved in to serve as studios for the major crafts disciplines. (As of today they remain "temporarily" in place).

IAIA opened in 1962 to some 140 carefully recruited students in the 10th, 11th, and 12th grades, with a contingent of post-high studio workers who were required to take only two academic courses at a post-secondary level. Emphasis was upon the secondary program, both in the balance of students and the nature of the academic curriculum offered.

The opening was auspicious, for a number of reasons. The Pueblos objected to the purpose to which the school was to be put, and to the fact that it would serve tribes from other areas, despite the fact that the land upon which the school was located, atypically, had been dedicated in trust to the Federal government to serve the educational needs of all Indian tribes; thus giving the Pueblos no prior special territorial claim to the institution such as that which would have been natural under different circumstances. Their cry at the time was to gain the facilities to be used for vocational training purposes. (A point which received major consideration of a compensatory nature, when some years later the ten million dollar Southwest Indian Technical Institute was built within the Pueblo environs of Albuquerque).

The progressive philosophy of the new school brought worry to conservatively minded patrons and some Indians who believed that its announced plans to encourage students to experiment in non-traditional areas of artistic development such as sculpture, creative writing, the performing arts, film training, photography, and new forms of painting was somehow wrong.

But, to the students who came, and to an enthusiastic faculty, the opening was exciting—for not only would Indian students of special artistic inclinations find a whole institution open to the advancement of their cultural traditions, much like other art schools that served the cultural needs within the major society, but here by example, was a demonstration by the Federal government of a major change in attitude regarding the value of cultural difference. Now, perhaps long-standing historical policies of deculturalization were coming to an end, and for the first time in history Indians would be allowed to reenter the cultural/arts stream that had flowed throughout their history for more than 10,000 years.

Perhaps it would be here that a new educational philosophy could begin to grow that would enable new generations of Indians in the utilization of the arts for the restoration of cultural pride, and the reconstruction of their tattered cultural base.

According to aims of the institution published its opening year, IAIA's goals far exceeded those of the mere teaching of arts and crafts:

"The underlying philosophy of the program is that unique cultural tradition can be honored and can be used creatively as the springboard to meaningful contemporary life . . . The Institute holds that cultural differences are a rich well-spring from which may be drawn new creative forces relevant to contemporary conditions and environments. We believe that, ultimately, by learning to link the best in Indian culture to contemporary life, the young Indian will be able to solve his own problems and enrich the world scene in the process."

Here would be the perfect laboratory to begin to address the problem of how the lasting values of traditions in the arts and related areas of the humanities could be sorted out for use far into the future:

"We do not believe it is possible for anyone to live realistically while shut in by outmoded tradition. We do believe that each generation must evolve its own art forms to reflect its own times and conditions, rather than turn to the hopeless prospect of mere remanipulation of the past. The Indian artist who draws on his own traditions to evolve new art forms learns to stand on his own feet artistically, avoiding stultifying clichés applied to Indian art by purists who, sometimes unwittingly, resent any evolution of forms, techniques, and technology in Indian Art . . . In general, the Institute plans its programs around the special needs of the individual, as best they can be determined. It attempts continuously to expand its understanding of student problems as they emanate from (his) cultural origins . . . The goal of the programs is to develop educational methods which will assist young Indian people to enter contemporary life with pride, poise, and confidence."

From this promising beginning in 1962 the school moved with efficiency and excitement through its first years, with the work of its students attracting widespread attention throughout the nation for its artistic validity and vitality in a number of fields: creative writing, the fine arts, the performing arts, and the crafts. But by 1967, due to the growing realization that it would be difficult to impact the world at a high-school level, and the facts that too few of the graduates from its high school program were moving into advanced work in the arts, and post-high school students were clamouring (sic) for transferable credits for their two years spent at the Institute, program directions were officially modified to include a greatly expanded mission at the professional level. With formal acceptance of the local administration's recommended expanded role for the Institute by the Commissioner of Indian Affairs, the Institute management team began moving toward its newly set goals in 1967. Sufficient headway was made of such a positive nature as to warrant the support of members of Congress. From a 1969 Senate Subcommittee on Indian Affairs:

"The Tragedy of Indian Education" came the following recommendation:

"33. The subcommittee recommends—
      The Institute of American Indian Arts at Santa Fe, New Mexico should be raised to the level of a 4-year college, supported by the Bureau of Indian Affairs. The Institute has had considerable success in instilling a cultural pride in Indian students by providing them with opportunities for creative expression.

The individual-oriented programs recognize the importance of a sense of identity. By becoming a college, the Institute could provide a college wide curriculum for Indians which considers their culture and history—something unique in higher education. The valuable lessons learned and put into practice by the Institute should be expanded into a college curriculum so that he Institute might become a model for colleges interested in developing innovative programs, such as in-teacher training which recognizes Indian needs."

In 1972, in response to broad public criticism leveled at its operation of boarding schools in general, the Director of Indian education called for the submission of 10-year plans—with accompanying rationale—in justification of their continues existence. IAIA submitted plans for a greatly increased role for itself as a major cultural institution:

"The Need for a National Cultural Center for American Indians

In the entire history of government programming and the varying philosophies under which assistance has been rendered to American Indians there has been a tragic omission of any major concern for the extension of the cultural aspects of Indian life. On the contrary, Indians have suffered hundreds of years of cultural decimation as the result of programs deliberately aimed toward the destruction of their cultural lifeways. The behavioral confusion resulting from efforts made to abolish them has caused generations of frustration to both Indians and their would be benefactors . . . It is predictable that tensions stemming from conditions of (preventable) cultural anomie will increase for generations ahead, unless specific institutions are created that can be used to guide the socio-cultural progression of Indian peoples . . . Failure to recognize the synergistic value of cultural well-being results in an unnecessary continuation of processes that tend to nullify the effective response of Indians to education, economic progress and personal stability . . . the Institute feels that it is now time to move from the secondary level to a college/professional level institution that can be continuously charges with the creation of (befitting) internal leadership in Indian cultural affairs."

Detailed long-range plans were submitted which included orderly development toward a third stage development in which IAIA could eventually realize its services to the Indian community in such areas as training of cultural "animateurs," arts educators and cultural research specialists, preparators of culturally relevant educational materials, writers and illustrator of text books and tribal histories; photo and video specialists; museologists, film directors, and technicians. It would continue its lead role in the grooming of performing artists, craftsmen, poets, authors, and journalists. In closely related realms, the expanded curriculum would include Linguistics, Indian tribal language development; Studies in Indian Religion, Philosophy, Indian Community Planning, Vernacular Architecture; and new roles for Indians in Environmental Development and Industry.

Unfortunately, the dream was not to be realized, even though the plan as projected was officially sanctioned by the Director of Indian Education, and was followed by orders to the Institute and the Division of School Facilities to curtail any plans for future expansion at the old site in favor of locating a new land area on which to begin a new and more suitable plant. But, following the actual selection of a new site, no further action transpired due to the fact that in 1973 the entire Bureau of Indian Affairs found itself plunged into a virtual state of dissolution as a result of chaotic changes that were thrust upon it by widespread negative publicity when the BIA offices were taken over by dissident Indians. In the shake-up, major shifts in personnel occurred that affected program continuity in offices raging from that of the Commissioner of Indian Affairs through certain offices at the Secretarial level. Personnel in Washington offices were drastically curtailed in number, with many workers in the office of Indian Education being transferred to field offices in the west.

Any ongoing progress that might have taken place in the Institute's planning came to a halt when, as a result of the turn-over in Washington, IAIA was shifted back to the Albuquerque Area Office where it languished in an atmosphere of non-support, culminating in refusal by the Area Director to approve the request of IAIA to seek accreditation by the North Central Accreditation Agency; and finally, in a 1974 recommendation that IAIA reduce its program aims and absorb the student body from the beleaguered Albuquerque Indian School. This latter move was counter-manded (sic) only after a great struggle on the part of the Institute's Native American Council of Regents, and intervention by Executive members of NCAI and the protests of sympathetic friends and institutions throughout America. In actuality the situation resulted in a special dividend, for out of the ashes came a formally bestowed Charter from the Commissioner of Indian Affairs for IAIA to proceed towards becoming an Associate of Fine Arts Degree granting institution.

But all was not well. In 1977, discouraged by the constricted situation posed by the Institute's serving under a regionally oriented supervisory office (the Albuquerque Area Office), and the belief that the Institute's higher education responsibilities would always be compromised, the Regents, joined with those of Haskell Indian Junior College and the Southwest Indian Polytechnic Institute (who were suffering similar problems), managed to have all three schools withdrawn from the supervision of their respective Area Offices and placed under a new Office of Higher Education in the Central Office. In actuality no such office had come into existence as late as 1979, and the Institute was placed once again under the tentative supervision of the Albuquerque Area, where it presently remains.

The Institute, dangled in a virtual no man's land in a saga of neglect, fell under a formula funding approach throughout the years which bore little relationship to its actual needs as an aspiring institution. Funding increases received have invariably been earmarked for coverage of the annual automatic cost of living increases for its staff, with no consideration for the exponentially rising increases in general operational costs—with the result that IAIA has been forced to feed off itself. In a practice of not filling vacancies as they occur, the Institute has managed to barely survive in a gradually declining situation in which it has forfeited course offerings in ten major disciplines: namely, Music, Drama, Weaving, Printed Textiles, Foundry, Commercial Art, Indian Jewelry, Creative writing (as a major emphasis), Traditional Techniques (Beadwork, Indian costumes, Ribbonwork, Leather, etc.), and Cinematography.

Safely assuming that for every course area that has been withdrawn that some 10 to 20 potential students no longer enter the Institute program, it can be posited that the lack of course offerings contributes to a drop in student enrollment of some 150 to 200 students, who either go elsewhere or forfeit their rights to training in the arts altogether.

No discussion of the Institute's problems is complete without addressing the history of its Native American Council of Regents. In keeping with announced policies that Indian people should be enabled to run their own institutions, the Native American Council of Regents, IAIA, was formed in 1972. The authorized constitutional structure of the Council allows for representation from each of the generally recognized major cultural regions of the Indian nation: The Southeast, and the Northeast, and Midwest woodland culture groups; the Great Plains, the Southern Plains, the Southwest, the Great Basin, the Far West, the Northwest, and Eskimo. In addition, a Member at Large, a full voting Student Representative, and a non-voting faculty member. The initiating charter members were duly appointed by the Commissioner of Indian Affairs. Upon granting of the Charter for the Institute to become a Associate Fine Arts Degree granting institution the Regents were legally empowered to assume joint responsibility for the operation of the Institute. But despite the above going facts, the Native American Council of Regents currently finds that BIA authorities at the highest levels refuse to meet with them in major decision matters presently facing the future of the Institute.

But despite all the problems faced by the Institute's Administration and massive erosion in student offerings, and a commensurate loss in enrollment, IAIA has nonetheless miraculously managed to merit the enthusiastic support of its student body, and that of the North Central Accrediting Association and the National Association of Schools of Art. Its first stage moves toward full accreditation are well underway. The performance record of Institute graduates who are now coming into their maturities as practicing artists is an impressive one, and serves as evidence of a new leadership movement in American Indian Art, reversing the sluggish conditions that characterized the field during the 1940s and 1950s. An invaluable and irreplaceable representative collection of contemporary artistic expressions in a variety of media not resides in the Museum of the school and is drawn upon constantly by other institutions, national and internationally.

Long recognized as being one of the most effective innovative arts education institutions in minority cultural development, the Institute received its most recent commendation at the international level when it was selected to appear in a UNESCO report, in collaboration with the Editors of *ART, The Journal of the International Association of Art*. IAIA was listed as one of seven noteworthy arts education institutions in the world. Countries represented were Hungary, Uganda, Japan, Upper Volta, Canada, The Netherlands, and the United States.

The following experts are taken from pages 6 and 8 of the 1979 UNESCO report, *Educating Artists, Craftsman, Designers*:

> The present document is intended for the member states of UNESCO and all educational bodies and authorities which may be in search of useful guide-lines for setting up new art schools, or institutions for the training of craftsmen and designers, or which feel that their art education structures are due for an overhaul . . . UNESCO and the International Association of Art conceive it as their function to search out new models among the most progressive which they believe it possible to find in the different continents of the world and exemplifying the different approaches to educational in the visual arts—to make these models available to all who wish to consult them . . . .
>
> The schools in this study present some of the art education programmes (sic) which are helping not only to prepare artists for this more socially oriented mission, but also to assist those dedicated to the visual arts to maintain the high standards inherited from the past while expressing an authentic contemporary culture.
>
> Teachers in art schools now insist that the greatest flexibility of expression and working conditions are essential for the realization of full creative potential. Others are conducting forward-looking experiments among minorities with a rich cultural heritage who to-day find themselves in a poor or depressed sub-culture. These experiments are no mere revival of bygone arts and crafts; they are a direct attack on one of the deep-seated problems of pluralistic societies.
>
> New educational ideas are also needed in countries whose arts underwent a long twilight of decline under colonial rule and are searching for ways to put to advantage their traditional artistic skills in the fluid conditions which often prevail in these new societies . . . .

In view of the foregoing circumstances it seems extremely ironical that the Parent Agency (BIA), who is ultimately responsible for the vulnerable position of IAIA, would support charges of an unjustifiable low level of enrollment and high per student cost, and use them to bring about its demise.

Except for finding a practical quick answer for easing the dire need of the Albuquerque Indian School for decent accommodations for its student body the present cannibalistic move to devour the Institute could be alleviated by reversing the conditions that have plagued IAIA for years. The solution to the case appears to be obvious:

Reinstate the missing curriculum offerings, install a viable management process under the aegis of a duly authorized Board of Regents, authorize an effective recruitment program to counter the damage, get the student enrollment up to 350 (275 on campus and 75 off)—by increasing the allocation of two million dollars per year. Such a move would result in the rehabilitation of the IAIA program at a level that should have taken place years in the past, and the Institute would be enabled to continue its positive directional moves along the lines originally plotted—at a per student cost of $5,714.29, plus plant maintenance expenses.

Such a solution would allow the Institute to move realistically towards its contemplated third stage in which it could finally begin to realize its potential service role in behalf of the Indian community and the Nation—a program from which could spring generations after generations of young people who would be well founded in the arts and related fields, and who could provide the new forms of Indian expressions that will be so badly needed for the actualization of the Indian culture into the millennia ahead. What will Indians of the future be without access to the ever evolving art forms that will be required to portray the distinctiveness of the Indian way as it defines itself into the Twenty-First Century?

Appendix 4

Statement of Mission
by
Dave Warren, PhD

Editor's Note:
The reorganization of IAIA as the Institute of American Indian Arts and Alaska Native Culture and Arts Development in 1986 was a watershed moment for the Institute. The congressional non-profit charter issued through the Higher Education Amendments of 1986 allowed IAIA to pursue its most coveted goal; baccalaureate accreditation. The following "Statement of Mission" was presented in "A Curriculum Prospectus for the Institute of American Indian and Alaska Native Arts and Culture" in 1989 and was the first attempt to build a new curriculum and vision for IAIA under its new organizational autonomy. Although some of the statements were not applied in the final mission statement, many of the points made in the document are the foundation of the current curriculum.

Institute of American Indian Arts and Alaska Native Culture and Arts Development

Statement of Mission
Compiled by Dave Warren, PhD

[The following statement on the mission of the Institute of American Indian and Alaska Native Culture and arts Development act is a summary of contributions from a specially selected committee, consisting of Dave Warren, James McGrath, Dr. Rina Swentzell, and Lloyd Kiva New, (Chair) . . .]

The Institute of American Indian and Alaska Native Culture and Arts Development . . . is a private, non-profit higher educational institution created by an Act of the United States Congress of the United States. The Institute is governed by a Board of Trustees, nominated by the President and confirmed by the United States Senate. Its 19 members include 13 voting members, a majority of whom must be Native Americans. Of the six nonvoting members, four are members of Congress.

Promote the preservation and development of Native American cultures and art forms.

Provide individual Native Americans from throughout the United States with an education of quality in the arts including the visual and performing arts, traditional crafts, cultural studies, architecture, museum management, literature in both its oral and written forms, history and humanities.

Recognize the need to educate its students in the practical application and vocational dimensions of such fields of study including business management for the arts particularly for the self-employed artist of craftsperson and the communications arts such as graphic and commercial art and film and video production.

Provide the services and offer appropriate degrees in an accredited higher education institution designed expressly to promote the conservation, reinvigoration and projection of the culture and arts of American Indians and Alaska Natives.

Incorporate Native American arts, culture, and world view into all its educational activities—in the fields of visual, performing, and craft arts, and continuing literature, oral and written.

Serve Native American people in their social and cultural development needs through cooperative institutional association with individuals and formal or informal Native American groups.

Engage in alliances with non-Indian individuals and organizations toward meeting common goals of the advancement of the social, cultural and economic goals of Native Americans as found to be within its mission.

Encourage scholars to investigate the role of the creative process. Native American art forms and cultural institutions in supporting and reinforcing group and individual pride and identity for all Native Americans.

Provide a forum for scholars from all academic disciplines and from all countries to conduct research into the meaning of Native American cultural institutions and patterns and their roles in the lives of both Native Americans and other Indigenous peoples.

Develop and sustain support for its activities from Native American tribal organizations and associations, private individuals, corporations and foundations from throughout the United States.

An understanding and appreciation of Native American culture is critically important to Native Americans, but has individuals and as people. While culture can be defined in many ways and differs in definition for the individual, it is vitally important to the well-being of the student. The arts are one way Native American cultures express themselves. Art is also a potent means of expression for the contemporary individual Native American. Art can be a part of the process the individual follows to gain a sense of identity, of individual power and personal potential. Art and culture are each aspects of a complex way of learning and can be used as a means to the study and mastery of other skills.

At the Institute, culture will be considered to be both foundation and perspective and it will be equipped with unique resources, for recognizing, understanding, and applying an individual's full potential in a continuous process of self-realization.

At the Institute the past is a point of departure for the formulation and emergence of the Institute as a new place of study, learning, exchange and exploration of ideas and ways of understanding a complex period in Native American society.

The Institute is an educational institution that includes but is not restricted to, the granting of arts and culture degrees, in any field appropriate to the needs of tribes and individual Native Americans. It will offer a comprehensive program of research and instructional programs all related to an understanding of the cultural arts in American Indian human and community growth and development.

The policy and programs of the Institute will demonstrate a responsiveness to the needs and concerns of Indian people, however tribally diverse and geographically dispersed they may be.

The Institute will deal sensibly and sensitively with the complexities of Native American arts and culture in a rapidly changing, highly complex Native American society.

The Institute will create a community of learners where past and present Native American personnel, and culture are explored and integrated, with references for the present and future needs of today's generation of Native Americans. Is a place where skills can be developed in order to communicate confidently and convey subtle understandings through creative expressions for the betterment of self, the Institute community, the native home community and the world at large.

The Institute will serve the needs of Native American peoples primarily by providing an educational program, including study, training, research, and student services to meet the unique social and cultural requirements of Native American youth. The Institute will assume educational responsibility for offering training of Native Americans through accredited programs at all levels appropriate to an institution of higher learning, using culture and the arts as a philosophy, pedagogy, and basis of teaching and learning.

The Institute will serve as a national and international center of education, cultural exchange, exhibitions and research. These activities will support its educational objectives including development and evaluation. And it is through them that the American Indian community and general public will learn of the nature and role of the Institute.

The Institute will offer service to the community through programs of technical assistance, institutional cooperation, collaboration and support.

The Institute's curriculum will be comprehensive and inclusive. It will reflect research in creative studies, multiple intelligences, culture and cognition, and the use of technology as both a medium of creative expression and a method of instruction. The curriculum will reflect the special capability of the Institute as a center for creativity, the exchange of ideas and methods of instruction, study, the training of Native American youth, exploration of integrated curriculums, and pedagogy including the studio arts, sciences, humanities, technology, and culture.

The curriculum will support and derive benefits from special programs such as national and international symposia, seminars, colloquia, and workshops employing the unique contributions of resident artists, humanists, philosophers, spiritual leaders and teachers from Native American communities, and other Indigenous peoples and members of the mainstream society.

The curriculum will incorporate special programs of remediation in reading, language comprehension and expression, computational and other skills in an integrated comprehensive program of study, student services, and research. All will be related to a core educational program to mutually reinforce student achievement and individual contribution to the overall educational process.

The curriculum will reflect an awareness of the particular social, cultural, medical, and psychological requirements of contemporary Native American society.

Appendix 5

"Plan 2015: Building a Foundation for the Next Fifty Years" As approved by the Board of Trustees November 6, 2010

Editor's Note:

The achievement of NCA and NASAD accreditation in 2001 marked the success of a thirty-year mission to make IAIA a four-year college. In an attempt to build upon the success and momentum garnered during the first decade of the 21st century, the IAIA Board of Trustees developed the following strategic plan in 2010 to strengthen and propel IAIA into a powerful position as the premier educational institution for American Indians.

Introduction

On August 6, 2010, the President's cabinet as well as representatives from student government, faculty, admissions, human resources and facilities met in an all-day retreat to review progress on the Plan 2012 priorities and to discuss revisions to Plan 2012. The planning group studied several Institutional Effectiveness models agreed to expand our current model to include outcomes for every department/unit that can be tracked and measured. Data results will be analyzed to find target areas for continuous quality improvement. The planning group also engaged in a study of current trends in higher education discussed areas where IAIA could provide better service to its students.

As a result, the planning group recommended no revisions to the vision and mission statements and only minor revisions in the mission objectives and core values statements. In addition, it was a consensus that five Strategic Themes will guide our work for the next five years and ensure IAIA's success for the next fifty years.

Moreover, workshops on assessment and establishing measurable objectives for the coming year were scheduled in August, September and October. Institutional priorities were established for the strategic themes and each division/department will develop annual work plans with outcomes measurable objectives for the 2010-2011 academic year reflecting the themes and priorities. Priorities will be established for each theme and department/units will develop annual work plans with measurable for the 2010-2011 academic year reflecting these five strategic themes and priorities.

Our Vision

To be the premier educational institution for Native arts and cultures.

Our Mission Statement

To empower creativity and leadership in Native arts and cultures through higher education, lifelong learning and outreach.

Our Mission Objectives

Prepare our students for success and leadership reflecting Native cultures and values.

Provide culturally based programs that fulfill the physical, social, emotional, intellectual and spiritual needs of our students

Offer the highest quality educational programs incorporating innovative teaching, critical inquiry and intergenerational learning

Provide training and outreach as a 1994 land grant institution that promotes a sense of place, tribal sovereignty and self-determination

Serve as a national center of excellence in contemporary Native arts and cultures through exhibitions, research, Indigenous exchange and other educational programs

Our Core Values

Collaboration, joining together for student success.
Excellence, upholding high standards for students, faculty and staff.
Creativity, encouraging fearless expression in art and life.
Respect, fostering an understanding of cultures, perspectives and identities.
Integrity, demanding honesty, accountability and responsibility to oneself and the world at large.

IAIA Strategic Planning Themes

The planning group established the following five themes to guide IAIA's planning establishing priorities work and developing new work plans: Enhancing Sustainability, Improving Communications, Creating a Culture of Evidence and Accountability, Improving Student Success, and Fostering a Community of Learning for all—Board, Administration, Faculty, Staff and Students.

Enhancing Sustainability

Sustainability is being effective stewards of IAIA's financial, human, physical and natural resources in ways that minimize impact on the environment and ensure the future viability of IAIA. Sustainability also pertains to being responsive and accountable to our students and various stakeholder groups through the use of technology, supporting Native arts and cultures and advancing the careers of IAIA students in the new economy.

Improving Communications

IAIA must increase its visibility and outreach to tribes, communities, alumni and local, state and federal governments. This will be accomplished through improving external communication, enhancing community service programs and scheduling campus events open to the larger community. Internal communications initiatives include team building, interdisciplinary conversations about student success efforts and student learning outcomes, recruitment and retention of students and faculty and staff, and listening to the voice of students.

Creating a Culture of Evidence and Accountability

IAIA will use technology to generate data to be used in decision making and budgeting processes. For example, student learning outcomes data will improve curriculum and classroom practices and also to re-allocate resources to those activities that advance the mission and programs of the institution. Creating a culture of evidence requires that IAIA set standards, expectations and evaluations for all divisions and departments of the institution.

Improving Student Success

Each unit has a responsibility to establish outcomes and measurable objectives that contribute to student success. Data will be used to track and retain students. For example, academic departments will determine student learning outcomes and objectives that are measurable and that proceed from a well-articulated philosophy of education. This philosophy of education will be shared by all units across the campus and will result in an environment that fosters learning and supports high quality teaching. Improving student success demands that students have access to technology and that all units encourage creativity.

Fostering a Community of Learners

Faculty, staff and administrators share the responsibility for creating a community that supports lifelong learning for all. The IAIA community strives to retain talent at all levels of the institution. Cross training, networking, professional development, service to the community and attention to health and wellness are all strategies to foster a learning community.

Notes

Chapter 1

1. Lloyd H. New, "Report on A Proposed Philosophical Approach to the Art Education Programs of the Institute of American Indian Arts, " (Santa Fe, 1962), 2, IAIA Archives.
2. Institute of American Indian Arts, "College Catalog, 2011-2012," (Santa Fe, 2011), 34.
3. Lloyd H. New, "Cultural Difference as a Basis for Creative Expression," (Santa Fe, 1964), 9, IAIA Archives.
4. New, "Proposed Philosophical Approach," 3.
5. IAIA, "2011-2012 College Catalog," 33.
6. Lloyd H. New, "The Institute of American Indian Arts, A Developing Institution," (Santa Fe, 1975), 7, IAIA Archives.
7. New, "Creative Expression," 1-2.
8. Ibid, 1-2.
9. New, "A Developing Institution," 8.
10. New, "Proposed Philosophical Approach," 3.
11. Lloyd Kiva New to Edith Crutcher, 31 December 1987, 24, Lloyd H. New Papers, IAIA Archives.
12. New, "A Developing Institution," 10-11.
13. New, "Proposed Philosophical Approach," 1.
14. IAIA, "2011-2012 College Catalog," 33-34.

Chapter 3

1. For insight into the developmental years of IAIA refer to Lloyd Kiva with Andreas Storrs Anderson and Sidney Little, "A Proposal for an Exploratory Workshop in Art for Talented Younger Indians," (Tucson, 15 Oct 1959), IAIA Archives, and Lloyd H. New, "Report on a Proposed Philosophical Approach to the Art Education Program of the Institute of American Indian Arts," (Santa Fe, 1962), IAIA Archives.
2. Lloyd H. New, "Report on a Proposed Philosophical Approach to the Art Education Program of the Institute of American Indian Arts," (Santa Fe, 1962), 2, IAIA Archives.
3. Ibid, 1.
4. Fritz Scholder, "The Native American and Contemporary Art: A Dilemma," in *Sharing a Heritage*, ed. Charlotte Heth, (Los Angeles: American Indian Studies Center, University of California, 1984), 61-63.
5. Vine Deloria Jr., *Custer Died for Your Sins: An Indian Manifesto*, (New York: Macmillan, 1969).
6. Robin Richman, "Rediscovery of the Redman," *Life*, (December 1967), 62-65.
7. Charlene Touchette with Suzanne Deats, *Ndn art*, (Albuquerque: Fresco Fine Art Publications, 2003).

8. Lowery Strokes Sims with Truman T. Lowe & Paul Chaat Smith, *Fritz Scholder: Indian not Indian*, (Munich; New York: Prestel, 2008).

Chapter 4

1. In 1961 George A. Boyce was hired by the Bureau of Indian Affairs as the first superintendent of IAIA. Formerly of the Intermountain Indian School in Brigham City, Utah, Boyce brought twenty-eight years of administrative BIA experience to IAIA. He formally retired in 1966.

2. Lloyd H. "Kiva" New (Cherokee) was hired as the first art director of IAIA in 1962. A successful fashion designer, New and his business associate, Charles Loloma (Hopi), had long dreamed of an art school for Native students. New was appointed superintendent (the title was later changed to president) in 1967 following the retirement of George Boyce and served in that position until his retirement in 1978. New would later come back to serve as interim president in 1988 during the reorganization of IAIA. New is generally considered the founder of the unique philosophical approach to art education used at the Institute.

3. During the late 1950s, the Rockefeller Foundation became deeply interested in American Indian art. Extensive research by the foundation led to the "Rockefeller Conference on Indian Art", held at the University of Arizona in March of 1959 and attended by thirty-one participants, including Lloyd New. As a result of the conference, a new exploratory workshop, the "Southwestern Indian Art Project" was created. The workshop hosted Indian youth from around the country during the summers of 1960 and 1961 and taught contemporary art forms and practices. Joy Gritton wrote, "contrary to popular perception, the Institute of American Indian Arts was not a direct outgrowth of the Southwestern Indian Art Project, but rather a parallel and contemporary development . . . ."

4. During the 1930s, the Santa Fe Indian School (SFIS) hosted *The Studio School* art program and produced an American Indian art aesthetic derived from student's cultural backgrounds. Prominent artists Allan Houser, Pablita Velarde, and Oscar Howe were students during the high period of the painting program. *Studio* director Dorothy Dunn retired in 1937, but other art instructors, namely Geronima Cruz Montoya and her assistants attempted to follow Dunn's goals until 1962. In the Fall of 1962, per the wishes of the BIA and under the advisement of the Indian Arts and Crafts Board, the IAIA program replaced the SFIS program and was assigned the physical property used by SFIS since 1890. Now under new leadership, IAIA took over the facilities and reestablished *The Studio* under different cultural and artistic goals and circumstances and helped it evolve into a vocational art center.

5. Intermountain Indian School in Brigham City, Utah opened in 1950 as a boarding school for Navajo students and was one of the largest schools in the BIA system. The influence of Intermountain on IAIA was evident in the early years, with former Intermountain employees George Boyce, Allan and Ana Houser, Oleta Mary, and Wilma Victor holding key positions in the new school. Intermountain closed in 1984.

6. Allan Houser (Warm Spring Chiracahua) followed George Boyce from Intermountain Indian School to join the faculty at IAIA in 1962. Houser taught sculpture and painting while continuing his successful career as an artist. Although he retired from teaching in 1975, Houser's profound influence on IAIA, its art, and its students continues to present day.

7. Charles Loloma (Hopi) was a successful educator, artist and jeweler and joined the IAIA faculty in 1962. He worked with Lloyd New in the Kiva Craft Center in Scottsdale in the 1950s and the Rockefeller project in Tucson and eventually joined New in Santa Fe to head the Plastic Arts and Student Sales departments. Loloma and New long shared a vision for an art school for Indian students and flourished during their time at IAIA.

8. Alongside her husband Charles, Otellie Loloma (Hopi) created sculpture and ceramic art at the Kiva Craft Center in Scottsdale in the 1950s and was an instructor for the Rockefeller project in 1961. Among the original IAIA faculty in 1962, Loloma was deeply influential in the ceramic arts program at IAIA and taught *Ceramic Sculpture, Painting, Basic Design*, and *Traditional Indian Dance* until her retirement in 1988.

9. Ralph Pardington graduated with an MFA in ceramics and sculpture from the Cranbrook Academy of Fine Art in 1962 and was hired to teach *Ceramic Sculpture* at IAIA the same year. In 1965, Pardington took over as chair of the Three-Dimensional Art Department and served IAIA in many capacities until his retirement in 1988.

10. Josephine Wapp (Comanche) was born in Oklahoma and received her BS from Oklahoma State University in 1959. Wapp taught at Chilocco Indian School and Intermountain School prior to her time teaching *Traditional Techniques, Traditional Indian Dance, Textiles*, and *Fashion Design* at IAIA. She retired from the Bureau of Indian Affairs in 1973 to continue her successful career as an authority on Indian arts and crafts techniques.

11. Louis Ballard (Cherokee-Quapaw) joined the arts faculty at IAIA in 1962 after receiving degrees in music theory from Oklahoma University and Tulsa University. Ballard was chair of the music and performing arts department and was responsible for much of the coursework in that area, including the E-Yah-Pah-Hah Chanters Chorus. Ballard left IAIA in 1975 and continued a successful career in music composition and performance until his death in 2007.

12. As an artist, Fritz Scholder is a famous American painter of the 20th century, but less is known about his career as an educator, having only taught *Advanced Painting* at IAIA from 1964 until 1968. Scholder attended the Rockefeller project as an advanced student in 1961 and was an assistant design instructor for the project in 1962.

13. Famed Native painter Kevin Red Star (Crow) was part of the first group of 150 students to enter IAIA and one of its most successful alumni. Red Star attended IAIA from 1962–1965 and continued his studies at the San Francisco Art Institute.

14. Oil painter and sculptor Earl Eder (Sioux) studied under Allan Houser at IAIA from 1962–1965 before receiving his BFA. from the San Francisco Art Institute in 1970.

15. In 1950, artist Lloyd H. "Kiva" New purchased a two acre field in Scottsdale, Arizona. By 1955, the complex named "The Kiva Shops" was one of the first and the most renowned of the studios in Scottsdale. The complex consisted of seven buildings where artists, including Lloyd "Kiva" New and Charles Loloma, created, displayed, and sold their works. "The Kiva Center" was recognized for its historic significance and gained historic preservation status in 2006.

16. After graduating from the Art Institute of Chicago with a graduate degree in arts education in 1938, Lloyd New took a job with the BIA, teaching at the Phoenix Indian Boarding School. New supervised young Indian artists in the illustration of bilingual textbooks for the Hopi and Navajo tribes.

17. Hildegard Thompson is seen by many as the 'grandmother' of IAIA. Around 1960, BIA education

Director Thompson was charged by then BIA commissioner Glen Emmons to investigate operations at the Santa Fe Indian School. According to a 1972 letter from George Boyce, Thompson was dissatisfied with the school, and pushed to establish a vocational art program (IAIA) to replace the existing curriculum at the Santa Fe Indian School. She was successful in obtaining a capitol sum from Congress and hired George Boyce to oversee the operation.

18. Royal Brown Hassrick worked for the government in many capacities between 1942 and 1948. Hassrick served as curator of the Southern Plains Indian Museum for the U.S. Department of Interior in Anadarko, Oklahoma from 1948-1952 and was assistant general manager of the Indian Arts and Crafts Board for the Department of Interior in Denver from 1952-1954. From 1955-1962, Hassrick served as curator of American Indian Art for the Denver Art Museum. Hassrick was an instrumental piece of the Indian Arts and Crafts Board and their involvement with IAIA.

19. The famous horror film actor Vincent Price was a strong supporter of IAIA. As a member of the Indian Arts and Crafts Board, Price was very active with the creative writing program. He established the *Vincent Price Awards for Creative Writing* in 1963 until 1970, and held annual poetry readings at IAIA in conjunction with the awards.

20. Rene d'Harnoncourt was the long time director of the Rockefeller funded Museum of Modern Art and at the time of the creation of IAIA also served as the chair of the Indian Arts and Crafts Board. d'Harnonecourt's opinion was very influential during the 1959 "Rockefeller Conference on Indian Art" and during subsequent developments leading up to 1962.

21. Rolland Meinholtz was the director of the drama department at IAIA from 1962-1972 and is credited as leading the direction of contemporary American Indian theatre in the 1960s.

22. Stewart Udall served three terms as a congressmen from Arizona, and served as Secretary of the Interior from 1961 to 1969, under Presidents John F. Kennedy and Lyndon B. Johnson.

23. Ermalee Webb Udall was the wife of Arizona politician Stewart Udall. Mrs. Udall was a staunch supporter of IAIA and was involved in garnering political support for the school in Washington.

24. *Cultural Followthrough* was a joint effort between the BIA Central Office, IAIA, and the Phoenix Area BIA Office initiated in 1970. The program supported the efforts of teachers to facilitate student art activities that used the national environment, tribal experiences, and tribal cultural heritage as significant and respected sources of self-identification and creative personal expression. The project supported a traveling art education van, a traveling children's exhibit, classroom demonstrations, teachers workshops, and three publications.

25. After years of attempts to remove IAIA from under the control of the BIA, the Higher Education Amendments of 1986 established the school under its now official title, the Institute of American and Alaskan Native Arts and Culture Development. Per the bill, as of June 1, 1988, IAIA was reorganized as a congressionally chartered non-profit entity and operated under the guidance of a Presidentially appointed board of trustees.

26. William Johnson was the first chairman of the IAIA board of trustees for the reorganized school. Initially contacted by Department of Interior political appointee Patricia Keyes, Johnson had been in charge of government programs for IBM since 1977.

27. When New and McGrath returned to IAIA during its transition, they encountered an accredited junior college, a status IAIA received in October, 1984, quite sometime after the two administrators had moved on. Both the Higher Learning Commission and National Association

of Schools of Art and Design accredited IAIA to grant two-year degrees. In 2001, IAIA was accredited to grant baccalaureate degrees in five separate degree areas.

28. In 1981, following years of congressional debate, IAIA was removed from the campus of the Santa Fe Indian School and took up rental property at the College of Santa Fe (CSF), now known as the Santa Fe University of Art and Design. IAIA operated the school in substandard facilities at CSF until 2001.

29. McGrath coordinated, designed, curated, and escorted the "Exhibition of American Indian Arts and Crafts" throughout Scotland, Berlin, Turkey, Argentina, Chile, and Mexico City between August 1966 and March 1969 for the U.S. Department of State. The exhibition was critically acclaimed, and featured the work of many IAIA students. It was considered to be instrumental in establishing contemporary Native art as an accepted international art medium.

30. Charles A. Dailey arrived at IAIA in November, 1971 after working at the Museum of New Mexico. He was charged with the oversight of the Museum Studies program as well as all museum operations and worked in that capacity until his retirement in 2007. Dailey still serves IAIA as Professor Emeritus of Museum Studies.

31. The IAIA *Honors Collection* was developed between 1962–1971 and is the backbone of the permanent collections of the Museum of Contemporary Native Art.

Chapter 6

1. A.T. Mann, *Sacred Landscapes*, (New York: Sterling Publishing, 2010)
2. Cardinal, Douglas J., "Institute of American Indian and Alaska Native Culture and Arts Development Campus Master Plan," (Santa Fe, 1993), 6, IAIA Archives.
3. Ibid, 7.
4. Lloyd H. New, "Report on a Proposed Philosophical Approach to the Art Education Program of the Institute of American Indian Arts," (Santa Fe, 1962), 2, IAIA Archives.
5. Lloyd Kiva with Andreas Storrs Anderson and Sidney Little, "A Proposal for an Exploratory Workshop in Art for Talented Younger Indians," (Tucson, 1959), 3, IAIA Archives.
6. Lloyd Kiva, "Comments on the Southwest Indian Arts and Crafts Project," (Tuscon, 1961), p. 3, IAIA Archives.
7. New, "Proposed Philosophy," 4.
8. New, "Proposed Philosophy," 1.
9. Cardinal, "Master Plan," 18.
10. Ibid, 18.
11. Ibid, 18.
12. Ibid, 19.
13. Ibid, 19.
14. Ibid, 18.
15. Loyd H. New, "Institute of American Indian Arts Unity Keynote Address," (speech presented to the Institute of American Indian Arts, Santa Fe, New Mexico December 12, 1998), 10, IAIA Archives.

Chapter 7

1. Lloyd Kiva with Andreas Storrs Anderson and Sidney Little, "A Proposal for an Exploratory Workshop in Art for Talented Younger Indians," (Tucson, 15 Oct 1959), 3-4, IAIA Archives.
2. Lloyd Kiva New, "Report at the Conclusion of the first six weeks" session of the Southwest Indian Arts and Crafts Workshop (Tuscon, 28 July 1960), 2, IAIA Archives.
3. Jay Scott, *Changing Woman: The Life and Art of Helen Hardin*, (Flagstaff: Northland Press, 1989).
4. Tim Troy, "The Institute Of American Indian Arts: Looking Back - Looking Forward," (1982), 12, IAIA Archives.
5. IAIA Staff, "IAIA Basic Statement of Purpose," (Santa Fe, 1964), 2-3, IAIA Archives.
6. Lloyd Kiva New, memorandum, "Comments on Southwest Indian Arts and Crafts Project Universtiy of Arizona . . . 2nd year, 1961," (Tuscon, 1961), 3, IAIA Archives.
7. Lloyd H. New, report submitted to the Special Sub-committee on Indian Education, U.S. Senate Committee on Labor and Public Welfare "The Role of IAIA in the Development of Indian Education and its Potential as a Major Cultural Institution," (Santa Fe, February 1969), 5, IAIA Archives.
8. Lloyd H. New, "The Institute of American Indian Arts, Some of its Goals, Problems, and Successes," (Santa Fe, 1979), 1, IAIA Archives.
9. Linda Lomahaftewa, phone interview by author, Santa Fe, 16 December 2011.
10. Ibid.
11. Lloyd H. New, "Potential As A Major Cultural Institution," 7.
12. Troy, Tim, "Looking Back - Looking Forward," 16.
13. Unknown, "Years Of Siege (The Decline of an Institution 1968-78)," manuscript drafted for inclusion into "The Institute of American Indian Arts: A United States Government Experiment in Culturally Related Education. A Report requested by The World Crafts Council for UNESCO," (Santa Fe, 1979), IAIA Archives.
14. Lloyd H. New, "Goals, Problems, and Successes," 6-8.
15. Lloyd Kiva New, "The Institute of American Indian Arts, A Developing Institution," (Santa Fe, 28 March 1975), 11, IAIA Archives.
16. Steven Kapelke with Dorothy Kostuch and Donald Sargeant, "Report of a Focused Visit to The Institute of American Indian and Alaska Native Culture and Arts Development" for the Higher Learning Commission North Central Association of Colleges and Schools, (Santa Fe, 8-9 October 2001), 4, IAIA Archives.
17. Charles A. Dailey, "History of the Institute of American Indian Arts Museum," manuscript draft, (Santa Fe, 1982), 7, IAIA Archives.
18. Lomahaftewa, interview.
19. Tim Troy, "Looking Back - Looking Forward," 18.
20. Ibid, 11.
21. Ibid, 24.
22 Robert Martin, interview by author, IAIA, Santa Fe, 6 October 2011.
23. Gregory A. Cajete with Larry Desjarlais, Charles Poitras, John Dixon, Junita Barry, and Linda Lomahaftewa, "Recommendations Concerning the Reorganization of IAIA," presented by the Academic Affairs Committee to the Institute of American Indian Arts Board of Trustees, Academic Affairs Committee (Santa Fe, 27 March 1987), 2, IAIA Archives.

24. Martin, interview.

25. National Association of Schools of Art & Design/North Central Association

26. Steven Kapelke et al., "Report of a Focused Visit," 12.

27. Martin, interview.

28. Institute of American Indian Arts, "Proposed Statement of Educational Philosophy," (Santa Fe, 24 April 1991), 1, IAIA Archives.

29. Martin, interview.

30. Steve Wall, interview by author, IAIA, Santa Fe, 6 October 2011.

31. Wall, interview.

32. Martin, interview.

33. Daryl Lucero, interview by author, IAIA, Santa Fe, 6 October 2011.

34. Martin, interview.

35. Hayes Lewis, interview by author, IAIA, Santa Fe, 6 October 2011.

36. Ibid.

37. Ibid.

38. Wall, interview.

39. Lomahaftewa, interview.

40. Lucero, interview.

41. Lewis, interview.

42. Crystal Worl, interview by author, IAIA, Santa Fe, 6 October 2011.

43. Ibid.

44. Ibid.

45. Lomahaftewa, interview.

46. Ibid.

47. Lucero, interview.

48. Ibid.

49. Wall, interview.

50. Ibid.

51. Lloyd Kiva with Andreas Storrs Anderson and Sidney Little, "A Proposal," 3-4.

52. Wall, interview.

53. Worl, interview.

54. Ibid.

Appendix 2

1. Adrian Parameter to Lloyd New, 28 December 1968, Lloyd H. New Papers, IAIA Archives.

2. Lloyd New to Adrian Parameter, 21 January 1969, Lloyd H. New Papers, IAIA Archives.

Selected Bibliography

The sources listed in this select bibliography are writings used by the authors to produce this book. However, this listing is by no means a complete record of all works consulted in the research. It is intended to be a convenient source for those interested in further study of education at IAIA. Finding aids for the various record groups and manuscript collections listed in the primary source section of the bibliography can be accessed on the Rocky Mountain Online Archive (rmoa.unm.edu). In some cases, digital copies of photographs and manuscripts can be accessed on the New Mexico Digital Collections website (econtent.unm.edu).

Primary Sources

Boyce, George A. "Learning And Living at IAIA." 1965. RG 02, IAIA Printed Matter. IAIA Archives, Santa Fe, New Mexico.

Cajete, Gregory A. with Larry Desjarlais, Charles Poitras, John Dixon, Junita Barry, and Linda Lomahaftewa. "Recommendations Concerning the Reorganization of IAIA." 1987. RG 01, IAIA Records Compiled by Chuck Dailey, SG-27. IAIA Archives, Santa Fe, New Mexico.

—— "A Curriculum Prospectus for the Institute of American Indian and Alaska Native Arts and Culture." 1989. MS 03, James A. McGrath Papers. IAIA Archives, Santa Fe, New Mexico.

Dailey, Charles A. "History of the Institute of American Indian Arts Museum." 1982. MS 15, Lloyd H. New Papers. IAIA Archives, Santa Fe, New Mexico.

Douglas J. Cardinal Architect Limited. "Institute of American Indian and Alaska Native Culture and Arts Development Campus Master Plan." 1993. MS 01, William Johnson Papers. IAIA Archives, Santa Fe, New Mexico.

Institute of American Indian Arts. "Proposed Statement of Educational Philosophy." 1991. RG 01, IAIA Records Compiled by Chuck Dailey, SG 31. IAIA Archives, Santa Fe, New Mexico.

—— "College Catalog, 2011-2012," 2011. RG 02, IAIA Printed Matter. IAIA Archives, Santa Fe, New Mexico.

—— "Status Study Report to the Accreditation Committee of the North Central Association of Colleges and Schools and the National Association of Schools of Art." 1977. RG 01, IAIA Records Compiled by Chuck Dailey, SG 17. IAIA Archives, Santa Fe, New Mexico.

Institute of American Indian Arts Staff. "IAIA Basic Statement of Purpose." 1964. RG 01, IAIA Records Compiled by Chuck Dailey, SG 08. IAIA Archives, Santa Fe, New Mexico.

Jeffries, Mackey. "Recommendations for Developing the Administrative Role in the Institute of American Indian Arts (Task Four of the Transition Evaluation)." Printed in "Research and Evaluation Report No. 17, Institute of American Indian Arts Transition Evaluation."

January 1973. RG 01, IAIA Records Compiled by Chuck Dailey, SG 14. IAIA Archives, Santa Fe, New Mexico.

Kapelke, Steven with Dorothy Kostuch and Donald Sargeant. "Report of a Focused Visit to the Institute of American Indian and Alaska Native Culture and Arts Development." Developed for the Higher Learning Commission North Central Association of Colleges and Schools. October 2001. RG 01, IAIA Records Compiled by Chuck Dailey, SG 41. IAIA Archives, Santa Fe, New Mexico.

Kiva, Lloyd with Andreas Storrs Anderson and Sidney Little. "A Proposal for an Exploratory Workshop in Art for Talented Younger Indians." October 1959. MS 15, Lloyd H. New Papers. IAIA Archives, Santa Fe, New Mexico.

—— "Comment on the Southwest Indian Arts and Crafts Project." 1961. MS 15, Lloyd H. New Papers. IAIA Archives, Santa Fe, New Mexico.

Native American Council of Regents. "The Future Institute of American Indian Arts and Culture: A Major Multi-phased National Cultural Advancement Center." 1977. MS 07, Winona Garmhausen Papers. IAIA Archives, Santa Fe, New Mexico.

New, Lloyd Kiva. "Report at the Conclusion of the First Six Weeks. " July 1960. MS 15, Lloyd H. New Papers. IAIA Archives, Santa Fe, New Mexico.

—— Memorandum. "Comments on Southwest Indian Arts and Crafts Project University of Arizona . . . 2nd year, 1961." 1961. MS 15, Lloyd H. New Papers. IAIA Archives, Santa Fe, New Mexico.

New, Lloyd H. "Report on a Proposed Philosophical Approach to the Art Education Programs of the Institute of American Indian Arts." 1962. MS 15, Lloyd H. New Papers. IAIA Archives, Santa Fe, New Mexico.

—— "Cultural Difference as a Basis for Creative Expression." 1964. MS 03, James A. McGrath Papers. IAIA Archives, Santa Fe, New Mexico.

—— "An Analysis of the Program of the Institute of American Indian Arts at the End of Its Fifth Year of Operation." 1967. RG 01, IAIA Records Compiled by Chuck Dailey, SG 07. IAIA Archives, Santa Fe, New Mexico.

—— Report submitted to the Special Sub-committee on Indian Education, U.S. Senate Committee on Labor and Public Welfare, "The Role of IAIA in the Development of Indian Education and its Potential as a Major Cultural Institution." 1969. RG 01, IAIA Records Compiled by Chuck Dailey, SG 09. IAIA Archives, Santa Fe, New Mexico.

—— "Progress Report: Institute of American Indian Arts, with Recommendations." 1970. MS 15, Lloyd H. New Papers. IAIA Archives, Santa Fe, New Mexico.

—— with James E. Hawkins and William J. Benham. "Research and Evaluation Report No. 17, Institute of American Indian Arts Transition Evaluation." January 1973. RG 01, IAIA Records Compiled by Chuck Dailey, SG 14. IAIA Archives, Santa Fe, New Mexico.

—— "The Institute of American Indian Arts, A Developing Institution." 1975. MS 15, Lloyd H. New Papers. IAIA Archives, Santa Fe, New Mexico.

—— "The Institute of American Indian Arts, Some of its Goals, Problems, and Successes." 1979. RG 01, IAIA Records Compiled by Chuck Dailey, SG 19. IAIA Archives, Santa Fe, New Mexico.

—— "Institute of American Indian Arts Unity Keynote Address." 12 December 1998. MS 15, Lloyd H. New Papers. IAIA Archives, Santa Fe, New Mexico.

Poitras, Charles. "Institute of American Indian Arts." Printed in "BIA College Management Operations Analysis for 1976," for Office of the Commission of Indian Affairs. 1977. MS 07, Winona Garmhausen Papers. IAIA Archives, Santa Fe, New Mexico.

Rainer, John C. with Popovi Da, Hellen Peterson, Anne M. Smith, Frank M. Tippetts, James P. Shannon and Tom Segundo. "A Special Report to the Commissioner of Indian Affairs, Mr. Louis R. Bruce." 1970. RG 01, IAIA Records Compiled by Chuck Dailey, SG 10. IAIA Archives, Santa Fe, New Mexico.

Senate Committee on Labor and Public Welfare, Special Subcommittee on Indian Education. "Indian Education: A National Tragedy-A National Challenge." 91st Cong., 1st sess. 1969. Rept. 91-501.

Southwest Planning & Marketing with Herzlich & Associates. *The Institute of American Indian Arts: Impact Assessment and Market Study.* 1996. MS 08, Robert Harcourt Papers. IAIA Archives, Santa Fe, New Mexico.

Tippeconnic, John W. Jr. "The Institute of American Indian Arts Background Information (Task One of Transition Evaluation)." Printed in "Research and Evaluation Report No. 17, Institute of American Indian Arts Transition Evaluation." January 1973. RG 01, IAIA Records Compiled by Chuck Dailey, SG 14. IAIA Archives, Santa Fe, New Mexico.

Troy, Tim. "The Institute of American Indian Arts: Looking Back—Looking Forward." 1982. RG 01, IAIA Records Compiled by Chuck Dailey, SG 22. IAIA Archives, Santa Fe, New Mexico.

Unknown. "Years of Siege (The Decline of an Institution 1968-78)." Manuscript drafted for inclusion into "The Institute of American Indian Arts: A United States Government Experiment in Culturally Related Education. A Report requested by The World Crafts Council for UNESCO." 1979. MS 15, Lloyd H. New Papers. IAIA Archives, Santa Fe, New Mexico.

West, W. Richard. "Program Evaluation: The Institute of American Indian Arts, Santa Fe, New Mexico." printed in "Research and Evaluation Report No. 17, Institute of American Indian Arts Transition Evaluation", January 1973. RG01, IAIA Records Compiled by Chuck Dailey, SG 14. IAIA Archives, Santa Fe, New Mexico.

Wiest, Kay V. Photograph Collection. MS 10. IAIA Archives, Santa Fe, New Mexico.

Yenawine, Bruce H. with Dr. Barbara Mickey, Dr. Paul Arnold, and Fr. Michael Roethler. "Report of a Visit to Institute of American Indian Art, Santa Fe, New Mexico." For the Institutions of Higher Education of the North Central Association of Colleges and Schools and the Commission on Accreditation of the National Association of Schools of Art and Design. 1984. RG 01, IAIA Records Compiled by Chuck Dailey, SG 24. IAIA Archives, Santa Fe, New Mexico.

Secondary Sources

Blank, Ruth. "The Development of an Instructional Materials Center at the Institute of American Indian Arts, Santa Fe, New Mexico, 1970." A thesis presented to the faculty of the Department of Librarianship, San Jose State College. In partial fulfillment of the requirements for the degree, Master of Arts, by Ruth Blank. N.p. June, 1971.

Boyer, Paul and the Carnegie Foundation for the Advancement of Teaching. *Native American Colleges: Progress and Prospects*. Princeton: Jossey-Bass Inc, 1997.

Carney, Cary Michael. *Native American Higher Education in the United States*. New Brunswick: Transaction Publishing, 1999.

Deloria, Vine Jr. *Custer Died for Your Sins: An Indian Manifesto*. New York: Macmillan, 1969.

Garmhausen, Winona. "History of Indian Arts Education in Santa Fe: The Institute of American Indian Arts with Historical Background 1890-1962." PhD Diss., University of New Mexico, 1982. MS 07, Winona Garmahausen Papers. IAIA Archives, Santa Fe, New Mexico.

Garmhausen, Winona. *History of Indian Arts Education in Santa Fe: The Institute of American Indian Arts with Historical Background 1890-1962*. Santa Fe: Sunstone Press, 1982.

Gritton, Joy L. *The Institute of American Indian Arts: Modernism and U.S. Indian Policy*. Albuquerque: University of New Mexico Press. 2000.

—— "Cross-Cultural Education vs. Modernist Imperialism: The Institute of American Indian Arts." *Art Journal* 51, no. 3 (1992): 28-35.

Hill, Rick with Nancy Marie Mitchell and Lloyd New. *Creativity is Our Tradition: Three Decades of Contemporary Indian Art at the Institute of American Indian Arts*. Santa Fe: Institute of American Indian Arts, 1992.

Mann, A.T. *Sacred Landscapes*. New York: Sterling Publishing, 2010.

Oppelt, Norman T. *The Tribally Controlled Indian College: The Beginnings of Self-Determination in American Indian Education*. Tsaile: Navajo Community College Press, 1990.

Scholder, Fritz. "The Native American and Contemporary Art: A Dilemma." in *Sharing a Heritage*, ed. Charlotte Heth, Los Angeles: American Indian Studies Center, University of California, 1984.

Scott, Jay. *Changing Woman: The Life and Art of Helen Hardin*, Flagstaff: Northland Press.1989.

Sims, Lowery Strokes with Truman T. Lowe and Paul Chaat Smith. *Fritz Scholder: Indian not Indian*. Munich; New York: Prestel, 2008.

Szasz, Margaret. *Education and the American Indian: The Road to Self-Determination, 1928-1973*. Albuquerque: University of New Mexico Press, 1974.

Touchette, Charlene with Suzanne Deats. *Ndn Art*. Albuquerque: Fresco Fine Art Publications, 2003.

Index

www.ingramcontent.com/pod-product-compliance
Lightning Source LLC
Chambersburg PA
CBHW020910180526
45163CB00007B/2690

* 9 7 8 0 8 6 5 3 4 9 1 3 1 *